FROM THE

A U.S. Foreign Policy Primer

G.T. Dempsey

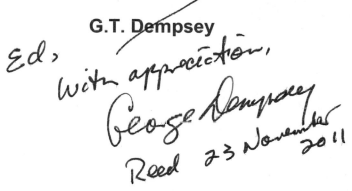

Ed,
with appreciation,
George Dempsey
Reed 23 November 2011

openrepublic.org

The Open Republic Institute
Dublin 4, Ireland

Published by Open Republic Institute Ltd.

Distributed by The Liffey Press

Printed by Colour Books Ltd. Dublin, Cover design by Jennifer Hord

ISBN: 1-904148-55-7

The Open Republic Institute

The Open Republic Institute (ORI) is Ireland's only platform for public policy discussion that is specifically interested in individual rights within the context of open society and open market ideas. The ORI works within a non-political framework to provide public policy analysis and new policy ideas to government, public representatives, civil servants, academics, students and citizens.

The ORI publishes the annual Economic Freedom of the World Report – in association with Canada's Fraser Institute – and is a member of the Economic Freedom Network – an international group of policy research institutes.

The ORI has no corporate policy views of its own. The views expressed in this book are the author's and not those of the Open Republic Institute.

For my children

And for my remaining friends in Ireland.

Memento – hae tibi erunt artes –
Pacique imponere morem....

Abbreviations

AFL-CIO	American Federation of Labor – Congress of Industrial Organizations
ASEAN	Association of Southeast Asian Nations
CERDS	Charter of Economic Rights and Duties of States
COCOM	Coordinating Committee (NATO)
CTV	Confederación de Trabajadores de Venezuela
DCM	Deputy Chief of Mission
DGB	Deutscher Gewerkschaftsbund
EC (EU)	European Community (now the European Union)
ECE	Economic Commission for Europe (UN)
ECST	European Convention on the Suppression of Terrorism
ETA	Euskadi Ta Askatasuna
FNV	Federatie Nederlandse Vakbeweging
FRAP	Frente Revolucionario Antifascista Patriótico
FSI	Foreign Service Institute
G-77	Group of 77
GRAPO	Grupo Revolucionario Antifascista Primero de Octubre
GSP	Generalized System of Preferences
HLM	High-Level Meeting (ECE)
IDB	Industrial Development Board (UNIDO)
IMF	International Monetary Fund
IRA	Irish Republican Army
NAFTA	North American Free Trade Agreement
NAM	Non-Aligned Movement
NATO	North Atlantic Treaty Organization
NIEO	New International Economic Order
NSC	National Security Council
OAS	Organization of American States
ODA	Official Development Assistance

OECD	Organization for Economic Cooperation and Development
OPEC	Organization of Petroleum Exporting Countries
PCE	Partido Comunista Español
PDVSA	Petróleos de Venezuela, S.A.
PFP	Partnership for Peace (NATO)
PSOE	Partido Socialista Obrero Español
RDS	Royal Dublin Society
RUC	Royal Ulster Constabulary
SDLP	Social Democratic and Labour Party (Northern Ireland)
SAE	Senior Advisers on Energy (ECE)
TIR	Transport International Routier (ECE)
UN	United Nations
UNCTAD	UN Conference on Trade and Development
UNIDO	UN Industrial Development Organization
UNSC	UN Security Council

Preface

Why I Did the Things I Did

I joined the American diplomatic service because I was seduced by George F. Kennan.[1] In my final months at Oxford, I went many afternoons to the fine library in Rhodes House and, sitting at the long wooden table by the window that looked out on the gardens towards Wadham College, read what books I could find about my country's Foreign Service. There I read the first volume of Kennan's memoirs. There I was seduced by his portrait of his own diplomatic career as one of intellectual commitment.

I was soon disabused of this notion that diplomacy, today, is an intellectual profession. My first shock came on arrival at the Foreign Service Institute. In those days, in June 1973, FSI was housed in a rather nondescript, high-rise office building in Roslyn, Virginia looking across the Potomac River to Georgetown and to the District of Columbia. It wasn't so much the tackiness of where I was to be introduced into diplomatic life which shocked me; it was the Institute's lack of a bookstore. Naively – as I came to realize – I had anticipated a somewhat seamless transition from graduate school at Oxford to another scholarly environment. After all, Kennan had written of his own formal introduction into diplomatic life as involving lecturers droning on about consular law and the proper drafting of diplomatic messages – certainly, not as enticing as his later studies in Russian language and history in Berlin, but still portending, I presumed, that my own initiation would likewise be

---

[1] An earlier version of this preface (together with chapter 7 and the Epilogue) was delivered, on 29 February 2000, as a paper to Dr Gary Murphy's seminar on international relations at the Business School of Dublin City University.

concentrated in readings in diplomatic history, customs, law and practices. I discovered, rather, that the several weeks of the modern-day Junior Officer Course were intended to introduce us to the bureaucracy of the Federal Government and that our reading material consisted of government publications. I don't want to overplay this. As I subsequently learned, many of the courses at FSI, such as those in area studies, involve extensive reading-lists of books and scholarly articles and lectures by academic specialists. And the intensive language courses – the true *raison d'être* of FSI's existence – are the best in the world. But no one would mistake it, at least in my days, for a university campus and the atmosphere was not one of intellectual curiosity but of getting 'read in'.

This isn't without its reasons. The American Foreign Service today feeds a near insatiable appetite on the part of a huge Federal Government for information specific to decision-making. And while you can prepare before you go to an overseas assignment – and the State Department will assign you perforce to the pertinent courses – your real learning comes at post. There, on the job, you develop the skills of a diplomat. There, at first hand, you come to know the country and to truly know its language and you gain the confidence of the country's citizens so that they confide in you. You so enter into the spirit of the foreign culture that you understand why things are done the way they are and what can be done and what can't be done, and you put all you learn and all your insights together and you write it so that those officials in Washington who know but little of the country will understand why it behaves as it does.

You are also, today, transferred every two or three or four years. The measured development and sequential assignments-in-area of specialists like Kennan no longer much exist (though the minority who are Arabists or Chinese or Japanese language specialists will disagree). Still, I found that, for most of us, 'scholar' and 'diplomat' were no longer synonymous – a reality which was physically brought home to me when I arrived at my second posting, in Vienna, in early 1978. I was dealing there with the United Nations and one day, not too many months after my arrival, I was asked by the embassy's administrative counselor to see what books my office could use from the embassy's library. They were dismantling it, having decided they could use the space for more immediate purposes. Until then, I hadn't even known there was a library at post. It had simply been an unmarked, locked room at the end of a corridor. I went along, as instructed, and what I found almost brought tears to my eyes. The American embassy in Vienna is itself housed in a lovely eighteenth-century baroque palace, with high ceilings and marble floors and gracious space in the rooms and corridors. The library, I discovered, was very much an integral part of such a building, with built-in wooden shelves stretching floor to high ceiling so that ladders set into metal runners were needed to reach the highest shelves. Down the middle of the sizeable room, there sat a heavy wooden reading-table with a half-dozen chairs and goose-neck reading lamps at each place. There were racks for magazines and journals and a librarian's desk and, standing next to the desk, the catalog file-cabinet with its ranks of drawers for the index cards. On the shelves were thousands of books. As I looked through them, I found that in many the book-plate reading 'Library of the Legation of the United States of America at Vienna, Austria' had been corrected by hand to read 'Embassy'. On the desk were the date-stamps and other paraphernalia of a librarian's daily work, left as they were when funding for embassy libraries was terminated by the State Department sometime in the mid-1960s.

My first posting had been Madrid where I had arrived in summer 1974 after my year of learning the bureaucracy and learning Spanish. I was there for just two years which is still, I believe, the standard junior officer first tour. Also, as is still standard, I served first as a vice consul, though my career specialization – my 'cone' – was political. After Madrid, I returned to the State Department where I served, for little over a year, as the analyst for Spanish affairs. I was assigned then to Bulgarian language training and began to think of a career in Eastern Europe, primarily for the continuity ('worldwide availability' is standardly taken by our personnel system to equate with finding warm bodies for vacancies). Any such thoughts, however, were terminated when the Bulgarian government declared me *persona non grata*. The State Department termed it 'reciprocal retribution' (we had denied a Bulgarian trade official a diplomatic visa and I was simply the next in line) and, as compensation for the five months of learning Bulgarian which would now be wasted, offered me Vienna. I was there until the summer of 1980. I then spent the academic year 1980-81 at Columbia University in New York, supposedly studying multilateral diplomacy in preparation for my next overseas assignment in Geneva, 1981-85, where I would also deal with the United Nations. After Geneva, I was the labor attaché in The Hague, 1985-87, and then the chief of the political section in Dublin, 1988-92. In between The Hague and Dublin, I had a second academic year assignment, this time as a sort of diplomat-in-residence at Reed College in Portland, Oregon. After Dublin, the harsh reality of 'worldwide availability' finally come home to roost and I was shipped off to Caracas. By then I was a Foreign Service Officer Class One (the equivalent, in military terms, of a colonel) and early retirement was an option. After two years in Caracas (to reach the minimum age of 50 years), I took it.

In fact, I had thought about early retirement from my very first posting. One of the reasons for that was the discrepancy I have described between the scholarly commitment of Kennan's time and the bureaucracy-mentality of mine. Another reason was also the lack – which I have hinted at – of a professional personnel system in the U.S. Foreign Service. Officers are not assigned on the basis of experience and performance and proven ability but simply availability. In order to get an assignment useful to your own career (as well as, in truth, to the Foreign Service), you have to use the 'old boys network' – assignments are controlled by the bureaus in the State Department and by embassies, not by central personnel – which means having someone senior in rank who knows you and thinks highly of your abilities and who is in a position to influence, if not determine, the assignment you're after. By the nature of the beast, as you are promoted up the ladder, there are fewer and fewer of these 'mentors' – the Foreign Service is pyramidal and officers senior to you keep disappearing through retirement. When it came time for me to leave Dublin, I looked around and, for the first time, there was nobody. Hence, Caracas.

Caracas, in itself, would have been sufficient to convince me to take early retirement but, if it had not, the ambassador, during my first year there, would have been. Oddly, he was a career diplomat. It's not that he was the first inadequate ambassador I had served under, but the others had all been political appointees.

The political appointment system in the American diplomatic service is notorious. Everyone deplores it and every president is equally culpable. If Eisenhower could appoint a Perle Mesta, Clinton could appoint a Pamela Harriman – being a political hostess in Washington is such ideal training, you see, to be an American diplomatic chief-of-mission. In some ways, though, this system could be considered appropriate, even essential, given the American system of government. In parliamentary governments, the politicians are all elected. In the American system, many are appointed. Cabinet members, in particular. They're businessmen and educators and lawyers and retired generals. Those who run our government are, in this way, truly representative of the realities of American society. So why not ambassadors as well? My own first ambassador had been a four-star admiral. Over the next two decades, I served under political and career ambassadors in about equal numbers. All of the political ambassadors were, with one flaming exception, considerate and personally pleasant. All, equally, did not know what they were doing. In classical terms, an embassy is personified as the mission of an ambassador. In modern usage, an embassy more standardly is taken to mean the office-building housing the mission's staff (more properly termed the chancery). In the American system, the modern usage is far more appropriate since, due to the large percentage of our ambassadors who are in place as a result of political patronage, the real work of diplomacy is carried on by the career staff. In many cases, this is done despite the best efforts of the political ambassador to have things done his (or her) way. Sadly, far too regularly, political ambassadors arrive at post determined to instill, in the embassy staff, a sense of personalized service to them and to their idea of how 'to get the job done'. They have no idea of the mandated workload of an embassy and they share the same ignorant contempt for diplomacy as a profession as do our presidents.[2] At

---

[2]George F. Kennan *At A Century's Ending* (New York, 1996), p. 34, speaking of Joseph Davies, the American ambassador in Moscow, 1936-38, '...a shallow and politically ambitious man who knows nothing about Russia – has no serious interest in it. His only real interest is in the publicity he can get at home. We are ashamed for him before our diplomatic colleagues, not because of his personal qualities or imperfections...but because of his obvious unfitness for the job. To us,

the end of the day, despite all the justified acknowlegments of such first-rate political ambassadors as Averell Harriman or David Bruce, it remains that the United States is the only serious country without a wholly career diplomatic service.

What follows in this book are not memoirs. Not having served as an ambassador, it would be presumptuous of me to do any such thing, though the different chapters rely heavily upon my personal experiences. I found, in looking back over my service in some six missions, that I had, as it happens, dealt with many of the concerns dominating American diplomacy in the latter half of the twentieth century: democratization, the economic development of the Third World, conflict (or rivalry) with the Soviet Union, ethnic politics and conflicts, war. A working title for this book as it developed could have been, 'Episodes in U.S. Foreign Relations Since Vietnam'. Each chapter constitutes a case-study from the perspective of a working-level professional diplomat. I am attempting to put a human face on what is far too standardly treated in soulless abstraction. My hope is that such an approach will help those who are not professional diplomats to understand the realities – the constraints and the possibilities and the impossibilities – with which we professionals have to contend in getting our jobs done. As my Introduction makes clear, clearing away myths is my first concern. Only by revealing the realities, can judgments of our performance be made true. And from my readers who would be critics of American foreign policy, I ask only that they make a good-faith effort to understand what we have done and why we have done so, and that they undertake this effort rationally – that is, that they base their

---

the Foreign Service officers stationed here, his having been sent out as our chief seems like a gesture of contempt on the president's part for us and our efforts...'
See also my article, 'It takes more than being Oirish to be a good US ambassador,' *Sunday Independent*, 12 July 1998.

examination on demonstrable facts and draw their conclusions from the facts in a fair-minded and logical manner.

*

I would like to thank Aengus Fanning, Willie Kealy, and Ronan Farren of the *Sunday Independent* and David Quinn, former editor of the *Irish Catholic,* for giving me the opportunity, on repeated occasions, to publish my views on many of the subjects addressed in this book. Thanks as well to the many friends who debated these issues with me: Professor Paul Arthur, Tony Brown, †Professor George Butterworth, Christopher Cahill, Dr Thomas Clonan, Joe Colgan, Margot Collins, Frances Daly, Eamon Delaney, Gryffyd Dempsey, Candace Dempsey-Aguiar, Colonel Ned Doyle, Brian Fallon, †Tom Flanagan, Professor Tom Garvin, Lt Col Ed Gormley, David Hanly, Professor George Huxley, Benedict Kiely, Morgan Kulla, Brian Lacey, Mary Lawlor, Conor Lenihan, T.D., Timothy J. Lynch, Desmond McDermott, Ambassador Philip McDonagh, Paul MacDonnell (of the Open Republic Institute), Stephen McKenna, Seán MacRéamoinn, Bill Millan, Marco Morais, Caitlin Morais-Dempsey, Dr Gary Murphy, Fr Seamus Murphy, S.J., †Louie O'Brien, Professor Eunan O'Halpin, May O'Riordan, Michael O'Riordan, †Tony O'Riordan, Brenda Power, Bill Prasifka, Matthew Russell, Jean Rylands, Dr Liberato Santoro-Brienza, Professor Edward Segel (of Reed College), Fr Tom Stack, Kent Steinkamp, Mary Ellen Synon, Fr Paul Tighe, Rebecca Tracy, Professor Robert Tracy, John Treacy, Mary White and †Dr Sean J. White.

*

Some of the material in this book has appeared in different versions, as follows: the Introduction as 'Myth-making and Missing the Point: Largely Irish Perceptions of American Foreign Policy,' *Irish Studies in International Affairs* 9 (1998), pp. 119-33; chapter 3 as 'Why Global Negotiations on Third World Economic Development Didn't Work', The Open Republic Institute (Dublin), 30 April 2001, at www.openrepublic.org; chapter 5 as 'Ireland and the Gulf War: A View from the American Embassy,' *The Recorder: The Journal of the American Irish Historical Society* 14/1 (2001), pp. 113-31; chapter 6 as 'The American Role in the Northern Ireland Peace Process,' *Irish Political Studies* 14 (1999), pp. 104-17; the Epilogue as 'American free lunch may have to be paid for,' *Sunday Independent* (Dublin), 27 May 2001; and the Postscript as 'Ireland and the Second Gulf War: Farewell to Foreign Affairs Fecklessness,' *The Recorder* 16/2 (2003), pp. 67-81. For permission to republish earlier material I am indebted to the editors of the journals concerned.

4 July 2002

Blackrock
County Dublin

Foreword

11 September 2001

"Yes, we could well have a retaliatory war.[3] President Bush has warned that those governments which host terrorists will be held as responsible as the terrorists themselves. And Nato has invoked the mutual defense response of its treaty – for the first time in its history – by determining that the terrorist attacks on the United States constitute an attack on all of its member-states.

Retribution is coming and when it does it will be inflicted by a united alliance and it will be horrific. And it will be sustained. American spokesmen, notably Secretary of State Colin Powell, have made it clear that this will be a campaign not just against the

---

[3]This, my first written response to the events of that day, appeared in the *Sunday Independent* on 16 September. An extract from it featured on the front-page of that issue. What took place that day was so singular that I have thought to reprint my article as a Foreword in order to convey the awful immediacy of not just the American reaction but of public Ireland's response to our reaction. That of the government and of the Irish people was generous and heartfelt and gratifying; that of the media – the *Sunday Independent* and local radio stations apart – was soul-wearying. On 12 September, I appeared on Pat Kenny's radio program on RTE. He opined that the American public would be 'baying for blood' and he compared the actions of the terrorists on the previous day to the war in Vietnam and to the bombing of Dresden. Hardly for the first time, I wondered why I even bothered. But I did, and over the next few months I contributed the following articles to the *Sunday Independent*: 'We don't need lectures on morality, thank you,' 23 September 2001; 'The myth of European superiority,' 30 September 2001; 'The rules of war, not law, are needed to fight terror,' 14 October 2001; 'Fighting the war from the radio studio,' 11 November 2001; 'The war pundits who are wrong and won't admit it,' 25 November 2001; 'At last we're all speaking the same language,' 9 December 2001; and 'US must beware of 'friend' and foe,' 20 January 2002.

perpetrators of Tuesday's atrocities but against all global terrorism.

The first target has already been identified as it becomes increasingly evident that Osama bin Laden was, indeed, the key responsible figure. His objectives are irrelevant – destabilizing moderate pro-U.S. Arab governments, driving the U.S. military from Saudi Arabia, punishing the U.S. for backing Israel – it matters not at all what that deranged mind thought were the reasons for his actions. What he made happen quite simply constituted acts of war driven by an irrational hatred of America.

It's not that there isn't still hope that war can be averted. But doing so requires the unyielding support of America's friends, as well as its allies – support for actions which could well involve the use of terrible force, not against conventional armies but against already impoverished countries. It will be harsh. It could be horrifying. But this time there will be no space for public Ireland to play its usual role of self-righteous posturing and condemnatory moralizing, for what took place in America on Tuesday was truly an attack on us all, on civilized society itself.

Fortunately, judging by the response of Irish political leaders – which has been magnificent – and by the heartfelt reactions of the Irish people, there is no fear of this. Ireland is standing 'shoulder to shoulder' with the U.S.

And, then, we have the *Irish Times*. Its editorial response to the atrocities, together with the op-ed opinion piece by its resident moralizer Fintan O'Toole, equated the American people with the terrorists: 'So arrogant and merciless...as blindly passionate as the emotions that led yesterday's killers'. Implicit in both pieces were the judgment that we brought it all on ourselves and the prediction that our response will be as 'savage' as the actions of the terrorists. And, surely, once we have responded, Vincent

Browne will pen one of his condemnations of us for war atrocities.[4]

What, then, about Irish radio and television? From a news point-of-view they can hardly be faulted. Unfortunately, on the talk-shows, rather than uniform rationality, we have had the ubiquitous Robert Fisk, once again spewing out his smokescreen of skewed assertions and sanctimonious indignation – all to argue that it's all the fault of Israel and, thus, of the United States for 'bankrolling' that 'brutal' state. If I heard the exchange correctly, Alan Dershowitz, on Wednesday's Last Word talk-show, called Fisk a 'bigot' and an 'anti-Semite'. Whereupon, Eamon Dunphy pulled the plug on him, saying he would not have Fisk insulted on his program.

Let us be clear about this. The Irish media, in general, bears their share of the responsibility for what happened in the United States. For far too long in this country there has been a prevailing view which denigrates and condemns and even vilifies American foreign policy. Many of these venomous falsehoods – such as claims that hundreds of thousands of Iraqi civilians were killed in the Gulf War – have continued to spill out over Irish airwaves this last week. The hatred of America which drove the suicidal terrorists doesn't flourish in a global vacumn.

Any society which glorifies suicide as a heroic act is a sick society. America suffered at the hands of such people before in the kamikaze attacks of Japanese militarism. And, in the present-day case of the Palestinian Arabs, their society has been made what it is by decades of being lied to by their leaders who, instead of reasoned argument, preach hatred and murder – lying and hatred given sustenance by those, in our societies, who practice a

---

[4]Which he promptly did; 'Afghans the victims of US terrorism,' *Irish Times*, 17 October 2001.

tolerance for terrorism. 'Oh,' they'll cry, 'of course it's terrible what they did, it's absolutely unacceptable, but you have to consider the cause.' And, then, they call for 'understanding'. This is no more than a witless pandering to Arab irrationality and intransigence.

We understand all too well the true causes of the violence. The Palestinians, and the Arab world in general, have had more than a half-century to come to terms with the existence of the Jewish state of Israel. Instead, they have answered every Israeli offer of a negotiated peace with violence. No appeal to the alleged misery of their lives in 'refugee camps' or to their anguish can change the simple truth that their situation is of their own making – compounded by the cynical mendacity of the Arab governments which have perpetuated their refugee status as a weapon against Israel. The world is full of refugees, tens of millions since World War II – the others, most suffering far greater hardships than any the Palestinian Arabs have witnessed, get on with their lives. The sole difference in Palestine is that the Jews are involved.[5]

So, here in Ireland, what's to be done? A bit of truth would help. For starters, there could be some honest articles on such contentious Middle Eastern issues involving the U.S. as the effects of depleted uranium used in shells fired by the allies during the Gulf War or the impact of the UN sanctions on Iraq.[6]

---

[5]Nothing of what I have said in this paragraph is news, at least not to anyone who cares to be rational; see Martha Gellhorn's October 1961 article for the *Atlantic Monthly*, reprinted in *The View from the Ground* (London: Granta Books, 1989), pp. 197-244.

[6]Precisely such an article did soon appear in the *Irish Times*: Kevin Myers' 'An Irishman's Diary' of 18 September 2001. That was a Tuesday. The previous evening on RTE's 'Questions & Answers' current-affairs talk-show, I had accused sections of the media of having 'lied' to the Irish people over, specifically, the effect of the UN sanctions on Iraq. While I can hardly claim credit for having

Neither, after all, involves rocket science: unless the laws of physics change, 'depleted' uranium cannot cause cancer; and documents, publicly available from the United Nations, establish that the oil-for-food program generates more than sufficient revenue to cover all of Iraq's needs in the areas of food, medicine, and infra-structural repairs. The blame lies entirely with Saddam Hussein who has deliberately underspent the monies available to his government from this program − by up to 50 percent − in order to exploit the continuing misery of his people to con the gullible into supporting his demand for a lifting of the sanctions.

No, this isn't about a failure of American foreign policy. This is about hate-mongering. President McAleese, in her truly affecting unscripted response on television to the tragedy, nailed the cause of the atrocities beyond cavil by anyone rational − it was 'crazed hatred unchecked'. Now is not the time for vacuous moralizing about dialogue rather than retaliation. It is the time for all of us to exhibit the resolve to check the evil of terrorism by holding those who preach and practice hatred to account. This is as clear as what needs to be done. Osama bin Laden is target number one and, if the Taliban leadership continue to shelter him, they become the target.

---

prompted Myers' article it was immensely gratifying to see him use the same blunt word to describe what has long been going on: 'Nor does [political immaturity] explain the frequency with which we not merely tolerate lies about the US, but actually revel in them: such risible canards as that...US policies are causing Iraqi children to die of hunger.... Iraqi children die because [Saddam] is diverting money to his army...' Two days later, on 20 September, the *Irish Times* printed an op-ed article by John Pilger − which had previously appeared solely in an online magazine − 'Islamic peoples are already victims of US military and financial power: US fundamentalism is the root cause of the horror inflicted on Washington and New York,' in which he regurgitated the litany of loathsome falsehoods about American foreign policy which he has been peddling for years.

By all means, talk first. And then, if the terrorists are not surrendered, war."

Introduction

Myth-making and Missing the Point

What follows may be taken as the personal *cri de coeur* of someone who, for more than two decades, was a professional American diplomat.[7] Most of my service was in Western Europe; four of those years, 1988-1992, were spent in Dublin where I served as First Secretary for Political Affairs.[8]

---

[7]An earlier version of this essay was delivered, on 13 March 1995, to the National Committee for the Study of International Affairs of the Royal Irish Academy, in the Physics Theatre of Newman House, Dublin.

[8]If the reader prefers, 'Ireland' as the subject of my study rather than the physical place – could be taken as a state-of-mind, as characteristic of that sort of mind-set determined to misrepresent American policies and actions which is yet prevalent, in the West, among the professional intellectuals (here I mean the writers and artists and the professors of English literature or linguistics or environmental studies or whatever, who, not just intelligent but also highly educated and conditioned to an intellectual arrogance, presume themselves intuitively possessed of policy insights and operational judgments superior to those of us who have actually worked as foreign affairs professionals, and – it goes without saying – possessed as well of a sense of justice indisputably morally superior to the bureaucratically-deadened souls of us diplomats). Certainly, since I first wrote the judgmental observations, trenchantly critical of wilful Irish misperceptions of American foreign policy, which follow in this Introduction and the succeeding chapters, and even more so since the years that I served in Dublin in official status, there has come about a decided shift in Ireland in the public representation of our foreign policy towards a basically reasoned and, at times, even appreciative accounting of what we do and why we do it. For the most part, then, public Ireland has traded in the mind-set of the *Berkeley Barb* for that of the *New York Times*. Still, this study has more than just historical value. Insofar as public Ireland's view of America is no longer so truly *sui generis*, then a critical evaluation of its continued failings – a failure, for instance, of empathetic consideration of the real constraints under which the U.S. needs operate – can

When I arrived for my posting at the American embassy in Dublin in the summer of 1988, it was with a sense of anticipation akin to one of homecoming. This was not the normal feeling one has on arriving at a new post, but I was one of the tens of millions of Americans with Irish ancestry. In my own case, the ancestry was too many generations in the past for me to still have family in Ireland but there were the stories my grandmother had had from her mother and there were the Irish-born priests and nuns at school. I had also visited Ireland twice and had found the people every bit as welcoming as their reputation would have it. More pertinent to me as a career diplomat were the numerous friendly and highly-productive working relationships I had enjoyed with Irish diplomats over the previous decade, most of which I had spent dealing with the United Nations. Consequently, I was stunned – there is no other word for it – when, but a few weeks after my arrival, I was hit by the sudden realization that the prevailing attitude in Ireland towards American foreign policy was not the friendly understanding and support I had every right to expect but overtly-expressed contempt.[9]

It was so pervasive that it seemed to emanate from the very lay of the land – so much so that the general lack of any factual basis for the condemnatory assumptions made no difference. We were bullies. We did evil and sinister things. Pleasure was taken over our failures and supposed defeats. The only words spoken

---

serve as a more general analysis of why American foreign policy is so often unfairly abused. See also n. 17 below for 'America' and 'anti-Americanism'.

[9]One factor giving rise to the disparagement of American foreign policy (which I won't be considering except in passing) is European cultural condescension. Though it is the very seed-bed of reflexive contempt for all things American, it is too generalized a phenomenon to receive detailed treatment in a study dedicated to the Irish context; see my articles, 'Never judge a W. Bush by his cover,' *Sunday Independent*, 24 June 2001; and 'The myth of European superiority,' *Sunday Independent*, 30 September 2001.

about us in the Dáil seemed to be ones of condemnation.[10] Indeed, on virtually every issue in international relations, the common parlance in the Dáil, in the newspapers, on radio and television, at cocktail parties was one of accusations and judgmental observations which found us in the wrong, usually wilfully in the wrong. We even enjoyed the singular pleasure of a regular demonstration each Saturday morning.[11]

---

[10]An exception was Austin Deasy, TD (see, for an example of his common sense and decency, 'US Embassy welcomes remarks by Donlon...,' *Irish Times*, 23 November 1989).

[11]The extent of the reflexive distaste for the American diplomatic presence in Ireland is fittingly illustrated by the comic saga of the embassy railings. Once erected, they were uniformly received as greatly enhancing both the attractiveness of the embassy and of the neighborhood. And, given that their visually-handsome aspect was readily apparent in the architect's renderings, you would think our decision at long-last (the embassy was built in 1964) to erect them would have been welcomed. Rather, from before my arrival and lasting throughout my four years at the embassy, our plans were bitterly opposed by the neighborhood associations and were regularly sneered at – by politicians from all parties – as reflecting a 'Fortress America' mentality. See, as typical, Eamon Delaney *Accidental Diplomat* (Dublin, 2001), p. 48: 'The US Embassy...is a monument to paranoia and perceived conspiracies, with cement-heavy flower pots to deter suicide bombers and an unhealthy desire to find out the names and occupations of the surrounding neighbors'. Delaney is writing of the time, 1987-88, when he was serving as a junior diplomat in that section of Protocol in Iveagh House which dealt with foreign embassy matters. Presumably, then, his mocking attitude reflected that of his superiors. Delaney seems to be saying, in effect, 'How dare the Americans protest concerns regarding their security in loveable Ireland? Sure, who would ever harm them here?' Well, let us remind him that this is an island with several thousand political murders to its recent credit, including one ambassador; that the murderers of that ambassador, the IRA, enjoy wide-spread if largely tacit support within Ireland and received their armament, including explosives, from the Libyan regime; that the presence in great numbers of Libyan 'students' in Ireland – as Delaney himself puts it (p. 50), 'very flush with cash and surprisingly active on behalf of their home regime' – was an open scandal; and, finally, that whatever the justification for short-sightedness at the time of his service in Protocol, he had, when he came to write his book, the still-fresh

Most distressing was that, in all this, there was no possibility of rational debate. The condemnatory attitude seemed to spring from the sort of fundamentalist convictions which no one amenable to debate – that is, anyone who was both fair-minded and knowledgeable about the given situation – would ever espouse.[12] I began to wonder if I had, somehow, wandered into a country which had suffered an invasion of body-snatchers from a planet peopled by time-warped 1960s radicals and Marxist revisionist historians.[13] Over the succeeding months, as I read

---

example of the bombings of two American embassies in friendly and neutral East African countries, with the loss of hundreds of lives. Some paranoia!

[12]For example, twice within the first month of my stay in Ireland, I was told by Irish people of the professional class that Colonel Gaddafi had supplied the IRA with Semtex and armaments in response to our bombing of Tripoli in April 1986 because the British government had permitted us to use our air bases in the UK to launch our strikes – the accusation being that Irish people were being blown up by the IRA because of our action against Libya. However, even at that time, it was already public knowledge that French judicial interrogation of the skipper of the Eksund had revealed that Gaddafi had sent a number of shipments of weapons and explosives, totaling over 100 tons, to the IRA *prior* to April 1986 (there were at least four major shipments, beginning in August 1985; see now Jim Cusack 'Arms from Libya...,' *Irish Times*, 27 June 2000). The willingness to believe bad of us was not deterred by mere facts. Similarly, I learned that my counsellor-level contacts at the Foreign Ministry uniformly believed that it was not the Libyans who were responsible for bombing the La Belle discothèque in West Berlin (the final justification President Reagan cited for ordering the bombing of Tripoli) but the Syrians. Even when I supplied them with documentation demonstrating that this version, which had been pushed by Channel 4, was a simple-minded confusion with a separate bombing in Berlin (which had, indeed, been carried out by Syrian agents), they continued to prefer the version condemnatory of us. I am sure that, even today, long after the opening of the Stasi files revealed documentary evidence of the Libyans' guilt (see Denis Staunton 'Five on trial for 1986 bombing of Berlin night club,' *Irish Times*, 19 November 1997), Iveagh House continues to believe we were in the wrong.

[13]Indeed, in what in retrospect served, ironically, as a pre-conditioning to these alarming revelations in Ireland, I served the year before my posting to Dublin as a diplomat-in-residence at Reed College in Portland, Oregon – a small

through the files in my office, I learned that this anti-American attitude within the Irish political class was not something new. My predecessors, for a decade and more back, had regularly reported on the pervasive antagonism we faced and had periodically attempted to analyze the reasons for it. Much of what follows replicates their puzzlement. Much, also, derives from previous efforts of mine to come to grips with this phenomenon.[14]

Whenever I raise the issue, the initial response is inevitably, Why bother? Why is it of any significance to take an honest look at how American foreign policy is misrepresented in Ireland? I recall the occasion when Ambassador Richard Moore organized drinks at his residence to discuss precisely this question. The Irish guests were all what are known as opinion-makers – all well-known media figures. The guest of honor was an American political commentator who was also an old friend of the ambassador's. He began the discussion by citing the Irish newspaper he had bought when he had landed at Shannon that morning. It was the early days of the Gulf War, and the newspaper had been replete with articles harshly critical of the U.S. He explained how shocked he had been by the condemnatory tone of the articles and how dismayed he was by what seemed to him their wilful inaccuracy and their malign bias. He had, he pointed out, thought he was coming to visit a friendly Western country. The Irish guests refused, at first, to

---

liberal-arts college long renowned for encouraging free-spirits among its student body and faculty alike. There, as well, I encountered a prevailing attitude (which passed beyond the boundary of intolerance towards any opposing views) of condemnation of the American government and all its works. It seemed a campus preserved in a time-warp from my years as an undergraduate at Berkeley where, off and on, I had experienced my Sixties.

[14]My articles, 'Irish Attitudes towards USA Foreign Policy,' *Studies* 82 (Autumn 1993), pp. 265-75, and 'Curse of anti-Americanism,' *Sunday Independent*, 21 May 1995.

acknowledge that any problem existed. He convinced them. They then queried why we would care. Do you have to be loved by everyone? one asked.

In the normal course of foreign policy formulation, such distorted versions of events do not, after all, enter into consideration – they exist in a sort of parallel world where real events are intertwined with supposed events and all are artfully rearranged to satisfy the needs of some deviate agenda. In normative contrast, those who actually deal seriously with foreign policy deal in a real-world agenda. However, Ireland *is* a small country. A real danger exists of foreign policy formulation coming detached from reality simply through personal friendships or, more likely, through faulty operation of the mechanisms by which Iveagh House liaises with international non-governmental organizations, particularly on human rights issues. Some Irish NGOs, some of the national solidarity support groups, for instance, ought to be kept at arm's length – their 'facts' are, at best, ideological manipulations; indeed, more often, they are quite simply figments of a politically psychopathic imagination. On the other hand, there are NGOs, such as Amnesty International, whose integrity and expertise can be irreproachable. It is essential, however, to keep very much in mind – in the forefront of official consideration of their reports and submissions – the fact of their structural bias; such organizations have been created, precisely, to criticize governmental actions.[15] As such, the manner of their presentation of any given situation is that of a lawyer's brief.

Factually erroneous views, or views so judgmentally exaggerated as to lose contact with what governments actually

---

[15]In a private conversation, Mary Lawlor, then-director of Amnesty International in Ireland, told me that their objective was to 'shame' governments into doing better.

have the power to effect, if allowed to stand uncontested, will pollute at the very source. Why bother? Because it is a proper concern of the U.S. if such views pass on to infect the body politic of the European Union. More immediately pertinent to an Irish audience, irrational views produce irrational foreign policy – the entire process is systemically damaged. Neutrality, as enunciated by de Valera, was a pragmatic policy, employed for certain achievable and practical-minded aims. What damage was done, though, to the perceptive equipment of generations of Irish through the self-righteous elevation of neutrality to a Holy Grail? The days of cost-free posturing on foreign policy issues are gone; the luxury of weakness has no place in the new Ireland.

The term applied to the phenomenon I am concerned with is 'anti-Americanism,' and it can be defined as criticism, extending to condemnation, of the U.S. driven by a distorted or factually untrue representation of events. In the specific area of foreign policy, it manifests itself as a reflexive tendency – tending towards a determination – to brush aside both complexities and simple truths and to cast the United States as a sinister agent.[16] While I believe the definition is precise, I remain unhappy with the term, 'anti-Americanism'. [17] Its conceptual impact is too sweeping, too inclusive, and too transparently at odds with the natural good will that characterizes the relationships of

---

[16]See chapter 4 below.

[17]Similarly, as with 'Ireland' in n. 8 above, 'America' – rather than that specific country – may be taken as the elephant-in-the-room *du jour*, the hegemon of this current time; and, accordingly, 'anti-Americanism' may be seen for what it is in cognitive and psychological terms: the irrational rejection of the modern-day world and its complexities, usually in favor of some mythical pastoral past or some unrealizable utopian future. It is no coincidence that the Greens have surpassed both the Socialists in being the number-one denouncer of U.S. foreign policy and the Ulster Unionists in saying 'no' (in the Greens' case, to anything modern).

Americans and Irish both at official level and between our
peoples. No American comes to Ireland and feels otherwise than
at home. More vexing, the term is too overbearing – parading a
self-centeredness, as though the rest of the world must be judged
by the quality of their love for us.

Nevertheless, the realities of our global influence are
unavoidable. The United States is, at least residually, the global
honest broker, and, indeed, more often of first, rather than last,
resort. International problems we would well leave to the
ministrations of others have a way of landing back in our laps –
the long festering of the break-up of the former Yugoslavia was
perhaps the most prominent of the most recent cases-in-point.[18]
And, sadly, the incidence of unfounded, unwarranted criticism of
U.S. foreign policy is all too easily demonstrated in Ireland.
There is an acceptance, here, of truly calumniatory accusations
about the U.S. which, if made about Ireland, would provoke
instantaneous outrage. John Pilger, for instance, can appear on
RTE radio news and claim, 'There are signs...' note the phrasing,
'There are signs that the Western powers are building up the
Khmer Rouge'. If you wait for the anchorman to ask the obvious
question of what evidence Pilger has for such a sinister assertion,
you'll wait in vain. Rather, what you will, eventually, hear the
presenter saying is that it was, after all, the Americans who
'created' the Khmer Rouge and who 'nurtured' them after the
Vietnamese invasion of Cambodia. That this is factual nonsense

---

[18]Needless to say, unfortunately, the conventional reaction in public Ireland to
our successful interventions in both Bosnia and Kosovo was one of sneering
abuse; see my articles, 'It's time for some straight talking,' *Sunday Independent*,
11 April 1999; and 'The real lessons of Bosnia and Kosovo,' *Sunday Independent*,
28 November 1999.

which is believed nowhere else in the civilized world doesn't matter.[19]

To take but a few illustrative instances over recent years of such factually-perverted condemnations of the U.S.'s record: we can begin with how the 20th anniversary of the fall of Saigon (at the end of April 1975) was represented in the Irish media.[20] Nowhere – literally – was there any consideration given to what twenty years of Communist rule had meant to the people of South Vietnam. There was no mention of the summary executions following the completion of the Communist conquest of the south. No mention of the 're-education' camps. No mention of the expulsion of the ethnic Chinese. No mention of the pervasive corruption throughout all levels of the Communist government. No mention of the economic stagnation and the deprivation of basic civil and human rights. Indeed, many commentators in Ireland would have you believe that the terrible sufferings of the boat people had never happened. Rather, the whole focus was on the evacuation of the city which was characterized as the final withdrawal of American troops. Media articles, even television reviews, were peppered with phrases like 'undignified last scramble' and 'shameful withdrawal'. An *Irish Times* editorial, in particular, was unambiguous: 'the evacuation of the last troops from the embattled U.S. embassy...the ignominious withdrawal of

---

[19]It certainly has never mattered to Pilger; see my review, 'John Pilger's lonely world,' *Sunday Independent*, 11 October 1998. One can learn everything one could care to know about Pilger's reportorial and analytical 'method' of 'pious rant and egregious falsehood' in his article on the 'realities' behind the Nato intervention in Kosovo, 'US and UK embark on new imperial expansion,' *Irish Times*, 27 March 1999, and Kevin Myers' adroit dissection of it, 'An Irishman's Diary,' *Irish Times*, 31 March 1999. Nevertheless, RTE continues to regard Pilger with collegial esteem; he was invited, for instance, to participate in a 'debate' on the Vietnam War on 28 April 2000.

[20]See chapter 7 below.

American troops 20 years ago'. Excuse me. There were no U.S. troops in Vietnam when Saigon fell. The very last U.S. combat forces had been withdrawn a full two years before. Marines had to be helicoptered in from aircraft carriers to assist the embassy's Marine guards in the evacuation. Painting the fall of Saigon as Yanks fleeing before the conquering North Vietnamese is, on the surface, simply to indulge in a sort of residual infantile leftism. The deeper question is why no one in Ireland seemed to notice, or care, about the falsehoods.

The war in Vietnam was also instanced by Fintan O'Toole in a column dismissing the right of the U.S. 'to exercize some kind of moral authority in the matter of war crimes' in Bosnia.[21] He cites, justifiably, the lax judicial treatment of Lt. William Calley, the officer in field command of the U.S. soldiers who carried out the massacre at My Lai. But any serious discussion of Calley's trial would have also placed it within its historical context, specifically the nature of the war conducted by the Viet Minh as well as the political firestorm raging back in America which distorted all consideration of the behavior of U.S. troops in Vietnam; and surely any serious commentator would have had the elemental willingness to point out that what happened at My Lai was the *only* such mass atrocity committed by an American unit during the entire war. The truth is that any fair-minded consideration of the American military performance in Vietnam would find the same professionalism and honor and integrity that we have adhered to in all our wars; and any fair-minded commentator would also find the norm to be that American soldiers who did commit crimes in Vietnam, including rape and murder, were arrested, tried, convicted, and sentenced to

---

[21]'The West is ill-suited to dole out justice for war crimes,' *Irish Times*, 25 August 1995.

draconian prison terms (the U. S. Code of Military Justice makes no concession to civilian norms of leniency). In contrast, summary executions, torture, mutilations and rule by terror were standard operating policy for the Viet Minh. These are facts which seem not just to have escaped Mr. O'Toole's notice, but have largely escaped Irish notice.

I recall, for instance, meeting an Irish stockbroker who had spent his summer holidays in Vietnam and how surprised he was to have encountered genuine friendliness everywhere from the South Vietnamese. 'But they thought I was an American,' he explained. I assured him that his experience had been a common one. Anyone taken for an American on visits to South Vietnam will find themselves treated with affection. The South Vietnamese have no difficulty putting consequential events in historical perspective. They know all too well the realities of two-plus decades of Communist rule. They also remember that it was not the Americans who were the aggressors in the war.

Still, the Vietnam war was a long time ago (as human awareness goes), and what I have cited, though egregiously biased, is not unique to Irish perceptions.[22] What, then, about two

---

[22]Generally speaking, the Vietnam war is still perceived as a particularly brutal war. Even for the many who reject the self-righteous leftist claims that it constituted 'imperialist' behavior by the U.S. and who believe, rather, that we became involved in defense of the South Vietnamese for honorable and justifiable reasons, the sheer level of destruction our fire-power inflicted is held to have exceeded any good that we could have achieved – see Robert S. McNamara *In Retrospect* (New York, 1995), pp. xvi-xvii and 269-70; and Joe Lee, 'The Cold War and the reversal of fortune,' *Sunday Tribune*, 26 September 1999. However, few would contest the rightness of our fighting in Korea, particularly in light of the vibrant democracy and economy which South Korea today enjoys (for all its adjustment problems) as compared to the wholesale devastation playing out in the North. Odd (isn't it?) how judgmental perceptions change, for by most standards – particularly those of civilian casualties, restraints on conduct of the war, and sheer destruction of the country – the Korean War was far more brutally-fought than

more recent instances of what are widely considered to be U.S. foreign policy successes – the restoration of democracy in Haiti and the political settlement in Bosnia? On the first, Conor Cruise O'Brien writes off President Clinton's determination to restore President Aristide as wholly hypocritical and motivated solely by a desire to terminate the arrival of Haitian refugees in Florida for fear of its impact on the Democratic vote on election day 1996.[23] This is, superficially, simply a rather silly misreading of the American political scene. It mirrors the constant reiteration, in Ireland, that Clinton got involved in the Northern Ireland conflict in order to win Irish American votes (note: there has not been a significant Irish American ethnic voting-bloc for decades).[24] At that level, Dr O'Brien's judgment can be lightly dismissed as the sort of off-the-wall accusation believed in only by out-of-sorts academics whose 1960s-style radicalism remains unreconstructed by reality – a sort of cognitive dissonance fueled by intellectual petulance.[25] Certainly, the truth is otherwise. President Aristide

---

was Vietnam. (To provide just a few examples, in its three years, Korea produced some one million killed in battle of whom 70 percent were civilians and 54,246 American; in the nine years of the American involvement in Vietnam, the corresponding figures were 1.5 million of whom 28 percent were civilians and 58,151 American; see James T. Patterson *Grand Expectations*, New York, 1996, pp. 207-8 and 595-96. The total deaths attributable to war causes are unknown; the standard estimates are 3 million in each war.) For a cogent overview of the biased historiography of the Vietnam War, see Stephen J. Morris 'A winnable war?' *Times Literary Supplement*, 24 March 2000, pp. 4-6.

[23] *On the Eve of the Millennium* (New York, 1995), pp. 89-90 and 135-36.

[24] See chapter 6 below.

[25] Dr O'Brien has often directed wilfully-biased and mean-spirited slurs at American foreign policy and American diplomats. For a vintage example, see his *Memoir: My Life and Themes* (Dublin, 1998), pp. 175-77, where he castigates American diplomats at the UN in the mid-1950s as 'arm-twisters' whose tactics to ensure favorable votes included 'bribery or blackmail;' of course, Dr O'Brien is unable to provide any examples of such criminal behavior and all his own encounters with American diplomats would appear, on his own recounting, to

used to take his cue from such academics who attack American 'imperialism'.[26] But then he learned first-hand the benefits and positive intent of the U.S.'s benevolent hegemony, and like other regional democratic leaders, such as Oscar Arias and the late José Napoleón Duarte, he was grateful. The truth is that the only way to stem Haitian involuntary emigration is by assisting the Haitian government to build a country politically and economically fit to live in – which is what the democratic countries of the Western Hemisphere, led by the U.S., are attempting to do. Unfortunately, the democratically-elected Aristide proved himself to be a Mugabe, rather than a Mandela, opting to govern in the same vein of corruption, brutality and incompetence as his dictatorial predecessors across the two centuries of democracy Haitian-style.

Similarly, on Bosnia, Garret FitzGerald lays the blame for years of brutal Serbian use of force on the U.S.[27] He argues that,

---

have been civil and devoted to policy discussions. Perhaps Dr O'Brien's intellectual *amour-propre* is such that he is incapable of believing that anyone who resists or counters his arguments could possibly be prompted by anything other than sinister motivations – certainly, on pp. 180-84, he slurs the motivations of the Irish UN ambassador, charging that Ambassador Boland engaged in 'mindless servitude to the dictates of the United States' for the sake of obtaining the presidency of the General Assembly (O'Brien's contention that such honors were reserved for members of permanent missions is wilfully-ignorant hogwash). Professor Joe Lee, 'Independence of mind in the emerging world order,' *Sunday Tribune*, 11 March 2001, characterizes 'the intensity of [Conor Cruise O'Brien's] animosity towards his two departmental colleagues, F.H. Boland and Eamon Kennedy [as] making the [Irish] delegation sound for all the world like a university department in exile....'

[26]Cf., Joseph Dunn *No Vipers in the Vatican* (Dublin, 1996), pp. 143-63, where Fr Dunn managed both to repeat Aristide's pre-presidential accusation that the U.S. was training the Haitian military (we weren't) and to bring President Aristide back from his three years of exile without mentioning that it was the U.S. which forced through his restoration to power!

[27]'US foreign policy to benefit from Clinton's second term,' *Irish Times*, 9 November 1996.

'several years' back, a peace agreement had been reached
between the warring parties but that the Clinton administration
encouraged the Bosnian government to 'toughen its stand,'
resulting in renewed Serbian aggression. He remarks, 'foreign
policy founded on righteous indignation, that takes insufficient
account of realities on the ground, ends up doing more harm than
good.' Dr FitzGerald would be well advised to heed his own
advice. Anyone who believes that the Serbs ever intended to
adhere to any of the multitude of agreements, truces, or ceasefires
that were brokered is operating from the planet of wishful
thinking. The only way to stop Serbian aggression was to
confront it militarily,[28] and this could only be done successfully
after the Croatian and Bosnian governments created, armed and
trained armies capable of doing so (which they did with covert
American assistance). The Serbians lifted their siege of Sarajevo
and grudgingly observed the Dayton Accords only because their
forces had been beaten on the ground. Arguing otherwise is one
thing; accusing the U.S. of responsibility for thousands of brutal
murders due to its 'connivance' in the destabilizing of an agreed
peace 'achievement' takes a goodly measure of blinkered
wilfullness.[29]

---

[28]As Kofi Annan's own self-critical report on the experience of Bosnia
acknowledged: 'In the end, these Bosnian Serb war aims were ultimately repulsed
on the battlefield, and not at the negotiating table' (quoted from 'Annan accepts
the UN must carry blame...,' *Irish Times*, 7 December 1999).

[29]William Shawcross *Deliver Us From Evil* (London, 2000), pp. 71-74, makes
the same argument concerning American culpability. However, what both
Shawcross and FitzGerald do not even allude to (deliberately so?) is the crucial
question of enforcement. The Vance-Owen peace plan divided Bosnia into ten
cantonments, each constituting an ethnically-homogeneous enclave. How on earth
were the Muslim and Croatian cantonments to be defended, scattered as they were
amongst Serbian cantonments? As Shawcross acknowledges (*ibid.*, pp. 162-66),
the viciously-aggressive Bosnian Serb nationalism was only checked by armed
force (in particular, the Croat offensive made possible by covert American

Lest these be considered idiosyncratic judgments, I should note that I will be repeating, over the ensuing pages and chapters, further examples, sufficient to demonstrate that, rather than idiosyncratic, they are sadly typical. More tellingly, we will see that the perceptions underlying them have affected Irish official policy. I am not, of course, arguing that this sort of irrational or distorted judgment is unique to the Irish. Anti-Americanism is a general phenomenon of the left (as well as of the lunatic right), and there are Americans like Noam Chomsky whose sole approach to American foreign policy is one of vitriolic condemnation.[30] However, in the United States, such figures are wholly on the fringe. No one who is seriously engaged in international affairs takes them seriously. For the most part, they are simply ignored (except by counter-culture fanatics and immature university undergraduates). On the other hand, in countries such as the Netherlands, anti-Americanism is, indeed, to be found in mainstream politics (as I will illustrate, below, by an incident involving the Dutch Labor Party). However, it does not dominate the foreign policy debate in those countries. This is the operative difference. In Ireland, it has and, to a significant degree, still does dominate the debate.[31] During both Gulf Wars, for

---

training; *ibid.*, p. 155) and then contained by the minatory enforcement powers given to IFOR by the Dayton Accords. (See also my review of Shawcross' book, *Sunday Independent*, 4 June 2000).

[30]In Ireland, Chomsky is regularly referred to as a 'trenchant critic' of American foreign policy or as a 'noted dissident'. He is nothing of the sort, for critics and dissidents operate in the realm of logic; Chomsky is a fantasist. To say that, in regard to American politics, Chomsky is a dissident is to claim that, in regard to astro-physics, astrologers are dissidents.

[31]This was the finding of former ambassador to the U.S., Sean Donlon, in his highly-controversial address to the Ireland-United States Chamber of Commerce on 21 November 1989; this address was reported, partially, in the *Irish Times*, 'Clergy's 'anti-Americanism' attacked,' 22 November 1989. (I praised his

instance, you would encounter in the Irish media daily and voluminous instances of condemnatory comments and judgments concerning the U.S. Nothing was said in Ireland which was not said elsewhere but, particularly during the first Gulf War, anti-Americanism colored virtually all that was said,[32] and the effect, officially, was that the government which was supportive of the U.S. position wanted simply to keep its head down.

In general, of course, official U.S.-Irish relations are rarely less than highly cordial. For instance, some years back while Ireland held the presidency of the EU, then-Foreign Minister Dick Spring effectively put paid to a row, supposedly brewing between the EU and the U.S. over the Clinton administration's punitive air attacks on Saddam Hussein's military (in response to Hussein's renewed aggression in Kurdistan), by terming the attacks 'justified'. On the other hand, it can be noted that, during the first Gulf War, Spring's Irish Labour Party was the only serious socialist or social democratic political party in Europe to oppose the coalition effort. Similarly, Ireland was the only country in the civilized world which did not support the coalition in that war – the only assistance lent by Ireland was to allow U.S. military transports to transit Shannon airport (and, as then-Taoiseach Charles Haughey complacently announced to the Dáil, the U.S. planes transiting Shannon were paying 'full commercial rates'). At the time – as during the second Gulf War – Irish attention seemed pre-occupied with questions of Ireland's neutrality, as though there was a moral case to be make in support of Saddam Hussein's contention that Western 'imperialism' was behind it all. Surely, here was a case of Irish perceptions of U.S. foreign policy motives producing cognitive dissonance in public

remarks, as reported in the *Irish Times* on 23 November.) On this, see further in the Epilogue below.

[32]See chapter 5 below.

debate. Indeed, it took the American deputy chief of mission to point out, publicly, that Ireland was not neutral in the first Gulf War, having supported the UN resolutions condemning the Iraqi aggression.

More recently, Ireland changed its vote from abstention to approval of the resolution, annually introduced by Cuba in the UN, condemning the U.S. embargo. This followed on condemnation of the U.S. policy in 'hearings' in the Oireachtas foreign affairs committee. According to news reports, there was, in these hearings, no consideration expressed of the repressive nature of the Castro regime.[33] There was no recognition of Castro's atrocious record of support for subversion in the Western Hemisphere (such as his support for guerrillas seeking to oust the social democratic government of Rómulo Betancourt in Venezuela) or of his sending abroad of Cuban troops, as Soviet surrogates, to prop up such bestial regimes as that of Mengistu in Ethiopia. There was no acknowledgment of the continual stream of refugees risking death or punitive jail sentences to flee Castro's Cuba – some estimates placing the number of refugees, over the four-plus decades of Castro's rule, as high as a tenth of the population of the island. Nor was there consideration of the legitimate concern of the American government to compel democratization in Cuba, if for no other reason than that the vast majority of those Cuban refugees have settled in the United States. At the very least, one might have expected an acknowledgment that the nations of the Western Hemisphere are united in demanding such a democratization on the grounds that

---

[33]See my articles, 'Religious persecution in Castro's Cuba,' *Irish Catholic*, 22 August 1996; 'Ritual rage over US Cuba action,' *Sunday Independent*, 22 December 1996; 'The harsh realities of Castro's Cuba,' *Sunday Independent*, 9 January 2000; and my review, 'Che, man and myth,' *Sunday Independent*, 13 July 1997.

the establishment and continuance of democratic government in each of the countries of the region is the legitimate concern of all the countries of the region. But we heard nothing of all this in the Oireachtas hearings. Rather, from deputies from all parties, we heard an excoriation of the U.S. policy of embargo as 'immoral, illegal, and bullying'. This is not a reasoned perception of foreign policy.[34]

Throughout my career as an American diplomat, I was struck by this standard readiness to personalize U.S. foreign policy, to depict our policy as determined to punish enemies, to portray us as focusing on vengeful pettiness – an attitude wholly alien to my own experiences when involved in the formulation of U.S. foreign policy. Perhaps I can best illustrate the dissembling nature of this phenomenon by recounting one incident where I was directly cognizant of our internal deliberations. When I arrived in The Hague in the summer of 1985 as the American labor attaché,

---

[34]In general, Irish commentators seem incapable of dealing rationally with the U.S.-Cuban relationship during any period. For a typical example of this cognitive disability, David Shanks, ('Some reflections on a "splendid little war,"' *Irish Times*, 5 December 1998), characterized our liberation of Cuba in 1898: 'The US had taken up arms using the rhetoric of anti-colonialism in support of separatist Cuban freedom fighters.... (After the war, the Cubans were duly cheated in true frontier fashion)'. What fantasy is this guy on about? Two rebellions by the Cubans against Spanish colonial rule (1868-78 and again from 1895) had been brutally put down by the Spanish (in the first an estimated 200,000 were killed; in the second the Spanish pioneered the use of the concentration camp to deny civilian support to the rebels). We invaded and defeated the Spanish. For just under four years (July 1898 to May 1902), a U.S. military government, with Cubans occupying most of the official posts, oversaw normalization, effecting numerous reforms, particularly in education and public sanitation (for one example, yellow fever, long endemic on the island, was eradicated). After negotiating a constitution, Cubans convened the first independent Cuban government on 20 May 1902. Cf., Tom Humphries, 'Time for US to stop its bullying and let Cuba live,' *Irish Times*, 28 December 1999, and my reply, 'The harsh realities of Castro's Cuba,' *Sunday Independent*, 9 January 2000.

one prime concern of my embassy was to cultivate improved relations with the Dutch Labor Party. My part of this concern lay with the major Dutch labor union federation whose president had recently stepped down preparatory to becoming deputy leader of the Labor Party. His political future seemed ordained for success and, indeed, he later became the Dutch prime minister. I soon learned, from my working-level contacts, that there was a great deal of resentment within the party directed at the U.S. government. The reason for the resentment – indeed, for accusations of bad faith on our part – was that we had, supposedly, blocked the otherwise sure election of a senior figure in the Dutch Labor Party as UN High Commissioner for Refugees. The argument ran that we had done so out of a desire to 'get even' because of a conflict, a year or so previously, between our then-ambassador and this senior politician, who was then serving as his country's foreign minister, over the right of Dutch demonstrators to hold demonstrations in front of the American consulate general in Amsterdam, demonstrations which involved hanging the U.S. president in effigy. Though the demonstrations were eventually halted – after considerable antagonism – my Dutch colleagues insisted that we had neither forgiven nor forgotten.

It happens that, prior to being stationed in The Hague, I served for four years in the U.S. Mission in Geneva. Though not involved normally in refugee affairs, I was a member of a working-group tasked with making recommendations concerning the pending vacancy for the High Commissioner for Refugees. This working-group was set up a full year before the vacancy would occur and before anyone, including the Dutch diplomat in question, had declared an interest in the job. We recommended that, rather than another diplomat, what was needed was a senior official with demonstrated managerial skills; and we identified, as

a candidate, such a senior official in the Red Cross. The State
Department accepted our recommendations, they became U.S.
policy, and our recommended candidate was, in due time, elected
by the member-states as the new High Commissioner. The point
of this anecdote is not the wisdom of our choice, or the lack of it,
but that the candidacy of the Dutch candidate was not 'blocked'
by the U.S. It was, in truth, never even considered. We already
had a candidate. Frustratingly, I was never able to convince my
Dutch contacts of the groundlessness of their resentment. They
were simply certain that they 'knew' the truth. In truth, they were
indulging in all-too-standard myth-making about the motivations
of U.S. foreign policy – sophomorically personalizing its
formulation in the way we have seen Conor Cruise O'Brien and
Garret FitzGerald and the members of the Oireachtas foreign
affairs committee do.

I would argue that if foreign observers feel compelled to put
U.S. foreign policy on a personalized basis they would do far
better to look to the American character. The mainstream analysis
of American foreign policy has long been that it is driven by a
cyclical dynamic of realism versus idealism. For instance, Henry
Kissinger in the defining chapter of his book *Diplomacy*
contrasted Theodore Roosevelt's power politics with Woodrow
Wilson's moralism: 'Roosevelt...insisted on an international role
for America...because a global balance of power was
inconceivable to him without American participation. For
Wilson...America had an obligation, not to the balance of power,
but to spread its principles throughout the world'.[35] It would be
impossible to deny that some of those who have been in charge of
American foreign policy have, indeed, adhered to what they felt
was a hard-nosed policy of pursuit of American 'interests' (a

---

[35] *Diplomacy* (New York, 1994), pp. 29-30.

Realpolitik); Kissinger himself would be the prime example. The result, inevitably, has been a degradation of America's standing in the world.

Americans – contrary to the conventional wisdom of pundits that they neither know of nor care about international affairs – very much want their country to be seen to be doing the right thing abroad.[36] Using covert operatives to produce the conditions for a coup in Chile or to mine harbors in Nicaragua is not the 'right thing' in the eyes of the ordinary American. Standing firm, however, very much is. It has been common to support the conventional pundit's analysis of the supposedly cyclical dynamic of American foreign policy by contrasting the 'idealism' of Jimmy Carter's emphasis on the priority of human rights with the 'realism' of Ronald Reagan's hard-nosed confrontation with the Soviet Union, particularly in defense spending. This was not an operating concept shared by those of us who served as professional American diplomats at the time. Regardless of what the Carter or Reagan partisans might proclaim, we saw the two administrations, rather, as an essential continuum – a view shared by the ordinary American. For both the diplomat and the man-on-the-street, Carter and Reagan, in what they did, acted upon the basic premise of American foreign policy which is one of supporting democracy (a formative norm which Kissinger never

---

[36]By way of belated reply to the query of the Irish opinion-maker which I cited at the beginning of this piece – 'Do you have to be loved by everyone?' – the answer is, 'In all fairness, that is a small-minded, if not calculatedly mean-spirited, attempt to belittle our real concern which is the wholly legitimate desire that, when we are doing the right thing, our actions be acknowledged as such and that, on all occasions, our motivations be judged fairly. We are only being human in so desiring'. As an example , see Ronan Fanning *Sunday Independent*, 25 January 1998, p. 15.

grasped[37]). If Reagan sought to out-spend the Soviets on defense, Carter achieved a commitment from the NATO member-states of an annual 3% real growth in defense spending. If Carter put human rights at the top of the agenda, Reagan achieved a personal initiative in establishing the National Endowment for Democracy, providing seed money for democratic institution-building in the developing world.

The point here is that, occasionally, pundits ought to step back from their cleverness and look at human realities. Foreign policy is conducted by human beings. Producing clever models where human beings are reduced to factors or baselessly depicted as behaving irrationally simply obscures the truth, no matter how good the 'copy' might be. If analysts would truly look to the American character, they would find that 'idealism' and 'realism' are not mutually exclusive. Indeed, by operating on the differing levels of thought and action, they are mutually reinforcing. Idealism springs from basic assumptions about the nature of man and of society. Realism involves a recognition of necessity, of the tangible forces of power, of resources and arms. Throughout World War II, for instance, Franklin Roosevelt pursued a consistent anti-colonial stance in planning for the post-war world. This very much reflected the basic assumptions imbibed in an American upbringing. The realities of war, however, compelled him to cede 'space' (if that is not a gross understating of the outcome) on this issue to the British, the French, the Dutch, the Soviets. More recently, then-President George Bush, in the first Gulf War, said that America was not so much defending vital oil supplies as acting on the principle of resisting aggression; and, as he and other members of his administration repeatedly reminded

---

[37]See my review of the third volume of Kissinger's memoirs, *Sunday Independent*, 27 June 1999.

us, the simple and self-evident truth, in this instance, was that the 'aggression' involved was the seizure of control of the vast oil resources of the Persian Gulf, which if let stand would make possible, indeed near certain, further aggression. Defeat of aggression equalled defense of oil; defense of a principle equalled defense of a key national interest. Idealism and realism.

The question I want to address now is why – why the readiness of so many in Ireland to ignore facts and condemn the U.S. and why the acceptance by so many more of such unjustifiable and usually malign accusations. I intend doing so by surveying the mental geography of present-day Ireland – or, at least, that part of it attuned to interest in international affairs. This is a treacherous essay. It is all too easy to fall into the sort of facile generalization about national psyches which I find so odious in others essaying an explanation of why we Americans do what we do. Still, my job, and my conditioning, as a professional diplomat for all those years was to so wholly enter into the essence of a foreign culture as to understand why things were done the way they were, to understand what could be done and what couldn't be done, and to write of my insights so that officials of my government who knew little of the country would understand why it behaved as it did. You may find me over-sensitive in the way anyone with a single focus might be. My observations may prove as transient as the weather. Still, my observations are of real, not imagined, happenings; and, at the end of the day, the weatherman does not invent the weather. I will begin my look at the motivations, and causes, of Irish anti-Americanism with some which are obvious, though ephemeral and not at all uniquely Irish; I will then turn to those which are lasting and truly Irish because they spring from enduring myths of national self-identity. Even the least reaction carries some cognitive ballast. But I intend my exposition to reflect a template where some reactions arise from passing grooves, others from the cut pattern.

The Irish are fond, rather too fond perhaps, of citing begrudgery as their national vice.[38] It can be a source of biting wit; it can also be a structural impediment to conditions becoming better than just passable. When we Americans encounter it, it takes two forms – spite and resentment. Spite in the simple sense is, I would argue, the single, most active energizer of anti-American protests in Ireland. This manifests itself as the need to, somehow, find fault. It can never be, for instance, that there are some problems for which there is no solution which can be imposed from the outside. And, when it comes to the U.S., it can never be that the Americans are unable to solve a problem; it 'must be' that we don't want to. Or, it can be spite of the damned-if-you-do, damned-if-you-don't variety – 'It's a dreadful situation, and you're guilty because you intervened in other peoples' business; and, if you didn't, you're guilty because you should have done something about it'. Perhaps the classic Irish example of this came during a debate in the Dáil on the first Gulf War when the then-spokesman on foreign affairs for the Labour Party, in the first half of his lengthy intervention, condemned the West led by the U.S. for intervening in a regional conflict and, in the second half of the intervention, condemned us all for not having imposed democracy on the countries of the region. In this sense, a good deal of Irish criticism of the American role in Europe would be motivated by spite: the malicious depiction of our every action, our every initiative – whether it's the Marshall Plan or the agreement with the then-Soviet Union which removed all intermediate-range nuclear missiles from Europe or our negotiating a resolution of the Bosnian war – as driven solely by

---

[38]See J.J. Lee *Ireland 1912-1985* (Cambridge, 1989), pp. 645-48.

self-interest.[39] Clearly, it does take an extraordinarily spiteful casuistry to so twist that agreement (by which the terrifyingly-destabilizing presence of SS-20s and Cruise missiles was eliminated) into a simple desire on our part to dominate Europe, and yet I have listened to a lecture by an Irish politician doing precisely that. That particular politician later became a minister.

Nevertheless, I would consider true spite as uncharacteristic of the generous Irish character. Rather, it is, in the political sense which is the proper subject of this study, the agitation of the ideologically bent – those whose cognitive equipment is in functional disorder. These can be readily identified by their argumentative methodology of distortion and evasion and condescending sneering. They will argue, for instance, that the allied bombing in Afghanistan resulted in a 'slaughter of the innocent,' relying on bogus exaggerations of civilian casualty figures, while they ignore the documented barbarities of the Taliban regime. They will distort the death-toll of the allied airstrikes on the retreating Iraqi army on the road from Kuwait City to Basra into tens of thousands, while claiming that this army column was simply ordinary Iraqis 'trying to get home'. This malign bias against the West in general and America in particular is so marked by a contemptuous disregard for simple common sense that one reaches for psychological explanations. Certainly, such fantasies derive not from rational thought but from irrational emotions, emotions that lead to claims that the greatest terrorist force in history has been, and remains, America. However, while I could name one or two Irishmen answering to this description – a certain maritime historian, for instance, or a wannabe Marxist revolutionary from Derry – these are just cranks

---

[39]Of course, confusing process with intent is hardly unique to Irish commentators; see my article 'Even friends must talk out difficulties,' (Portland) *Oregonian*, 7 March 1988.

who write letters to The *Irish Times*. They don't rate in the ranks of Irish punditry; they wield no influence. Ireland cannot boast (or despair) of the lunacy of a homegrown Noam Chomsky.

Resentment, on the other hand, affects even the sane. 'Bullying' – believe it or not – is the accusation which crops up handily whenever the U.S. runs foul of a core Irish national interest. Witness, for instance, the Irish minister of commerce and industry – otherwise justly known for his measured political judgment and his courage in standing against tribal shibboleths – who twice accused us of 'bullying' when we were but fighting our corner over the agricultural reform measures of the Uruguay Round.[40] It may be that resentment is more prevalent here in Ireland than elsewhere; Ireland *is* a small country. Any of us who are younger brothers will recognize the naturalness of the reaction. Outbursts of Irish resentment of the U.S. in particular are also natural. Overall, the relationship of the U.S. and Ireland is generosity heavily weighted in Ireland's favor, but unreasonable resentment is inherent in families.

After begrudgery, the second leading source of anti-Americanism in Ireland, pervasively present in the lay of the land, is misinformation. The classic example here would be U.S. foreign policy in Central America,[41] though this is a dispute largely now in the past (but raised by Garret FitzGerald in that article concerning the U.S. role in Bosnia which I cited in the text above – he actually managed to recall the European condemnation of the use of military force in that region without

---

[40]See both chapter 3 below and the Epilogue.

[41]For a prime example of wilful distortion of both facts and logic in this area, see Sean Cronin 'Clinton dithers on new policy for Central America,' *Irish Times*, 1 April 1995 (and my reply, 'US Central American policy widely misunderstood,' *Irish Times*, 15 April 1995).

once even alluding to what the Soviets were up to there).[42] In truth, our policy in Central America has consistently been straightforward: to restrain repression, whether from the right or the left, and to nurture democracy. The means we have sometimes employed have been tortuous, but not incommensurate with the tortured history of most of the countries of the region. Democracy, after all, had seldom been more than an aspiration in Latin American political culture.[43] Inequalities remain deeply embedded. These realities – of both the indigenous conditions and of our policy – were widely recognized elsewhere (in particular, as I noted above, by the democratic leaders of the region). But not in Ireland. Here, our policy was simply represented as support for right-wing governments repressive of their peoples.

I would argue that the culprit behind this vicious misrepresentation was (and remains) misinformation. One layer, the supporting bedrock so to speak, was a certain historical ignorance – by this I do not mean ignorance of the facts of history but the ignoring of history's relevance. Citing instances of American behavior in the Caribbean or Central America before

---

[42]In a separate article ('Ireland should not remain in post-Cold War isolation,' *Irish Times*, 23 November 1996), Dr FitzGerald wonders how it came to pass that, on the question of joining the Partnership for Peace, Ireland could find itself isolated with only Tajikestan among all the countries of northern Eurasia also refusing to join: the 'fact is that this is a completely self-inflicted wound, a product of a crazy brand of Irish neutralism....' The remainder of the article is a detailed review of the many positive joint exercises and cooperative ventures (such as IFOR) conducted by the PFP consequent upon 'US initiatives'. He laments that Ireland is 'spurning this chance to play our part in what is self-evidently the greatest peace-creating initiative the world has known'. But, given Dr FitzGerald's own condemnatory track-record, is it any wonder that the Irish public has been so badly misled on the motivations of U.S. foreign policy?

[43]See chapter 2 below; and my review, 'Dictatorship runs in their blood,' *Sunday Independent*, 30 July 2000.

World War II or during the early years of the Cold War is irrelevant to today. What was acceptable Great Power behavior – indeed, the internationally-mandated norm of behavior – is not just unacceptable in today's post-colonial world, it is literally unimaginable. It enters into no calculation in today's State Department or Pentagon or White House. For instance, President McKinley in 1898 decided that the United States would have to take possession of the Philippines out of a sense of responsibility. Having shattered Spanish power there, our departure would have left the islands the subject of a struggle between England and Germany over their possession.[44] But, while motivated by this American consideration, McKinley could only have given his belief the effect he did in a time when such behavior was the norm for a Great Power – in a time when wars of conquest were, as they had been throughout mankind's historical existence, commonplace and legitimate, and colonialism was considered desirable. In today's world, President Clinton, even with the blessings of the world community, resisted for two years, in the face of continuous accusations of vacillation and weakness, the sending of an occupying force to restore democracy in Haiti. Times change. While motivations may remain constant, the contextual reality in which they are interpreted and implemented evolves. Idealism and realism.

Similarly with Cold War-induced behavior. The CIA-involvement in the overthrow of Arbenz in Guatemala in 1954, for instance, took place, and could only have taken place, in the conflict-spawned atmosphere of the Cold War, within that first post-war decade which, among other brutal events, had witnessed the extension of Communist rule over country after country, the

---

[44]And, eventually, the Japanese as well; see George F. Kennan *American Diplomacy* (Expanded ed., Chicago, 1984), pp. 16-17.

bloody repression of worker revolts in East Germany and Poland, the attempted strangling of West Berlin, and the bitter war in Korea.[45] It is a fundamental error of historical understanding to indifferently transpose events from one era to another distinct in accepted understanding of obligatory international behavior. Levels of enlightenment do change. Today, for instance, states have obligations towards each other concerning the environment and human rights (to cite but two areas) which would have been inconceivable in 1954. Indeed, the countries of the Western Hemisphere have now added to their own regional agenda of inter-state concern the new item of governmental corruption, as *the* obstacle to social justice. Before meaningful and useful judgments can be drawn, consequential events must be placed in a historical perspective.

More directly pertinent to the Irish perception of our policy in Central America, however, was a more immediate level of misinformation – the depiction of American embassies in the region as engaged in sinister support of right-wing forces. Having spent two years, at the end of my professional career, at the American embassy in Venezuela, I must say that when I encounter this sort of characterization of U.S. policy I feel as though I am looking into one of those distorting mirrors you find in amusement parks – the elements of reality are there but the reflection does not represent reality. Perhaps a better analogy could be drawn from the favorite science fiction reading of my sons when they were teenagers. Sci-fi stories frequently feature parallel worlds – a world of artfully rearranged reality existing parallel to the real world, into which persons could step when reality was too much to bear, or perhaps simply too mundane. In

---

[45]See my review, 'The century that killed the Utopian dream,' *Sunday Independent*, 27 February 2000.

the world of American foreign policy where reasons for decisions are normally mundane, a parallel world of sinister dimensions has often been evoked. It is a world where our foreign policy is defined by the overthrow of Mossadegh in Iran and Arbenz in Guatemala.[46] Where it is accepted that we 'pushed' Castro into the arms of the Soviets. Where our involvement in Vietnam was quite simply 'imperialistic'. The reality is different.

My first posting in the U.S. Foreign Service was Madrid where I arrived a little over a year before Franco died.[47] At the time of his death, I was the junior officer in the embassy's political section. Both before Franco's death and for the ten months or so that I remained in Madrid after his death, I participated in numerous internal embassy discussions concerning our role in post-Franco Spain. The sole focus of these discussions was how best we could support, and protect, a democratization process in Spain. That democratization was the only acceptable

---

[46]Both of these cases – fixtures in the cosmology of self-righteous leftists – are, in fact, classic examples of historiographical irony: acclaimed on the one-hand by conservatives as CIA victories and seized on on the other by liberals as proof-positive of the sinister nature of American foreign policy, they are neither. Rather, they constitute clinical examples of the institutional mendacity of the CIA. In Iran in 1953, Mossadegh was overthrown in the same fashion as the Shah several decades later; quite simply, he lacked the support in the military necessary to withstand the massive street demonstrations against his regime (the Iranian high-command being particularly horrified by Mossadegh's tactics of playing footsie with the Soviet Union in his dispute with the British over the Anglo-Iranian Oil Company). The claim by the CIA operative, Kermit Roosevelt, to have orchestrated it all was never more than a manifestly absurd case of braggadocio (see Barry Rubin *Paved with Good Intentions: The American Experience and Iran*, Oxford, 1980, pp. 54-90, particularly 88-89). Similarly, in Guatemala in 1954, Arbenz fell victim to the sort of power-struggle among fellow military officers which has plagued Latin American political history. The taking-of-credit for the coup by the CIA was bald-faced lying to Eisenhower (see Theodore Draper 'Is the CIA necessary?' *New York Review of Books* 44/13, 1997, pp. 18ff.).

[47]See chapter 1 below.

future for Spain was a given, though it was by no means a foregone conclusion that democratization would succeed or that it would even be embarked upon. The generals still held the high ground on the political landscape. As I say, I was the junior officer present in these intra-embassy discussions. The other embassy officers involved, up to the ambassador, had, by that time, already served 15 or 20 or more years in our diplomatic service. Most of them had served extensively in Latin America. Where, I could have asked myself, had all this supposedly reflexive American support for right-wing dictators gone? But that would have been a question out of the parallel world – a parallel world where, uniquely, the United States is depicted as the all-powerful determinant of events and where the real world of a particular country's own history, its own political and cultural and economic and social inheritance, is submerged to the point of being ignored.[48]

Another, and wholly fraternal, phenomenon from the parallel world is the perverse transformation of attempts by us to rectify abuses into responsibility for the abuses themselves. Some such transformations are simply bizarre, such as the standard supporting accusation, in positing our 'responsibility' for the antagonism between the U.S. and Castro's Cuba, that the Mafia controlled gambling and prostitution in Havana before Castro took power – an accusation levelled as though the Mafia were a department of the U.S. Federal Government, rather than an international criminal organization which we, and many other countries, have been attempting to eradicate for decades. A more integral example of this phenomenon would derive from our

---

[48]Cf., John Lewis Gaddis *Strategies of Containment* (New York, 1982), pp. 337-39; and my articles, 'When in doubt, blame the Americans,' *Sunday Independent*, 22 November 1998; and 'Pinochet: the battle of justice versus democracy,' *Sunday Independent*, 28 March 1999.

relationship with the military in many Latin American countries. Our attempts, through training, to enhance professionalism, ethical behavior, and respect for democracy in these military forces, are portrayed as responsibility for the death squads and for atrocities such as the massacre of the inhabitants of a village carried out by an American-trained battalion in El Salvador (Fintan O'Toole has just such a weasel-worded accusation in the article I cited above). One particular target has long been the U.S. Army's School of the Americas, which provides courses, particularly at the field staff level, for Latin American military officers. Periodically, there have been attempts by U.S. congressmen to abolish this school which they dub the 'School of Dictators'. Typically, in any newspaper article dealing with this issue, there will be a graphic showing a half-dozen or so Latin American military officers who had attended the School of the Americas, or another U.S. military course, and returned to their countries to become military strongmen. A more meaningful graphic would depict the hundreds, indeed thousands, of Latin American military officers who returned home from U.S. military training to perform with high professionalism and full support for democracy – precisely what occurred during the two military coup attempts in Venezuela in 1992. These were the first such attempts since the restoration of democracy in Venezuela in 1958. In both – and both involved bloody street-fighting – dozens of Venezuelan military officers who had attended U.S. military schools at some time in their careers fought, successfully, to put down the coups and to defend their democratic government (and this despite a widespread approbation by the Venezuelan public of the objectives of those who had attempted the coups).[49]

---

[49]See chapter 2 below.

The obvious point I am making is that we must look beyond the individuals and the aberrations and seek the patterns if we are seriously seeking to characterize any policy, particularly its motivations. This is in addition to maintaining a historical perspective. Those who characterize U.S. foreign policy by citing a litany of aberrations — particularly if this is a litany of supposed CIA operations — are simply missing the point. The CIA is not and never has been central to the formulation or implementation of U.S. foreign policy. In real world terms, it constitutes, far too often, a structural aberration. In 1996, for instance, the State Department, prompted by the U.S. Congress, uncovered an attempt by CIA officers to cover up for contacts (snitches) of theirs in Guatemala (one was a Guatemalan colonel) who were implicated in murder and who the CIA officers concerned knew were so implicated. In covering up, the CIA officers lied to the American ambassador and to Congressional investigators. Once the facts were uncovered, the CIA officers involved were disciplined; the two most senior were fired. In terms of U.S. policy towards Guatemala, then, there is no other way to fairly describe this CIA activity than as an aberration. In all fairness, a real world observer, in seeking a paradigm for our policy in that country, would look, rather, towards our reaction, in the spring of 1993, to the attempt by the general then serving as president to dissolve parliament in an auto-coup similar to that which President Fujimori had pulled off in Peru some years previously. Hemispheric reaction was immediate. The Organization of American States, with the U.S. in the lead, issued denunciations and convoked a ministerial to coordinate a response. Within days, the general had backed down. He withdrew his tanks from around the parliament building, and he was himself removed from office. Democratic institutions were restored. This is the perspective — of a hemisphere-wide consensus on democracy — from which to

view U.S. policy in the region; it is the perspective common to all
the professionals seriously engaged in the region, whether
diplomats, government officials, aid workers, journalists, or
academics.

But it was not the way American policy there was viewed in
Ireland. No one in Ireland would have ever credited the U.S. with
support for democracy anywhere in Latin America. Why? For the
answer we must look to the source of the received view in
Ireland: the Catholic religious who worked in the region, the
missionary priests, nuns, and brothers – a phenomenon noted by
many neutral observers. These are people whose dedication is
unquestionable, and yet their depiction of what we were doing
was flatly false.[50] This is troubling. I must say that I am

---

[50]The standard-bearer for this paradoxical mixture of sincerity and culpable
naiveté could be the late Fr Joe Dunn whose Radharc/RTE documentaries were so
influential in establishing, in Ireland, the received view of American foreign
policy, particularly in Central America. In his book, *No Lions in the Hierarchy*
(Dublin, 1994), which was derived from his experiences in making some '350
films in 75 countries,' he characterizes the U.S. (p. 171) as 'consistently' opposing
by whatever means necessary 'social revolution' throughout the world, with
emphasis on Central America. Why did he believe this? According to his own
words (p. 92), it was because 'pretty well all the religious I ever met in Central
America were unsympathetic, to say the least, to US/papal policy' – he had earlier
linked Pope John Paul II and the U.S. as being 'on the side of reaction'. In the first
instance, this is an unfortunately all-too-typical example of the naive, basically-
romanticized view of 'revolution' and what it meant in the twentieth century held
by radicalized religious. In truth, his unthinking equation of Marxism with
'reform' is as intellectually disingenuous as his blithe dismissal of the pope's
moral rejection of Marxism (born, let us remember, out of lived experience) as no
more than an 'antipathy' is disreputable. In the second instance, and more
pertinent to my concerns, there was the altogether dubious basis of his judgmental
characterizations of U.S. foreign policy: talking with the same sort of
ideologically-blinkered religious as he mixed with at home. He evidences no
contact whatsoever, at any time in his career, with U.S. officials or aid workers or
labor unionists or any other Americans striving to assist in the development of

intimidated by the need to offer an explanation. What we see, up front, is their commitment, their palpable concern to rectify abuses and to allay human suffering. What we often neglect, I would suggest, are the cognitive patterns within which their compassion seeks solutions. The long years of their training are passed within an authoritarian environment, and their education is framed by theological certitudes, a sort of pseudo – or quasi-scientific framework for all else. I do not mean, by this, to in any way contemn religious truth; I note only that such truth, however elegant or persuasive the reasoning, is not susceptible of empirical proof. Such an education predisposes one to solutions deriving from infallible authority; it does not necessarily condition one to appreciate the compromises and hard slog of fallible democracy.[51]

When I was the political officer at the American embassy in Dublin, I wrote, on the occasion of a new Irish foreign minister taking office consequent on the elections in the summer of 1989, an overview of Irish foreign policy, aimed at informing my government of what we could expect. One structural problem we identified was the small circle of those who actually had a hand in formulating Irish foreign policy. Very much on the plus side was the exceptionally high quality of Irish diplomats. On the down side, I argued, was the almost complete lack of fora for informed public debate. There was not, then, even a parliamentary foreign affairs committee, much less any Irish equivalent of the numerous world affairs councils to be found in cities throughout the United States. As a career diplomat, I must confess to a certain

---

just, prosperous and democratic societies; and yet he felt qualified to judge (and condemn) us.

[51]Cf. the similar observations by Tom Garvin *1922: The Birth of Irish Democracy* (Dublin, 1996), pp. 34-35; and my article 'Is the Church out-of-step with the real World?' *Irish Catholic*, 20 August 1998.

empathetic envy of my Irish colleagues' absence of any obligation to appear before a legislative committee. Still, public pressure, uninformed by reasoned debate, can be pernicious. In this connection, I recall Hubert Butler's account of his attendance in Dublin in the early 1950s at a meeting of a then-existing Foreign Affairs Association, at a time when he was concerned to make publicly known the truth about the wartime Croatian government repression and attempted forced conversion of Jews and Orthodox Serbs. He was effectively silenced by the Catholic orthodoxy of that time.[52] For some time, now, the neo-orthodoxy of Latin American Catholicism has been to make the sort of common cause with Marxists in characterizing U.S. foreign policy that I have described above.[53] More than one scholar has termed Marxism a Christian heresy, with its own infallible interpretation of history and its own foreordained redemption,[54] and its powers of attraction have certainly been apparent, from the worker-priests in France on to *Sandinismo* in Nicaragua. I will leave it to others to offer what explanations they can for this perverse phenomenon; I will only note here the obvious that, while overt devotion to Marxist tenets is hardly a normative factor in Irish public life, there are many operating assumptions, Marxist in origin, which pass unremarked in Irish public discourse.[55]

---

[52]See Hubert Butler *The Sub-Prefect Should Have Held His Tongue and Other Essays* ed. R.F. Foster (London, 1990), pp. 271-82, esp. 273-74.

[53]See my article, 'Liberation theology's false gods,' *Irish Catholic*, 12 October 2000.

[54]For example, Reinhold Niebuhr *Moral Man and Immoral Society* (New York, 1932), pp. 155-56 (one of the few sensible observations or assertions in this seriously hare-brained book). See also Thomas Merton *The Springs of Contemplation* (New York, 1992), pp. 84-85.

[55]Marxism, in all its insidious manifestations, is a second factor conducive to a reflexive anti-Americanism which I won't be considering except in passing,

I turn now to my final two suggested motivations of anti-Americanism in Ireland – self-justification and realistic self-awareness – both, I would argue, deriving from Irish myths of national self-identity. By 'myths,' I do not necessarily mean something untrue. National myths are the stories or beliefs by which we express, most meaningfully, the ideals by which we live our national lives; they are the manifestation of a nation's consciousness.[56] In Tudor-Stuart England, for instance, legal antiquarians developed the Anglo-Saxon myth of a primitive Germanic democracy, born deep in the continental forests and transplanted to their island-nation. This was no bad thing. Though not historically valid, the myth empowered the long evolution of constitutional rule in England.[57]

In Ireland, self-justification as a motivating force in foreign affairs arises from the complex of national myths encapsulated in what is called 'neutrality'. Scholars can point out that independent Ireland has never truly been neutral because it has never met the international legal definitions of neutrality, as

---

since, like European cultural condescension (see n. 9 above), it is too generalized a phenomenon on the anti-American scene to be particularly illuminating about Irish responses. As elsewhere, what passes for its philosophy determines the positions of those in Ireland formally on the Left and its corruption of modern-day political discourse – e.g., treating Socialism as naturally occupying the moral high-ground – frames the general political/economic debate in Ireland almost without challenge. For instance, not even those Irish politicians dedicated to fiscal conservatism dare confront directly the operating contention that domestic economic progress depends on 'closing the equality gap'.

[56]Cf., T.W. Moody 'Irish History and Irish Mythology,' *Interpreting Irish History* ed. Ciaran Brady (Dublin, 1994), pp. 71-86 (see also the characterization of Moody's stance by the editor, pp. 7-8).

[57]Indeed, this myth of the Saxon origin of English liberties and, specifically, of the state as founded on the rights of man, by resonating in the mind of Thomas Jefferson, found echo in the American Declaration of Independence; see Jefferson's letter of 25 October 1825.

Sweden or Switzerland has – even in World War II, Ireland was not a neutral, but, rather, a non-belligerent. It can readily be acknowledged that, during the Cold War, Ireland was, as Taoiseach after Taoiseach pointed out, not ideologically neutral. Still, the myths persist.[58] During the first Gulf War, as I pointed out above, it took the deputy chief of mission at the American embassy to point out publicly that Ireland was not neutral since it had accepted the UN resolutions on that war. Pretending that abstention would be somehow nobler was not so much self-justification as self-deception. Humbuggery is not statesmanship. I don't want to belabor the self-justificatory aspects of this supposed neutrality. Irish neutrality is a subject for debate by the Irish themselves. I will just note, finally, that high-mindedness is as useful in international crises as wishful thinking.[59]

---

[58]Never more so than during the run-up to the second referendum on the Nice Treaty in the fall of 2002, when, in order to secure the needed result, the Fianna Fail/Progressive Democrat government engaged in po-faced pandering to 'neutrality' as a core Irish value. Still, there is hope; see Brenda Power 'There's no such thing as neutrality,' *Sunday Tribune*, 20 October 2002; and David Quinn 'The shame of neutrality in the war against terrorism,' *Sunday Times*, 20 October 2002.

[59]The most pervasive manifestation of this high-minded self-justificatory tendency takes the form of blaming the U.S. for whatever particular international problem is under discussion or ridiculing U.S. efforts to remedy the problem as hopelessly (or hypocritically) inadequate in order to magnify the role 'little Ireland' can play. Irish relief agencies have long relied on this technique to provoke contributions, saying in effect: 'We have to shoulder the burden because those evil (or ignorant or indifferent or cruel) Americans won't and, besides, they caused all the problems to start with'. Two articles which appeared in the *Irish Times* on the same day (26 January 2002) well illustrate this approach: Paul Cullen 'US takes eyes off AIDS to concentrate on the war,' and Tom O'Dea 'An Irishman's Diary'. The title given to the first accurately reflects the article's central judgment as given in its conclusion: 'Yet it may take the end of the war in Afghanistan for the US to address its responsibilities elsewhere in the world.' However, nowhere in the article, between the title and the final sentence, is there

any mention whatsoever of the specifics of what the U.S. is doing, or failing to do, in the international battle against AIDS; rather, we read, 'Happily, in Ireland, UNAIDS is pushing an open door.... Ireland...distinguishes itself by having a thought-out strategy to support HIV/AIDS programmes in badly affected countries'. Selfish America, plucky little Ireland. Similarly, O'Dea, writing on the flood-tide of judicial and parliamentary inquiries into corruption in virtually every sphere of Irish public life, seeks to seize the moral high ground by claiming that 'our parliamentary committees could teach an ethical thing or two to Congressional committees in the US....' His case-in-point? Arthur Miller's treatment by the House Un-American Activities Committee (the best part of a half-century ago!!). His account, which takes up the bulk of his article, is riven throughout with factual errors, including invoking the poisonous legacy of Senator Joe McCarthy (Senators do *not* run House committees) and claiming that Miller was 'liable to a year in prison' (This is not true. His actual sentence for contempt was a 30-day suspended sentence). But, then, O'Dea's version of what took place in America at that time never rises above the commonplaces of the wilfully wooly-headed Left. Indeed, the consensus today is that the hearings by the HUAC and similar measures did more damage to civil liberties than could possibly be justified by eliminating Communist Party subversive activities on behalf of the Soviet Union. But such subversion did take place. And Miller was hauled before the HUAC to be named and shamed because, by lending his prestigious name to myriad Communist Party and Communist-front events, he had greatly assisted their fund-raising (much as the extravagantly-paid screenwriters and actors in Hollywood did by paying Party dues), money which underwrote such subversive actions as the boycotting by Communist-controlled longshoremen unions of ships assigned to transport Marshall Plan aid to post-war Europe. (See Miller's testimony in Eric Bentley, ed. *Thirty Years of Treason*, New York, 1971, pp. 789-825. See also my review in the *Sunday Independent*, 31 December 1995, of the *Secret World of American Communism* ed. Harvey Klehr *et al.*, Yale University Press, 1995.) But the truth wouldn't satisfy the need to feel better about Ireland's self-induced travails by painting us Americans as bad people. Even Sean Donlon, the former ambassador who spoke out so trenchantly against anti-Americanism, has fallen into this trap. In an article on the need for the West to support Montenegro in the post-Kosovo war period, 'Montenegro still suffers...,' *Irish Times*, 29 July 1999, he lays the blame for this small country's woes on the U.S., citing as proof an unsubstantiated, unsourced assertion: 'A senior US diplomat is even reported' to have ominously and cold-bloodedly reminded the Montenegran president of the fate of Hungary in 1956, should Montenegro seek to separate from its federal union with Serbia. At best, this is cheap. It proves nothing but that

There is, finally, Ireland's realistic self-awareness of its vulnerabilities as a small country. Enmeshed with this consciousness are a myriad of myths of centuries of colonial oppression (remember that I pointed out that myths are not necessarily fictitious). Such myths, whether true or false, do animate, however. An awareness of the innate condition of small countries can produce a realistic and empathetic understanding and support for other small countries caught up in a power struggle with a larger country. This is an intuitive point-of-view difficult, if not impossible, for someone from a large country to share. In many ways, it is an invaluable leavening of otherwise heavy-handed large-country domination of events. The nuclear non-proliferation treaty came about, after all, as a consequence of an Irish initiative.

It can also, however, mislead a small country into a blinkered view; a psychological transference can take place. A case-in-point could well be the long stand-off between Libya and the U.S. (and also, of course, the U.K.) over the two Libyan officials indicted in the Pan Am 103 bombing. It is natural for an Irishman to feel a certain sympathy for a small country threatened by the concerted power of large countries; it is, however, unnatural to indulge in a sort of transference of identities. The Gaddafi regime argued for years that it could not legally hand over the two for trial in the U.S. or Scotland because it had no extradition treaty with either. Ireland's history of extraditions of 'political' offenders to the U.K. is also troubled. The two situations, however, were never even remotely the same. Regardless of the rhetoric thrown around by right-wing Tories, Ireland is not a safe-haven for terrorists, while the Libyan claim was aimed at producing precisely that

---

even a well-intentioned, highly-experienced and intelligent Irish statesman cannot escape his Irish conditioning.

result. The IRA are not Irish government agents; Libyan intelligence officers are, regardless of whom those responsible for the Pam Am bombing may have been ultimately acting on behalf of. The traditional safeguard for a small country of strict adherence to international law can never be permitted to be perverted by a legalistic pretext – to have allowed Libya's argument to stand as justified would have been to condone international lawlessness.[60]

What, then, of my own country's national myth? The American Republic appeared on the international scene as a decided outsider, as well as an innovation. John Quincy Adams, while serving as secretary of state, said in an address delivered on 4 July 1821 that America was 'the well-wisher to the freedom and independence of all,' but he warned against going 'abroad, in search of monsters to destroy'. Regularly, in the twentieth century, the monsters came looking for us. Our response has been a positive one, for world peace and justice and progress. Certainly, we have, at times, been too conscious of our strength and too trusting in our sense of generosity and have been led astray by our innate belief that we can translate our own political success into solving other peoples' problems. The late Senator Fulbright, in setting out the reasons for his coming to oppose the American take-over of the prosecution of the Vietnam War, termed this complex, the 'arrogance of power'. I like to believe that it is more innocent. I trust, rather, in the judgment of the greatest of our twentieth-century diplomats, George F. Kennan:[61]

---

[60]On this whole matter of the causes of perceptual errors in foreign affairs, see Robert Jervis *Perception and Misperception in International Politics* (Princeton, 1976).

[61]*American Diplomacy* (Expanded ed., Chicago, 1984), pp. 168-69. See also Kennan's conclusions in his *Realities of American Foreign Policy* (Princeton, 1954), pp. 61-62.

The...world can be thankful that if a great world power had to arise on this magnificent North American territory in the last three centuries..., it was one as peaceably and generously minded as this one.

One

Democracy 1: The Democratization of Franco's Spain

I arrived in Madrid in the summer of 1974.[62] The first year of my two-year tour at the American embassy was, professionally, uneventful. Like all first-tour American Foreign Service officers, I was serving as a vice consul, visiting Americans in Spanish prisons and issuing tourist visas. While enjoying life in Madrid, my work simply served to convince me that consular work was not something I wanted to do for a career.[63] Then, in October 1975, came a stroke of luck. Ambassador Wells Stabler, in anticipation of the difficult transition that would follow Franco's eventual demise, had long been attempting to re-inforce the embassy's political section. Bureaucratic changes are incremental affairs. Two new positions were approved but only one, a senior position, was to be filled immediately. The other, that of junior officer in the section, would not be filled until the following summer. In the meanwhile, via an informal internal embassy arrangement, I was plucked out of the consular section to break the new position in.

I felt I had arrived. It had been easy to fall in love with Madrid. I had come from two years at Oxford and I knew London and Paris. I had lived, as well, in San Francisco and Boston and Washington, D.C. Still, Madrid was a revelation. It was beautiful

---

[62]An earlier version of this essay was delivered, on 26 March 2001, to the National Committee for the Study of International Affairs of the Royal Irish Academy at Academy House, Dublin.

[63]See my article, 'A Consuling Day,' (Madrid) *Guidepost* 904 (1975), pp. 12-13.

and it was exciting. It was a gracious city with an innate vibrancy *en la calle*. For the first three months, while we searched for an apartment, we lived in a modern hotel about fifteen minutes walk from the American embassy. Early each morning that summer, I crossed the wide Plaza Colón and turned up Calle Serrano. It was a long street lined with plane trees and shops. There was early morning traffic and that sense of calm that comes with the morning light in Spain. The shops along Serrano were expensive. It was the center of the Salamanca *barrio* where those supporters of Franco who were trapped in Madrid had survived during the Civil War. It was said that it was the only quarter of Madrid that the Nationalist artillery had not fired on. What I mostly noticed were the beautiful young Spanish women. There seemed to be an unfair number of them, and all of them flashed smiles when they saw you looking at them. For an American, this was, at least initially, disconcerting. They actually smiled back, even while holding lovingly to the arm of their boyfriend. There was a saying in the embassy that you fell in love twice every block.

It was easy, then, to feel that you were living in a cosmopolitan, modern capital. There were few overt signs that it might be otherwise. Certainly, if you read through the daily newspapers as I did, it was – more than anything else – the dullness that came through. Rather than news reports, you found tediously-worded political essays on the true significance of Franco's 'institutions'. But if you were alert to what was not said you could sense the abyss beyond the dullness. Police actions were reported in curt paragraphs. I remember one news item which reported the shooting, the night before, of a Madrid city policeman and a subway policeman by a *guardia civil* (a member of the somewhat notorious national police force which had been created in the nineteenth century as a rural constabulary; a commonly-heard joke was that their patent-leather caps were flat on the back to make it easier to put them up against the wall when the revolution came). The whole story was less than a hundred words; no explanation was given for the shootings; there were no follow-up stories. On the buses, there were seats reserved for *los caballeros mutilados de la guerra*. You didn't need to ask which side they had fought on. In the Retiro Park, where I went with my children as often as I was free, there were signs designating certain recreation areas as constructed due to one *sindicato* or another – all state-controlled 'unions'. But it was easy to let these small intrusions fade into the background of a city full of life. It was easy to sit at a table at one of the *kioscos* in the Retiro and drink a beer while my children played on the hard-packed sand piling up mounds of horse chestnuts. It was easy, as well, to let the present and the recent past dissolve in historical resonances. We lived in an apartment on the second floor of a turn-of-the-century apartment building whose portal opened onto the corner of Avenida Felipe II and Calle Narvaez (named for the general who founded the *Guardia Civil*). Just down the wide avenue was a sports arena which occupied the circle where, previously, the *plaza monumental de toros* had been when Hemingway first came to Spain to see bullfights. My own apartment building sat on what had been the first playing field of the great Real Madrid football club. On Saturdays, I would cross the street with my older son, then just beginning school, and take the subway to the Puerta del Sol stop in the center of old Madrid. We would come up out of the old smell of the subway and turn into the Calle Victoria where I would buy my bullfight ticket for Sunday. Inevitably, there would be men leaning against the walls of the buildings along the narrow street, smoking thin cigars while their shoes were being shined. We would stop into one of the many small bars where I would buy my son a pastry and myself a *caña*. It seemed there couldn't be a city where it was simpler to enjoy life.

Still, there were the names of certain streets – Generalissimo and General Mola and Avenida de José Antonio – and there was the huge, red-painted emblem of the Yoke-and-Arrows stretched up the frontage of the *Movimiento* headquarters on Calle Alcalá and, giving the city a rather old-fashioned air, there were the cinemas. Spaniards, at least *madrileños*, loved going to the cinema. The city was full of old-style movie palaces seating hundreds and most nights they were packed. Not content with movie posters, the Spanish mounted, on the facades of their cinemas, huge mock-ups of scenes from the main feature, 20-foot high visions of Hollywood glory painted on plywood in flat garish colors. One such cinema fronted on the Plaza Colón and, in those early months, I passed it each morning and evening. During that entire time, the featured film was *Mogambo* and the heroic-sized images were of Clark Gable and Ava Gardner. It was being treated as a first-run film in the Madrid of 1974.

A few weeks after I started my new job in the political section, Franco died. It was a fascinating time to be an American political officer in Spain. It's not that I was involved in high-level affairs. Most of my time was spent digesting and writing up summaries and analyses of the policy documents being spewed out by the multitude of new political 'associations' (political 'parties,' *per se*, were still not legal). In those days, sending reports by telegram was still a laborious affair since our communicators had to physically type the approved text into their machines for them to be encoded and transmitted. Consequently, telegrams (or cables, as the Foreign Service referred to them) were restricted by the ambassador to no more than four double-spaced pages. Many of my reports ran to multiple pages and were, thus, sent by airgram (though typed on a special form, airgrams were essentially single-spaced essays sent in hard-copy via the diplomatic pouch – producing them made me feel like a graduate student). I also translated and analyzed the various convoluted 'reform' bills the first post-Franco government was grudgingly grinding out.

I was, however, regularly included in the lunches with opposition figures which were hosted by the ambassador or his deputy (in American parlance, the deputy chief of mission, or DCM). Sitting at the formally-set dining table (albeit at the far end) with figures like Joaquín Ruíz Giménez or José María Gil Robles and listening to them expound on how they saw democratization coming to Spain made even a cynic (and those of us who had come through the '60s in universities like Berkeley were professed cynics) feel like he was participating in history in the making.

I was also regularly a participant in in-house discussions on what role the U.S. should play in affairs. The sole focus of these discussions – in the political section, in the DCM's office, in the ambassador's office, in general staff meetings – was how the U.S. could support the democratization process.[64] There was no

---

[64]This occasions a look at how the Irish perceived our involvement in the post-Franco transition period, as an example of that lack of empathy which can prevail in Ireland for the consequential implications and the constraints under which the U.S., as a great power, is compelled to act. Indeed, regularly, the Irish response to our actions amounts to a refusal to set aside preconceptions and to 'think' about what the U.S., in any given hard-choices situation, is actually attempting to do. Though I wasn't even vaguely aware of it at the time, Garret FitzGerald, while serving as foreign minister, raised our Spanish policy with Henry Kissinger. In his memoirs (*All in A Life*, Dublin, 1991, pp. 180-81), he describes a meeting with Kissinger in October 1975 during which he contested the wisdom of the 'recent agreement with General Franco's government renewing US bases in Spain,' arguing that 'the signature of the bases agreement with the Franco regime in what were clearly its closing stages (Franco was known to be dying) could have counter-productive consequences as Spain moved back to democracy....' First of all (as I will detail below), the negotiations for this particular renewal of our bases agreement with Spain were not completed at the

discussion of there being any other acceptable alternative. In all the many discussions I participated in or knew about, I remember only one dissenting remark. Once, when we were preparing for the final negotiating sessions on renewal of our bases agreement with Spain (more on this below) and were fine-tuning how to best present the renewal as an overt act of support for democratization, the CIA representative present observed, 'I don't know about you guys, but I want to keep a strong ally'. 'So do we,' responded the DCM and the discussion continued.

In retrospect, the CIA representative's remark may not have had the retrograde import which I felt it had at the time. Certainly, no one else in the meeting seemed to much notice anything untoward about it. Our policy was that a strong ally of the United States was a democratic ally. Still, it stuck in my mind as a paradigm of the attitude common to all the many CIA officers I would encounter over the following two decades of my career in some five additional diplomatic missions. Outsiders

---

time of FitzGerald's call on Kissinger; the new agreement (upgraded to treaty status) would not be signed until the end of January 1976 (as a junior diplomat, I participated in the final negotiating sessions as a note-taker) – this was some two months after Franco's death. More significant, though, would be the obvious question of why, on this issue of intimate concern to us and where he could have had no particular knowledge of the strategy of our policy in bolstering the democratic forces in Spain, a strategy in which the renewal of the bases agreement (and its upgrading to treaty status) played a key role in helping to bring the Spanish generals on board, Dr FitzGerald didn't simply ask Kissinger for a briefing on U.S. policy. But, then, in the sixteen years between that meeting and the publication of his memoirs – a period in which the U.S. policy proved correct (once in power, even the previously-doctrinaire Socialists recognized the virtues of NATO membership for Spain) – Dr FitzGerald apparently never re-visited the issue. Indeed, despite being surprised and clearly discomfited at being made publicly aware of the actual chronology of events, Dr FitzGerald continued to argue his case ('Still, I remember it [the American policy on renewal of the bases agreement] was highly controversial!') during the Q&A period following my reading of this paper to the Royal Irish Academy.

don't realize how little we American diplomats have to do with the CIA, even those stationed in our midst. They are, truly, secretive. There's a reserve, even with the sociable ones, and most of us, in any case, want to have as little to do with them as possible, suspecting ulterior motives to any sociability on their parts. Officially, it's as though we're working for different governments, so little do we know of what they're doing. I often wondered how much even the ambassador knew.

It wasn't just their secretive behavior that made them off-putting. Their attitude was always, if mostly unstated, that they were the only true patriots. They saw themselves as the last guarantors of America, not just against us wooly-headed diplomats but even, or perhaps especially, against intrusive and dangerously-independent Congressmen and their staffs. This dismissive attitude towards us didn't go down particularly well with those of us who had spent our time in the military and were all too aware of their ambivalent performance in Vietnam.

As my involvement with Spain continued (on leaving Madrid in summer 1976, I was assigned as the analyst for Spanish affairs in the Bureau of Intelligence and Research in the State Department), I came to see the mental construct of the CIA officers I met as the equivalent of that of the Spanish generals. The generals too saw themselves as the ultimate guarantors of the state, to the extent of also arrogating to themselves the right to decide when the government in power ought to be removed as constituting a deadly danger to the 'integrity' of the state. Of course, none of the CIA officers I met or the CIA as an institution has ever acted in such a Praetorian Guard manner. They just gave me the impression they wouldn't mind doing so.

The Spanish generals, however, were a concern, even *the* concern. I was given a watching-brief on the extreme right – Blas Piñar's *Fuerza Nueva* and the myriad minuscule groupings the

Falange had splintered into. I followed their activities and threats through their publications and through press reports. This ran directly counter to the acquired instincts of a diplomat, particularly a political officer, that nothing substituted for personal contact. But we could not and would not deal directly with these people. They were outside the democratic pale. In the streets, their bully boys, the *guerrilleros del Cristo el Rey*, took particular delight in attacking students.

The real concern of the embassy were those certain elements on the far right which passed, at least institutionally, as democratic but which were determined to resist the coming of genuine democracy to Spain. Though unorganized, these disparate elements were well-labeled, by a leading Spanish journalist, as the 'bunker'. Included were certain iconic figures of the right, such as the long-time minister and at-that-time head of the Civil War veterans association, José Antonio Girón, and Francoist true-believers such as Franco's last prime minister, Carlos Arias Navarro. Most of all, though, we were concerned about the generals. At that time, all of the generals and all of the colonels on active service had entered the military either before or during the Civil War. They were imbued with the traditional Spanish military belief in their fundamental mission of safeguarding the Spanish state in all its integrity, re-inforced by four decades of anti-democratic Francoist rhetoric. Seemingly on a daily basis, one or the other of the four military ministers who sat in the cabinet would reiterate the military's adamant opposition to Communism, separatism, and threats to public order (that a number of the generals publicly labeled the 'International Freemasonry Conspiracy' a major threat to Spain amply illustrated the potential for danger in their mind-sets).[65] Lurking always in the background was the historical reality that, before the Franco era, Spanish army commanders frequently intervened to check perceived government abuses or to replace the government in power.

The procedure became virtually institutionalized as the *pronunciamiento* and gave its name to an era of Spanish political history. The military remained very much the ultimate arbiter of power.

Facing them was the newly-legal democratic opposition. Throughout the Franco period, political parties were anathema. It was a fundamental article of Franco-faith that the primary cause of the anarchy which Spain – according to the Nationalists – had fallen into in the 1930s was the inherent divisiveness of partisan politics. Hence, the abolition of political parties. In the immediate post-Franco period (the period while I was still in Madrid), transitional measures were enacted which allowed for political 'associations' – these measures were bound up with all sorts of legalistic restrictions in an attempt to make the 'associations' seem not to be 'parties' which of course everyone knew they actually were. It was very much part-and-parcel of the shadow-boxing of the time. The situation dramatically changed when the king dismissed Arias Navarro and brought in Adolfo Suarez to bring about genuine political reform.

Our concern was to support the measured approach to democratization demonstrated by the king. We were very much concerned that the opposition in their united calls for a *ruptura*

---

[65] A potential realized in the attempted military coup attempt of February 1981. The general who ordered his tanks onto the streets of Valencia, Lt. Gen. Milans del Bosch (a noted *ultra* and scion of a military dynasty with a propensity to rebellion), had previously commanded the Armored Division at Brunete (but 20 miles from Madrid!).

pactada – a dissolution of the Franco parliament and the election of a constituent assembly to write a new constitution – were badly misjudging the political situation and almost inviting a military intervention. Indeed, it would seem that that was the actual intention of the Communists; it was almost as though the Communists foresaw that, in a truly democratic Spain, they would become all but irrelevant. At the time, though, the democratic opposition – from right-wing Christian Democrats to radical-left Socialists – was united in viewing the legalization of the Spanish Communist Party (the PCE) as the litmus test of the democratic reform process. The Communists still carried great prestige for having consistently provided the leading opposition to Francoism, both outside and inside Spain, for four decades (the effective development, for example, of *de facto* trade unions from the late 1950s on – the *comisiones obreras* – was largely the work of Communist militants). The long-time PCE leader, Santiago Carrillo, was also the darling of liberal commentators on Spanish affairs due to his leading role in the evolution of Eurocommunism, overtly moderate rather than hard-line, reformist rather than revolutionary, and independent (not to say, critical) of the Soviet Union.[66] The legalization of the PCE had become, then, an issue of European legitimacy. The Socialists needed it for that reason (their mentors, the West German DGB, were especially adamant, though we ourselves were underwhelmed by their reasoning, given the PCE's rather casual democratic credentials); and Prime Minister Suarez needed it to ensure the participation of the Socialists in democratic elections. There could not be a more significant break with Francoism or a more normative signal of a pluralist future. Certainly, the

---

[66]Eusebio Mujal-León *Communism and Political Change in Spain* (Indiana, 1983), *passim*; and Raymond Carr and Juan Pablo Fusi *España, de la dictadura a la democracia* (Barcelona, 1979), pp. 219-21.

Communists played it for all it was worth – one provocative action followed another, many seemingly with military sensitivities as the target (here, perhaps most significantly, were their studied attempts to belittle the king as a political lightweight with a short future, stridently comparing him to Caetano, the Portuguese leader who had attempted to maintain the dictatorship after the death of Salazar). At times, we felt as though too many of the leading, and younger, opposition leaders were ignoring the surviving Civil War passions. It was almost as though, not having lived through the period themselves, they didn't really believe it mattered. They ignored the message of the official version of Spanish historiography that the Civil War had been a crusade against Communism, writing off the legacy of hatred of the 'Reds' as just another piece of Francoist propaganda. To them it was, literally, history, not the red flag to the generals which we were afraid it could be. It didn't help that Carrillo was widely believed to have been implicated in the Civil War atrocity of Paracuellos (thousands of Nationalist prisoners being held in Madrid were massacred at this village just outside the city when they were being transferred).

Sometimes, though, I could see the opposition's view of the rightist threat. Shortly before Franco died, there had been a demonstration in front of the Portuguese embassy which was just down the hill from the American embassy. The day before, the Spanish embassy in Lisbon had been burnt by protestors angered by Franco's execution of ETA and FRAP terrorists (long a fellow rightist dictatorship, Portugal had had its democratic revolution the year before). In Madrid, the counter-demonstration was conducted by *falangistas*. I went down to watch it with another young officer from the embassy. It seemed something out of a 1930s newsreel – the protestors wearing blue shirts and black berets, their right arms stretched up in the fascist salute, singing the Falangist hymn, *Cara al sol* – except that, now, they were all middle-aged. Afterwards, walking back up the hill, we realized that we were in amongst the protestors and that some were giving us angry looks. It seemed they were on their way to protest in front of the British ambassador's residence (which sat contiguous to the American embassy) and, hearing the two of us speaking English, apparently thought we were Brits. We assured them we were American. They smiled. We got into our embassy's parking lot and, from behind the barred gate, watched the protestors shouting insults at the British ambassador's lovely mansion. When they passed by us, they applauded. 'Isn't it great,' my friend said, 'having fascists for friends'. It was hard to take such people seriously. I could see, then, why the Socialists and the others seemed to write them off. Still, I wasn't so sanguine. They might be historical anachronisms but they were long used to having things political their own way. They made me, at least, nervous.

Fortunately, the Socialists (or, that is, the dominant party led by Felipe Gonzalez – the historical PSOE having split into a number of groupings over the decades of its illegal existence), despite the occasional rhetorical outburst, understood that the king and his new government were genuine democrats. We ourselves knew of Suarez' reasoned commitment to orderly democratization from our own regular meetings with him, from long before he became prime minister. We took every opportunity to say so to opposition leaders, particularly the Socialists. They never pushed Suarez beyond what he could deliver and, in the end, they opted for elections with or without the PCE (perhaps this decision was made easier by Carrillo also having betrayed the PSOE – while acting as head of the war-time PSOE youth wing, he revealed himself to have been a long-time Communist when he led his group into the PCE). In the event, the

PCE was legalized and participated and was duly consigned to the dustbin of history by the Spanish electorate (it turned out that the Spanish people just weren't interested in wasting votes on an outdated, not to say discredited, ideology, however trendy some tried to make it). At the time, though, it seemed the crucial issue and when Suarez pushed the legalization through there were genuine fears that the military would act. Somehow, their reaction was contained – a couple of resignations and a statement of 'revulsion'. No one has yet, to my knowledge, adequately explained why the generals caved in. It may just be that four decades of Franco's deliberate neglect of the military estate had left them politically deflated – they didn't know how to react except with rhetorical denunciations. Certainly, the lack of triumphalism by the PSOE and others also played a role in playing down the crisis. As did the determination of the king. That democratization was successfully achieved, if painfully gradually at times, owes everything to the king, his government and the cooperation of the responsible opposition. Throughout, the policy of the American embassy was to use all contacts to counsel moderation, caution and perseverance.[67] I believe that, in doing so, we were on the side of the angels.

Given our long-standing military relationship with Spain (the first bases agreement was reached in 1953), much of our moderating and supportive influence lay with the Spanish military. On a day-to-day basis, our own military (both at our bases and in our military advisory group stationed at Spanish military headquarters) carried the message. Their efforts were re-inforced by the embassy's Counselor for Political-Military

---

[67]Cf. Samuel D. Eaton *The Forces of Freedom in Spain, 1974-1979* (Stanford, 1981), pp. 30 and 44-45. Sam Eaton was the DCM during my two years at the American embassy in Madrid.

Affairs (the senior position which Ambassador Stabler had had established) who, among other items, delivered many a speech, in Spanish, to military gatherings.

Fortuitously, there was also the final negotiations for the renewal of the bases agreement. This had been due for its regular five-yearly renewal in 1973 but the negotiations had fallen apart over Spanish demands for greatly increased military assistance. There was also a Spanish desire for an enhanced security guarantee. While Franco was alive, there had been no question of Spain being accepted by the European countries as a member of NATO. Nor would there be that possibility until Spain was fully democratized. Our concern was, one, to use the renewal to emphasize that it constituted support for the democratization process and, two, to ensure that it contributed to the professionalization of the Spanish military (here, the working theory was that a military fully occupied with professional tasks would be less occupied with theological issues of safeguarding the integrity of the state – in essence, the same thinking that led the Socialists, once they had come to power in the 1980s, to completely reverse their opposition to the Spanish entry into NATO).

The first objective was met, in part, by the elevation of the agreement from an executive agreement (which needed only the approval of the president) to a treaty (which had to be ratified by the Senate). In ratifying it, the Senate formally expressed its hopes that the treaty would 'serve to support and foster Spain's progress towards free institutions...' Our second objective was furthered by increasing the military assistance in areas of modernized warfare (an advanced fighter squadron, for instance) which also allowed the Spanish government to claim, for public newspaper headlines, that they had obtained a billion dollars in exchange for the renewal.

A mythology has grown up around the U.S.-Spanish bases agreement. Or, rather, leftist political commentators have deliberately sought to use the history of the agreement to further discredit the Franco period. According to this mythology, Franco sold off Spanish national sovereignty to keep himself in power by obtaining American support. The argument goes that there was little, if any, reciprocity in the agreement: that is, the U.S. could freely use the bases while it was under no commitment to come to the aid of Spain should Spain be attacked.[68] This is nonsense on several levels.

First on the specific level of the agreement itself, the bases could only be used in the event of an all-out attack on the West by the Soviet Union; this was specifically spelled out in the agreement from its first incarnation. Indeed, the very rationale behind our seeking the bases back at the beginning of the 1950s was precisely to serve as a redoubt for re-grouping and launching a counter-attack should the Soviet Union launch such an assault.[69] And should the Soviet Union do so, there was no doubt – particularly not at the time of the initial agreement in 1953 when, supposedly, Franco sold the pass – that Spain would be high on the list of Soviet targets (let us try, after all, to remember the

---

[68]This myth-making argument is set forth in greatest detail in Angel Viñas *Los pactos secretos de Franco con Estados Unidos: Bases, ayuda económica, recortes de soberanía* (Barcelona, 1981).

[69]Prior to first arriving in Spain in the summer of 1974, I had been detailed for several months to help out on the Spanish Desk in the State Department. One of my tasks was to research in the archives of the Department the original negotiations in 1953 (more background information was felt necessary in light of the failure of the 1973 plenipotentiary session); one discovery I made was that the original desire of our Air Force was to obtain rights to up to a dozen bomber bases; the strategic thinking was, in the event of an all-out Soviet assault, to use Spain in the role that England had played in World War II – an unsinkable aircraft carrier.

history of the Spanish Civil War). In other words, there was no question of Spain *becoming* a Soviet target as a consequence of its military relationship with the U.S.[70]

The agreement allowed for no other use of the bases (e.g., the re-fuelling of planes headed to re-supply Israel in the Yom Kippur War). If the Spanish government ever felt that this prohibition had been breached, their option was to take physical control of the bases. Legally, the bases were always Spanish bases on which American military personnel were stationed; and, in practical terms, access to the bases was controlled by Spanish military police (as anyone could have seen by simply driving up to the gates). Should anyone doubt the integrity of these arrangements, they should talk to some of the high-ranking American military who, on official visits, were refused entry to the bases because they had neglected to obtain the proper pass (NATO passes didn't work!).

It is true that the U.S. acquired no obligation to come to Spain's assistance should she be otherwise attacked (by Morocco, for instance). But, then, Spain incurred no obligation to come to the assistance of the U.S. should we be attacked by anyone other than the Soviet Union (by Mexico?). And, finally, the security guarantee in the agreement – that is, the mutual defense commitment – was modelled on that contained in NATO. Contrary to popular belief, the mutual defense commitment in

---

[70]This did not, however, prevent the Spanish negotiators, particularly the military representatives such as Lt. Gen. Gutiérrez Mellado, from attempting to use as bargaining leverage (particularly on the issue of an enhanced security guarantee) Soviet 'concern' with the presence of U.S. nuclear submarines at the naval base at Rota (indeed, they even frequently invoked the presence of the five tankers at Torrejón Air Force Base on the grounds that they could be used to re-fuel nuclear bombers!).

NATO is not automatic either, though practical command structures ensure that it is all but.

Franco didn't sell off national sovereignty; he actually struck a rather astute bargain. As for the idea of his surviving due to American support, I don't imagine this needs refutation for any sensible person. Franco stayed in power for nearly four decades because there was no domestic opposition capable of ousting him. It's a bit much of the Spanish left to blame the international community in general or the U.S. in particular for their own failure to organize an effective opposition (or even any organized opposition, given their splintering propensities).

This whole claim is but a local manifestation of the general tendency to use weasal-worded terms in passing judgment on the U.S.'s relationships with various countries, particularly in the post-war world. Words like 'support' or even 'control'. No, we did not 'support' the Franco regime. We dealt with a government in *de facto* control of a country – that is, with the situation as it existed – in order to meet the transcending need of the defense of the West. We didn't create the situation. Nor, more pertinently, was there anything we could do to effect a proximate change. Democratization is not, in the normal course of events, a process that can be imposed from the outside. In Spain, as in her Hispanic offspring in Latin America, democracy has rarely been more than an aspiration throughout her political history. Democracy failed to take root in the 1930s for multiple reasons. If I can suggest one, it was the parlous state of democracy in Europe in general in those inter-war years. 'Organic democracy' (that is, fascism) occupied the political high ground. In contrast, democracy did take root post-Franco, buoyed up – indeed, made to seem inevitable – by the general condition of democracy throughout Western Europe and by Spain's own transparent need to integrate with democratic Europe.

Indeed, much of this integration had taken place long before Franco's death. Others, far more knowledgeable than I about modern Spain, have spelled out how the Spanish economy and society had slipped, by almost imperceptible degrees, into modern Europe.[71] Could any other outcome be possible in a country visited annually by Western European tourists in numbers doubling its population? Even to a junior diplomat, in the Madrid of 1974 it was obvious that there was no longer the dictatorship (*dictadura*) of the past, but a *dictablanda*. A cliché? Yes, but also a reality. In his own (I am sure, inadvertent) way, Franco largely prepared the ground for the replacement of his institutions by genuine democracy. Prosperity and democracy are mutually reinforcing.[72]

Rhetoric tends, by its nature, to become overheated. There are those – more numerous the farther right you look – who will still tell you that the Spain of those years either side of Franco's death was on the verge of anarchy. They will cite the terrorist outrages and the repressive counter-measures of the regime, particularly the executions. Certainly, when you were on the streets you began to look around you for any nearby presence of a policeman – urban guerrillas, first the FRAP and then GRAPO, had taken to murdering policemen in drive-by shootings and you didn't want to find yourself in the crossfire. Certainly, rightist death-squads hit back; several labor lawyers were murdered one night in the worst such atrocity during this period (responsibility was claimed by a self-styled 'Apostolic Anti-Communist Alliance'). And certainly the hard right screamed that the worst days of the Second Republic had returned with all that implied for the 'need' for the military to re-assert control. But in the 1930s, it was

---

[71]Cf., Richard Gunther *Public Policy in a No-Party State* (Berkeley, 1980).

[72]Cf. John F. Coverdale *The Political Transformation of Spain after Franco* (New York, 1979), pp. 1-4.

government forces who paid visits in the night to take their selected victims for a *paseo*. The apartment from which Calvo Sotelo had been lifted was but two blocks over from the American embassy and there was a marble plaque by its entrance.[73] There was also a marble plaque on the wall of the Jesuit church where Carrero Blanco had gone to mass each morning until that December morning in 1973 when ETA terrorists had blown him up, using so much dynamite in the huge crater they had managed to tunnel out under the street that his car was blown up and over the roof of the three-story church, coming to rest, pan-caked, on a second-story balcony of the inside courtyard of the adjoining rectory.[74] This was one parallel street over from the American embassy and, when I was newly-arrived, Spanish employees in the consular section told me about the explosion. At first, they had all believed that it was a gas explosion (Madrid was plagued with such accidents – the keystones over the majestic entrances of the apartment buildings put up around the turn of the century, like mine, proudly bore engraved in the granite, *Gas a cada piso*, but this extensive, century-old gas network had badly decayed and it was common to see newspaper photographs of the latest *socavón*). Many of our employees had had their cars parked along the street. All had been damaged. Those parked in the center of the block where the explosion had occurred had disappeared into the crater.

One thing I noted was how many of our employees had their own cars. And they all owned their own apartments, even the younger ones who had only been working for a few years. As

---

[73]The murder by government police in July 1936 of José Calvo Sotelo, parliamentary leader of the rightist opposition, was the culminating act of violence leading up to the outbreak of the Civil War.

[74]Admiral Luís Carrero Blanco was Franco's long-time strongman in government; he was prime minister at the time of his assassination.

soon as they had permanent employment, they were able to take out mortgages. I don't remember that any of them had anything particularly good to say about Franco but then political conversations were not common. Most seemed as apolitical as the average American. Some analysts argued that the general economic prosperity which had been reached under Franco's rule had transformed the hitherto political volatility of the Spaniards into a state of political complacency. So long as the living conditions of the working class continued to improve, the argument went, there would be no great political agitation. The bread-and-circuses of Rome had become the *piso y coche* of Franco. I felt that the apoliticism of the average Spaniard was due more to the deliberate policy of political apathy which Franco pursued. His *Movimiento* had been deliberately gutted of any real ideological fervor so that genuinely socially-radical *falangistas* like Dionisio Ridruejo could but protest their lack of influence (and be treated as regime pets). Insofar as it contributed to the demise of the divisive passions of the Civil War, this was all to the good. But the total suppression of street-level politics also stultified the normal development of any grass-roots pressure in reaction to governmental inaction – such as, for instance, environmental activism: the legendary crystal clarity of Madrid's skies had become, in the winter, the second circle of hell from the coal-burning furnaces of a city of apartment buildings. The odd day, when the depression lifted and the skies cleared so that the edges of buildings stood out in the cold as though etched in steel, was all that much more saddening. Just in the normal run of daily life, Franco did have a lot to answer for.

Still, when Franco died, the public response was surprising to many of us, certainly it was to me. We had always largely written off the mass demonstrations orchestrated in support of Franco. The Plaza de Oriente had been filled with thousands just weeks before Franco died. They had been gathered to support Franco during the international uproar over the executions, for terrorist offenses, of five members of ETA and FRAP. Even on television, the frailty of the old man was obvious (it was said that his prolonged exposure, that day, to a chill October wind hastened his final illness). And, while the crowd was duly enthusiastic, we all knew that they were largely government employees given the day off to go to the demonstration, those from outside Madrid having been bussed in and provided with a box lunch. But no one organized the demonstration when Franco died. His body was laid out to rest in state in the Palacio de Oriente and for days Spaniards filed past. The line stretched, literally, for miles. I went out to look. Four abreast, moving forward slowly, for hours in a bitterly cold and wet November. An estimated half-a-million Spaniards passed by Franco's dead body. What this signified, I didn't know then and I don't know now. But it could not just have been curiosity.[75] I watched the funeral on television. The heavy stone slab sealing his grave in the marble floor of the basilica in the Valle de los Caídos had to be rolled slowly into place on metal pipes. There was an inexorability about it as it sank into place. Immediately, the joke went around that it was to prevent Franco from climbing out when, as everyone fully expected, he returned from the dead.

---

[75]Cf., Paul Preston *Franco* (London, 1993), pp. 779-80.

Two

Democracy 2: The Democracy of Venezuela

I spent two years at the American embassy in Caracas, at the very end of my diplomatic career.[76] Indeed, being assigned to Caracas largely determined my decision to take early retirement. After spending two decades dealing with Western Europe, I was shipped off to a region I had neither expertise nor interest in. In terms of both my career and the needs of the Foreign Service, it was a throw-away assignment. Unfortunately, it was all too typical of the way assignments are mostly made. Rather than matching my onward assignment to my experience, I was selected for posting to Caracas simply because I had previously once served as a labor attaché (in The Hague) and because I spoke Spanish.

My Spanish was, of course, from my time as the junior officer in the Political Section in Madrid. During my service there, as Franco came to die, a name was coined to denote those with vested interests in resisting genuine democratization in Spain. Evoking images of Hitler's last redoubt, these diehards were termed the 'bunker'. As I was to learn when I reached Caracas, there's a 'bunker' in Venezuelan political life as well. This one, however, is a genuinely physical bunker, at least in appearance. It's the nickname, used by supporters and opponents alike, for the central headquarters in Caracas of *Acción Democrática*, the long-dominant political party in Venezuela. In Spain, the 'bunker' had

---

[76]An earlier version of this essay was delivered, on 24 March 1999, to Professor Eunan O'Halpin's seminar on Latin America in the world order at Dublin City University.

stood for the opposition to democracy; in Venezuela, it represented the core of what passed for democracy. This symbolic distinction only increased my disenchantment with my new assignment. I decided that I'd had enough of being a professional in a career service which didn't have a professional personnel system. Caracas itself served to confirm the wisdom of my decision.

I didn't care for the city or for the people. If Madrid can best be described, in one word, as vibrant, the word I settled on for Caracas was vulgar. It oughtn't to be. The city is sited in a long and narrow mountain valley with the huge green mass of the Avila mountain closing the valley off on the north side. Those in the embassy who traveled widely in the country (and most did) described the rest of the country as even more spectacularly beautiful than the setting of Caracas. Lush tropical foliage and a climate as near to perfection as possible. The old center of the city could also lull a visitor into believing that Venezuela was a real country. Here you find the serenity of the Plaza Bolívar with the cathedral and the capitol building, all creamy white walls and gold trim, with sun-drenched and tranquil interior courtyards. These monumental public institutions evoke a Spanish colonial past that was never quite that grand. Some even claim that, in truth, there's no distinctive indigenous culture in Venezuela nor any true national identity; indeed, that it's never been more than a culturally-impoverished province of Gran Colombia. Sufficient proof of these assertions, they argue, can be found in the ill-bred Spanish spoken in Caracas as compared to the purity of the pronunciation found in Bogotá.

But Venezuela possessed great oil wealth. This was, paradoxically, its undoing – a judgment repeated daily by Venezuelan politicians and journalists. Despite my jaundiced disposition towards the country and all its works, I was encouraged by the critical freedom of their political journalists. Rather too regularly, however, this degenerated into a mocking licence, and the journalists' lack of respect for institutions was just another manifestation of the basic vulgarity of Venezuelan public life. To give one example: I once attended the opening of the judicial year. This is a most solemn occasion, with the justices of the Venezuelan Supreme Court presiding and with a select audience directly facing their judicial bench – judges in their robes, the diplomatic corps, former presidents in the places of honor in the front row. One of the justices is designated to deliver not an anodyne keynote address but a learned lecture on a legal subject. And in the space between the semi-circular judicial bench and the first row of the eminent guests gather the journalists – not just the television crews there to film it all, but any journalist who happens along, chatting to each other, greeting each other with *abrazos* and kisses, smoking, blissfully (or scornfully) unaware of the solemnity of the occasion and of the efforts of the lecturing justice to be heard. For this poor *norteamericano*, it was an object lesson in the deficiencies of democracy Latin American style.

But, if they lack any intuitive grasp of the civic decencies of democracy, Venezuelan journalists have no doubts about the core problem afflicting their country; nor do they have any doubts about who's to blame. Pervasive corruption is the problem and heading the list of the culpable is the Venezuelan political class (writ large). For an American political officer who had, as I had, long served in Western Europe, it was a perverse pleasure to read the daily newspapers. Fierce in their criticisms of the failings of Venezuelan politics, the Venezuelan journalists didn't look for external scapegoats. They didn't blame the *Yanquis*.[77] They blamed themselves. I found this refreshing.

I should make clear why, precisely, I found this Venezuelan self-judgmental attitude so refreshing. It happened that, at the time I was finally settling into Caracas, I was reading proof on an article to be published in the Irish Jesuit journal, *Studies*.[78] This was my initial article discussing the disturbing phenomenon in Ireland of anti-Americanism. In regard to Latin America, this attitude typically laid all the blame for the woes in that region on the U.S.'s 'immoral' foreign policy. Indeed, the major focus of condemnation of us, in the years immediately preceding my arrival in Dublin in 1988, had been our policy in Central America, particularly during Reagan's presidency. However, during the four years I served as the Political Officer at the embassy in Dublin, the most vicious single outburst of anti-Americanism came in the autumn of 1989 sparked by a UN resolution concerning a political solution in Cambodia. Uniformly, politicians, journalists, academics – the political class generally – accused us of wanting the Khmer Rouge to return to power. That there was no evidence to support this assertion, and abundant evidence to refute it, mattered not at all – we were judged guilty of abusive great power behavior, of 'cynical complicity in genocide'. So pervasively was this condemnatory assertion stated that it is still difficult to find any Irish person, who pays any attention to international affairs, who would not

---

[77] A realistic attitude not shared – need we add? – by the Irish; see as typical Vincent Browne 'Thorn in the side of new world order,' *Irish Times*, 10 April 2002, where he predicts an intervention, 'covertly or otherwise,' by the U.S. in Venezuela.

[78] My article, 'Irish Attitudes towards USA Foreign Policy,' *Studies* 82 (Autumn 1993), pp. 265-75.

believe it to be simple fact that the U.S. 'supported' the Khmer Rouge, though they might admit not knowing just how.

Those with rather more knowledge make much of the U.S. vote for the Democratic Coalition (which included the Khmer Rouge) retaining the UN seat for Cambodia. At the very least, they claim, this provided the Khmer Rouge with 'political legitimacy'. Such an argument was not just weasal-worded; it also constituted conceptual nonsense as it simply ignored all the real-world consequential aspects of UN votes. For starters, it self-righteously ignored the reality that workable (as well as just) solutions in this world often involve dealing with distasteful people (Sinn Féin *et al.*?). Additionally, it ignored our reiterated declarations – given as explanations-of-vote (an official UN mechanism) – condemning the Khmer Rouge and putting formally on record our adamant opposition to any return to power by them. Nor, for that matter, did it in any way acknowledge that what we did in connection with this and similar votes on Cambodia was mirrored by an overwhelming majority at the UN – 124 member-states on this particular vote in 1989, most pertinently Ireland![79]

Perhaps most distressing from the perspective of rational consideration of international affairs, this condemnatory Irish attitude, in singling out the U.S., simply ignored the facts of the origins of this resolution, a process in which the U.S., at best, played but a marginal role. It was, after all, Prince Sihanouk who established the Democratic Coalition as the Cambodian government-in-exile and who formed an alliance with the Khmer Rouge in opposition to the Vietnamese-installed puppet government in Phnom Penh. And it was also Cambodia's

---

[79]I deal with the reaction of the Irish government to all this public outrage in chapter 5 below.

democratic southeast Asian neighbors (the ASEAN countries) which devised the prevailing strategy that this resolution represented within the UN – a strategy intended, in the first instance, to compel the Vietnamese to withdraw their army of occupation. This would be followed by UN-supervised elections and pacification efforts. A key element in this strategy was that, since the Khmer Rouge could not be defeated militarily (if the Vietnamese army could not do so, then who could?), they were to be neutralized (by keeping them on board in the Democratic Coalition) and, in the subsequent general elections, discredited by popular vote. The validity of the UN strategy has been borne out by its overall success.[80] Nevertheless, in the eyes of public Ireland, we still stand guilty as charged. As a prime example of cognitive dissonance – that is, the determination to believe what one wants despite the facts – this cannot be bettered.[81]

Sadly, all these factors of factual ignorance and wilful self-deception which formed widespread Irish belief concerning our

---

[80]A judgment which most commentators, I believe, would still support despite the mini-civil war between the two co-prime ministers, which broke out in July 1997 (it would seem that Hun Sen, once a Khmer Rouge warlord and then the Vietnamese-installed puppet prime minister, has still not learned even the rudiments of democracy). For a succinct (and wonderfully descriptive) account of the UN operation in Cambodia, see William Shawcross *Deliver Us From Evil*, pp. 33-43, 53-64, 74-77, 84-89, 95-98, and 182-86; see also my review, *Sunday Independent*, 4 June 2000.

[81]A couldn't-be-bettered example of precisely this is Michael Holmes 'Ireland and USA Foreign Policy: A Reply to George Dempsey,' *Studies* 83 (Summer 1994), pp. 208-9. Holmes does acknowledge that it 'would be wrong to describe US policy as being pro-Khmer Rouge,' but only after a page of selective or specious argumentation, full of weasel words such as 'indirect...support' and 'some responsibility,' designed to demonstrate that the U.S. deserved criticism of the sort handed out to it in Ireland; most tellingly, Holmes simply ignores the facts and realities which I have set out and which anyone seriously considering the issue would be concerned with.

policy towards Cambodia operated generally in forming Irish
attitudes towards U.S. foreign policy throughout the world – that
we could act out of generosity or a good-faith desire to help was
discounted out-of-hand and a mean-spirited motivation was
sought. Largely an attitude of the radical left in other countries, it
was long mainstream in Ireland – at least until President Clinton's
involvement in the Northern Ireland peace process. Now, this
phenomenon has, to a good degree, largely gone underground.
But it hasn't gone away. Despite its inherent illogicality, it
remains a resistant strain in the psyche of that tranche of public
Ireland interested in international affairs, particularly those who
concern themselves with Latin America.

Two more recent examples concerning this region will
illustrate this abiding compulsion, even in otherwise objective
accounts, to find some way, however unfair or factually
inaccurate, to blame the U.S. (or, at least, to cast a condemnatory
sneer in our direction). The first (both articles are from The *Irish
Times*) provides a fair-minded account of present-day Paraguay.[82]
But in speaking of the former dictator, General Stroessner, the
writer comments, 'In 1965 he sent Paraguayan forces to help the
US army in its invasion of the Dominican Republic in support of
a beleaguered right-wing military government there'. No. The
facts are otherwise. Two years previous to 1965, a military coup
had, indeed, unseated Juan Bosch, who had been democratically
elected following the assassination of the dictator Rafael Trujillo.
And the military elements which subsequently revolted against
this military government in April 1965 did announce their support
for restoring Bosch to office. But neither side held the balance of
power. A full-scale civil war threatened and the lives of civilians

---

[82]Hugh O'Shaughnessy 'Plucky Paraguay may be most corrupt country on
planet,' *Irish Times*, 4 February 1999.

could not be guaranteed. President Lyndon Johnson sent American military forces to forestall this potential catastrophe by establishing and holding a security zone between the two warring parties. This intervention was subsequently endorsed by the Organization of American States which, within a week, had dispatched an Inter-American peace force under the command of a Brazilian general. The American military units in the country came under this general's command and units from other hemispheric countries (such as police from Costa Rica) were sent. A truce was negotiated by the OAS and, a year later, democratic elections were held. Democracy in the Dominican Republic was preserved by our actions.

The second article deals with the Summit of the Americas which was held in Miami in December 1994.[83] The writer comments, 'Now the old Big Brother relationship, in which successive US presidents claimed and exercised the right to intervene at will in Latin-American republics, has been redefined, in the words of President Clinton, as a "Partnership for Prosperity." Only Cuba was left out but it was made clear that once its citizens are given the vote, it will be welcome to join'. I wouldn't necessarily agree with the economic analysis the writer provides in the rest of this article but it constitutes fair argument and, most pertinently, the writer characterizes the American motivations behind the Summit of the Americas in a fair-minded manner. Still, the 'Big Brother' tag is as needlessly snide as the claim that American presidents intervened at will is historically untrue. An objective report on this Inter-American summit would also have noted that sharing honors with free trade on its agenda was the new goal of 'good governance' – the decision that honest

---

[83]Peadar Kirby 'First world makes free trade rules – but keeps up its protectionism,' *Irish Times*, 17 December 1994.

and efficient government in each of the member-states was rightfully the concern of all the states in the hemisphere. I will return to this issue at the end of this chapter. In the meanwhile, this brings us back to Venezuela.

When you first come into Caracas, it appears a very modern, even cosmopolitan city. If you are lucky enough to first come into it at night, then, as you approach the city on the long drive in from the international airport on the Caribbean coast, you see the hills laced, in the black tropical night, with long strings of brilliant white lights. In harsh contrast, in the daytime, you see that the hills are covered with shanty-towns, terraces of shacks with corrugated roofs and cement-block walls and dirt streets. These are the *barrios* where the working-class of Caracas live. (For all the time I was in Caracas, this so-different usage of *barrio* from the neutral meaning it had in Madrid was a daily jolt.)

Those of us in the embassy lived, of course, in luxury apartments in the exclusive districts of the city, mostly high up the hillside on the slopes of the Monte Avila. For most of us, we lived in apartments which we could never have afforded to rent back home in America. There was no alternative. The middle-class apartments of Caracas were scarcely fit to live in and the middle-class districts of the city were far too dangerous. Every week-end in Caracas, at least two dozen people were murdered, mostly in the *barrios*, in shoot-outs between gangs. But no district was entirely safe, and many were killed by the police who could kill with impunity.[84]

In embassy circles, I met many American and British expatriates who had long lived in Caracas. Most were retired oil

---

[84]Cf. Sister Stanislaus Kennedy, 'A country living its own worst nightmare,' *Irish Times*, 17 October 1996.

executives. All lamented the deterioration in daily life. They described a Caracas of the 1950s and '60s which had been a slow-moving and pleasant city, little removed from its past of coffee plantations within the city limits. A city where, as in Madrid, street life came alive in the long balmy evenings. In the Caracas of the 1990s, no one walked the streets at night, and you lived in apartment buildings with armed guards at the electronically-controlled heavy-metal gates and in apartments with bars on the windows and multi-lock front doors with steel cores. I finally realized how serious it all was when I saw the doors advertised as 'meeting the highest Israeli security standards'.[85] What went wrong? According to the Venezuelans themselves, it was their massive oil wealth and the particular way their 'democratic' political system functioned.

For most of its history, Venezuela suffered the common fate of Latin American countries of one military dictatorship succeeding another and usually doing so in bloody fashion. Caracas was the birthplace of Simón Bolívar, the great *Libertador* of northern South America from Spanish rule. Styled the George Washington of Latin America, he emulated Washington only in the success of his generalship, not in political wisdom. In fairness to Bolívar, the political deck was stacked against any leader in nineteenth-century Latin America who might wish to create a genuine democracy. For this, there needs first be a popular appreciation of the essential virtues and restraints of democratic behavior and that has only begun to emerge in Latin America, on the whole, in the last decade or two.

In 1958, those who did wish to bring democracy to Venezuela ousted the last military dictator (who went off to exile in Franco's

---

[85]Another aspect which struck me was the near-total absence of sidewalk cafes; for a city with such a climate, this was a sign of something gone badly wrong.

Spain). Among them were such as Rómulo Betancourt and Rafael
Caldera, genuine democrats who, above all, were determined that,
this time, there would be no repetition of the disaster of 1948
when their first attempt to bring about a democratically-elected
government had ended in another military coup. They agreed, in
the 'Pacto del Punto Fijo' (named after the resort town where it
was negotiated), that, regardless of which party might hold
power, all parties would benefit from the 'spoils' – there would
be an agreed sharing-out of appointments and of government
largesse. Over the succeeding decades, genuinely free elections
were regularly held and power changed hands. *Acción
Democrática* won most of the presidential elections, but not all of
them, and minority parties were able to win congressional seats
and play a meaningful role in governing the country.
Significantly, the military retired respectably into the background
of civic life.

For four decades, Venezuela seemed to have successfully
escaped the nightmare of military strongmen and to have become
a country apart from the dreadful norm of Latin American
politics.[86] Jack Kennedy regularly cited Rómulo Betancourt as the
model Latin American statesman, a president who came to power
democratically, ruled democratically, and departed,
democratically, from office at the end of his term. Two decades
on from Betancourt's term in office, it was another Venezuelan
president, Carlos Andrés Pérez (known and referred to by all as

---

[86]To reiterate the basic home-truth, so standardly disregarded in Ireland (as
elsewhere): cruelty, venality, and political chaos are indigenous to Latin America
(as are such virtues as honor and valor); there is no need to look to outsiders to
blame for their shaping influences in Latin America's political history. Indeed,
Bolívar himself has been identified as seminally responsible for the legacy of
murderous strongman-rule and the legitimation of rule-by-atrocity; see Robert
Harvey *Liberators* (London, 2000), pp. 112-13, and my review, *Sunday
Independent*, 30 July 2000.

CAP), to whom we turned to put pressure on the Sandinistas to hold genuinely free elections in Nicaragua. CAP had the incontestably democratic credentials to do so. He was a legitimate power on the hemispheric stage and a voice within the Socialist International who could tell the Spanish and the Swedes what the Sandinistas were really up to and be listened to (though it took the best part of a decade before such European 'like-minded' countries would admit the reality that had been staring them in the face).

CAP, however, was also personally corrupt. He is said to have counseled the newly-elected Socialist president of Peru, Alan García, to steal all he needed in the first year on the theory that it would soon be forgotten so long as you then proceeded to notch up some presidential achievements. It was a theory which had, apparently, worked for CAP himself. When I arrived in Caracas in 1992, he was in office as the first democratic Venezuelan president to be elected to a second term (Venezuelan presidents could not succeed themselves; CAP's own first term had ended in 1979).

CAP was not the only Venezuelan president to be personally corrupt but those who were honest were the exception in Venezuelan political life as a whole. Corruption was pervasive. Politicians lived on graft, the generals were kept happy by kick-backs on contracts, the labor unions were co-opted by kick-backs on collective bargaining agreements and seats in the Congress. My primary responsibility was liaison with the CTV, the major Venezuelan labor federation. Once this had been a key job within the embassy. Much of Venezuela's economic and social legislation was written by the CTV; all of it had been vetted by them. The head of the CTV's international bureau also served as the director of international affairs for the social democratic *Acción Democrática*. So important internationally was the CTV, that the AFL-CIO based a representative in Caracas.[87] By the time I arrived, however, its influence was gone along with the oil revenue which had funded it all; now the CTV was on the outs with a president of its own party who wanted to rein in inflation.[88]

For decades, though, corruption was seen as an equitable distributive mechanism which provided everybody with a piece of the oil pie. Keeping it turning over smoothly were the political party machines. They permeated every aspect of Venezuelan life. As long as oil revenue provided the wherewithal to grease the system, all went swimmingly. Corruption was the glue which held society and politics together. As Betancourt, now an ex-president, lamented in 1978, Venezuela had become 'una sociedad de cómplices'. For decades, the federal budget underwrote an artificially-favorable exchange rate between the *bolívar* and the dollar, and Venezuelans, on shopping trips to Miami, were supposedly known as 'da me dos' ('give me two') for their free-spending ways. In macro-economic terms, Venezuela experienced massive growth without development. A hinterland of great agricultural and mineral potential was left largely unexploited. The marginalized migrated to Caracas. The capital's population grew exponentially in decades – from a half-

---

[87]The founders of the CTV were genuine heroes who had fought street battles with the military dictatorships (as well as with the Communists); its genial slide into co-opted corruption confronted the AFL-CIO with a dilemma. Internationally, the CTV was still a stalwart of free labor union development (its role in Nicaragua was vital); this international collegiality prevented the AFL-CIO from reaching out to reform labor movements within Venezuela. Given the long and heroic role of the AFL-CIO in promoting free labor unions throughout Latin America, this hurt.

[88]Its own president, Antonio Ríos, was also awaiting trial for graft and fraud; bizarrely, an assassination attempt was made on him – he was wounded but not fatally. Apparently, the motivation was that Ríos had become a symbol of corruption; the CTV tried to claim that Ríos was a victim of an international conspiracy against labor unionism.

million to, perhaps, six million (census figures, like virtually all other statistics in Venezuela, are lacking or amount to guess-work). At least half this population lived outside the formal economy. In the mid-1980s, it finally all imploded with the collapse of the real value of oil on the global market.

Life caught up with Venezuela. In their free-spending decades, Venezuelans didn't bother with maintenance. If something deteriorated, their attitude was to build another. When I arrived, Caracas was a city literally falling apart. The exterior walls of buildings were raw concrete marred with water streaks from the torrential rains that came in their season. The streets and the highway system that ran the length of the city were scary to drive on – missing guard rails and pot holes and, scariest of all, sprung storm drains. Because of the tropical rainstorms, storm drains were essential and crossed every downhill street at regular intervals. The metal rails of the drain-covers would, as is the wont of material objects, break after prolonged use. Rather than being replaced, a stick would be stuck upright to mark the danger so that cars would not lose a tire in the gap – some lasted years so that, even on the freeway, cars habitually slowed to pass around certain spots even long after the repair was eventually made.

But perhaps the purest, certainly the most towering, symbol of this era of economic irresponsibility was the Hotel Humboldt. Sited on the highest summit of the Avila, this ultra-modern, multi-story edifice is a magnificent sight from anywhere in the city below. A suspension-cablecar line had been built to lift guests and visitors swiftly up to the hotel (and, I was told, a second line was to take passengers down the other side to the resort hotels on the Caribbean). But the hotel was never opened for guests (not economically viable), and the *teleférico* had been broken for years. The hotel was still serviced. You could visit it if you had a four-wheel drive vehicle which could make it up the other side of the mountain. Rumor had it that the only regular users were the generals who had the occasional private bash there.

Though corrupt, CAP was not stupid.[89] He was, indeed, a highly intelligent and dedicated politician. On taking office the second time, he instituted a new regime of fiscal austerity. It was long past time to get Venezuela's budgetary house in order and CAP's measures were only logical. Unfortunately, he instituted his new measures within months of his inauguration – a ceremony so lavish that it was popularly termed his 'coronation' – and, doubly unfortunately, a key measure was a rise in the price of public transport. In the long era of falling real incomes, one saving grace for the Venezuelan man-in-the-street had long been cheap public transport; the proposed price rise, particularly combined with projected price rises for basic foodstuffs, meant that even middle-class Venezuelans could often not make ends meet. Additionally, and perhaps more important in terms of the Venezuelan psyche, Venezuelans had come to consider cheap gasoline as a birthright (gasoline was actually sold below production costs). The result was an explosion — hundreds, perhaps well over a thousand, were killed by the security forces in street riots. CAP became a hate figure.

Long before my arrival in 1992, rationality had departed the Venezuelan political scene. The sole focus was on getting rid of CAP. The politicians wanted to do it constitutionally or, at least, in some way that could be argued to be constitutional (when they finally did remove him from office, it was very much a case of rough justice, with the Congress essentially making up the Constitution as they went along). But, by the time they acted, the

---

[89]Though his insensitivity and arrogance extended to his flaunting an 'official' mistress.

rest of the people had long since ceased to care how they did it. There was a military coup attempt in February 1992, the first since 1948. It enjoyed widespread popular support, for the motives of its leaders if not for their methods. After it was defeated, the imprisoned leaders became folk-heroes.[90] And everyone began waiting for another coup. A few months after I arrived, in November 1992, the second attempt occurred. I watched much of the fighting from the windows of the Political Section in the embassy as rebel planes bombed the government troops attempting to re-take the headquarters of the Venezuelan Air Force (which was located in central Caracas about half-a-mile from the American embassy). On both occasions, particularly the first, CAP proved to be a man of genuine courage – the coupsters were out to kill him. In February, they missed him by minutes. In November, the day after the coup was put down, in a final gesture of defiance, some rebels 'bombed' the presidential palace with hand grenades (!). CAP still didn't seem, however, to understand the mood of the country. Everything was blamed on him.

It was easy to see why. All public services were gone to hell.[91] The judicial system barely functioned. Inherited from the Spanish system where everything was done in writing and the

---

[90]The astonishing popularity of the leader of the coup, Lt Col Hugo Chávez, was well illustrated by his election as president in December 1998!!

[91]Virtually the only state institution which functioned efficiently was the state petroleum company (PDVSA), a product of the nationalization in 1975 of the Venezuelan oil industry which had been developed by American oil companies – English remained its working language. A sign of the chaos or incompetence elsewhere was that, when the government decided to look into voting machines – after the disastrously chaotic and fraud-plagued local elections in December 1992 (with the multiplicity of small parties, each of which was represented on the ballot with its own logo as well as the name of its candidate, a Venezuelan paper ballot was the size of a circus poster and even more colorful) – the task was given to PDVSA.

judicial process moved forward in set stages each of which had its own lengthy written requirements, the system had nearly collapsed under the weight of a growth in crime while resources remained static (even a normal growth would have done it in, but crime in Caracas had grown exponentially). Court clerks barely had typewriters, much less computers (the World Bank was preparing a grant to computerize the central criminal courts). Underpaid, understaffed, overburdened, and facing the physical impossibility of ever actually catching up with their workload, court staff were receptive targets for bribes from anyone who wanted to see their case finally come to court (this included those who knew they would be convicted, since those arrested for crimes remained imprisoned on remand until trial, sometimes for years, without that time counting against their final sentence). Venezuelan prisons were considered the worst in Latin America (this was a common judgment, confirmed to me by experienced American consular officers who had spent their careers in the continent). Schools were without supplies, with teachers regularly on strike over wages which were insufficient for even a basic existence. Hospitals were stripped of supplies and equipment, stolen by doctors and nurses to re-sell in order to get enough to live on. The police did what they wanted. None of them was ever charged. Even the honest ones were largely ineffectual, since they received little or no training (the U.S. Department of Justice was conducting, during my time in Caracas, a series of seminars teaching the police such fundamentals as how to collect evidence and how to take notes that could be used in court – as well as how to conduct the questioning of suspects without resorting to beatings). The middle class had almost lost hope – their children could no longer expect to attend the private schools their parents had or get well-paying jobs as their parents had or buy an apartment like the one they had grown up in. In the midst of all this privation and decline, there was massive construction – of new luxury apartment buildings, funded by the laundering of drug money mostly coming in from neighboring Colombia. CAP was a culprit and he became the symbol of all that had gone wrong.

Where were we in all of this? Long, long before the first military coup attempt, the embassy had been reporting the time-bomb of corruption ticking away in Venezuelan society. No one in Venezuela much cared. Recall Betancourt's lament. After the coup attempts, they began to care. We also took on a new major objective – safeguarding Venezuelan democracy by letting everyone know who counted that a coup attempt, no matter who was behind it, would not be acceptable to the U.S. Great pains were taken on the exact terms of our standard message and on how it would be delivered. It was mostly done so in private exchanges to avoid the appearance of our acting in some sort of pro-consular fashion, though it was, on appropriate occasions, delivered publicly so that there would be no doubts (this was largely a typical damned-if-we-did, damned-if-we-didn't scenario – if we did, we were interfering in domestic affairs and acting the *Yanqui* bully; if we didn't, we were giving a green light).[92] In terminology, we focused on opposition to 'extra-constitutional' measures. If Venezuelan democracy was a facade, it was a

---

[92]This wasn't just our being paranoid; precisely this happened when a new defense minister (an admiral who, I might note, was a submariner trained in West Germany) made a private visit to Washington, D.C. and was invited to pay a call at the State Department. We were disturbed by his references to necessity sometimes overriding constitutions (he actually cited Abraham Lincoln's suspension of habeas corpus) and we told him so (we specifically rejected his analogy). Nevertheless, the Venezuelan newspapers were soon full of speculation that he had gone to get the 'green light'.

workable facade which, if preserved, could house a genuine democracy.[93]

The first notice I had of the November coup attempt arrived in the form of a Mirage jet-fighter. I had come awake in the early morning, aware that it was barely light and aware that I had been hearing gunfire that seemed heavier than normal (gunfire at night was frequent in Caracas). I went out to my living room in time to see a Mirage fighter blast across the sky, seemingly lower than my apartment which sat halfway up the Avila. I turned on the radio to hear ex-President Caldera proclaiming that 'la violencia no sirve para nada'. As I drove into the embassy, I passed many people on the streets, many holding pistols, but good-natured and joking as though it were a holiday. Early on, we issued a press release condemning the coup attempt. I didn't feel all that secure about that public gesture. Our embassy was a landmark building and it turned out that the pilots flying the Mirage fighters were rebels. Early that afternoon, shortly after the gunfire had died out as the last rebel troops surrendered, a Mirage jet buzzed the embassy; the sonic boom sounded like a thousand-pound bomb had gone off in the street outside.

You'll commonly hear, in countries like Ireland, that the U.S. dominates countries like Venezuela and that, in particular, our military runs their affairs. Venezuela is one of the larger and more significant of Latin American countries; in Caribbean terms, it is a local great power and has the full complement of military – an army, navy, air force and even a paramilitary national guard. While the cars on the streets are predominantly American and even carry American-style license plates, it's not the same in the military. They have French jet-fighters, German submarines and

---

[93]An additional problem was that Venezuelan political life was largely a gerontocracy; virtually all the politicians involved in drafting the new constitution of 1961 were still in office in the early-1990s.

Italian frigates. Their small arms are mostly Brazilian-made; the police carry Israeli and Austrian weapons. In all this, Venezuela mirrors the situation throughout Latin America. And if you say they don't need so much military, you'll have to talk to them. When we proposed a new strategic objective, within Inter-American defense cooperation, of a massive reduction in the standing military in Latin American countries (a reduction that would match our own in percentage terms), we were greeted with howls of outrage at this attempt to emasculate them.

We had much better luck with another initiative. Good governance. This would put governmental corruption on the inter-hemispheric agenda. Human rights were already there (as were trade and environmental issues). And the countries of the hemisphere had, a few years previously, formally agreed that it was now the legitimate concern of all the countries of the hemisphere that each maintain a democratic form of government. Governmental corruption as *the* obstacle to economic and social and political development was next. To this end, as I noted at the beginning of this chapter, a major step was reached at the Summit of the Americas held in Miami in December 1994, attended by all the democratic countries of the western hemisphere. Notably, this inclusive gathering left only Castro at home – a hero to gullible Europeans, a pariah to his Latin American presidential colleagues.

Within Venezuela, there were, of course, many honest men struggling to turn around a situation that seems almost hopeless. Rafael Caldera, the grand old man of Venezuelan democracy and once again elected its president in December 1993, was one. But his efforts and those of the others have largely been hamstrung by the refusal of the Venezuelan political class to give up its perks. Recall Betancourt's lament. A shining exception was *Causa R* (the Radical Cause). Condemned by the establishment as radical socialists, they were, in our view, reformists – trade unionists who simply wanted a square (and honest) deal for the workers which would also enable the industry concerned to prosper; public servants (such as Caracas Mayor Aristóbulo Istúriz) who wanted people to take responsibility for their actions in return for decent streets and schools and hospitals; internationalists who expected Venezuela to act as a responsible democracy and pay its debts (though, once in power, they would attempt to make those who stole the money pay it back). For them, taxes were an obligation and a tool, not a weapon. We did so much to encourage them that, during the presidential election in 1993, it was widely believed that the U.S. embassy was 'conspiring' to bring the *Causa R* candidate to power. When the American ambassador protested in a call on the presidential candidate of *Acción Democrática* that this was nonsense, the reply was, 'Así se dice en la calle'. I find this a delicious irony: Imperialist Uncle Sam and the Radical Cause arm-in-arm![94]

---

[94]For a similar debunking of self-righteous leftist assertions concerning U.S. policy in Latin America, see my article, 'The facts about 'Plan Colombia'', *Irish Catholic*, 7 September 2000.

Three

Economics 1: Economic Development and Global Negotiations

Since the ending of the Cold War and the consequent discarding of state socialism and its verities, there has been a sea-change in the terms of the international debate regarding the economic development of the Third World (indeed, this term itself is past its shelf-life, given the disappearance of the Second World that the Communist states constituted).[95] For the first time in nearly a generation, those involved directly in economic development issues are talking rationally about what must be done; the rhetoric of accusation is largely gone. This new civility is due to two fundamental paradigm-shifts: first, the command economy model – statist and centrally-planned – has been wholly discredited, and, second, there is increasing recognition that economic development, driven by economic liberalization, is indivisible from democracy and the protection of human rights. There is no alternative to liberal democracy.

For those of us involved in Third World economic development issues at the height of the New International Economic Order (NIEO) mindlessness, this is a welcome, and nearly unbelievable, change. Not that all is sweetness and light. While the professionals are reading, mostly, from the same page, pundits can still regularly be found indulging in what can, most fittingly, be described as the 'mythology of aid': the contention that the commitment of a developed country to alleviating Third

---

[95]An earlier version of this study was presented, in the fall of 1980, at Adjunct Professor John Stremlau's colloquium on the foreign policies of developing countries, School of International Affairs, Columbia University, New York.

World underdevelopment is measured by the amount of money it gives in direct aid – that is, its level of official development assistance (ODA). Regularly, for instance, there will be stories in the media about the need for Ireland to raise its ODA to the 'UN target' of 0.7 percent of GNP. The government junior minister concerned, of whatever party, will piously re-pledge the government's commitment to progress towards this hallowed goal. And snippish comments about the failure of the United States to even approach this goal will again be trotted out (though it is never mentioned that the United States explicitly rejects both the legitimacy and the validity of any such target). We need to be clear about this. Humanitarian or disaster-relief aid is one thing; the international community must and does always respond to calamity. But aid for economic development is something else altogether. At best, ODA is a palliative. At worst (as the dominant analysis of developing-country economic-theorists has long insisted), it creates a destructive dependency (*dependencia*), undermining indigenous initiative and perpetuating a begging-bowl economy.[96] Standardly – and despite the best efforts of donor countries – ODA re-inforces the control of corrupt local elites and existing inequities.[97]

---

[96]This is the rational side of the 'dependency' analysis; see Hedley Bull *The Anarchical Society* (New York, 1977), p. 88. The irrational – and by far the more vocal – side claims, as enunciated by Raul Prebisch, that dependency is actually and calculatedly forced upon the developing countries by the developed, with ODA as one weapon in the North's arsenal (along with foreign direct investment!); see David Landes *The Wealth and Poverty of Nations* (London, 1998), pp. 327-28 (and my review, *Sunday Independent*, 26 July 1998).

[97]Gerald M. Meier *Leading Issues in Economic Development* (Oxford, 1984), pp. 295-97, and Joan Spero *The Politics of International Economic Relations* (New York, 1977), pp. 141-45.

These realities, amply documented, have not, however, punctured the fatuous rhetoric of true-believers.[98] They are quite fond, for instance, of pinpointing Third World debt as *the* obstacle to development. Some of these pundits have actually cited the Old Testament prohibition of usury as a model for the forgiveness of developing-country debt, just as we have witnessed the Jubilee 2000 publicity campaign similarly calling on Biblical precedents. I suppose that, as well as a model for international financial flows, we should also turn to the archaic society of the Bible for models of public sanitation and racial equality (not to speak of international peace). More seriously, critics damn the World Bank and the International Monetary Fund for forcing Third World governments to slash social spending to balance their books. No, these UN bodies are not ogres, brutally victimizing indebted Third World countries. The parties responsible for the harsh choices are the national

---

[98]For an all-too-typical example of this sort of emotion-driven non-thinking on macro-economic development, see Dr Anthony Clare 'Rich man, poor man, beggarman, grief,' *Sunday Independent*, 18 July 1999. This article is, as is usual with such arguments, premised on the deliberate and polemical confusion of economic development (which is an absolute measurement) with 'world income distribution' (which is relative), unsurprisingly, then, the solution it proposes is one of re-distribution via increased national ODA. Emotion-laden phrases include 'greater selfishness' and 'relentless pursuit of wealth'. This is all particularly unfortunate because the good doctor does recognize that 'competitive markets best guarantee efficient production and economic growth'. However, instead of following the real-world logic of wealth-generation and then simply arguing the patently-obvious need for spending on effective social programs, he indulges in guilt-inducement and the pseudo-economics of the zero-sum fallacy that the developing countries are poor because we are rich and, therefore, they can only develop if we become poorer by donating a fixed percentage of our wealth to them (the 'black baby' syndrome). It is not surprising, then, that the thrust of his argument is that social deprivation is actually caused by economic growth – 'We need to balance concern for profits with concern for people'. Yes, let's all sneer at profit-making businessmen. But, then, Dr Clare is a psychiatrist.

governments themselves. Ineptitude plays a part in their poor performance in delivering public services; corruption plays a much larger role. Local government corruption, not international debt, is the key obstacle to Third World development.[99] And the solution is the integration of the developing countries into the world market.[100]

Logically, then, the measure of a developed country's true commitment here is measured not by its level of ODA, but by the openness of its markets to Third World products and the incentives it provides to Third World countries to export to it.[101] As Peter Sutherland has appositely noted, the aid regime of the European Union (the Lomé Convention) has failed 'in its objectives of...promoting social and economic development [because its] aid and trade provisions...restricted African countries to the export of certain primary commodities...'[102] We would all do far better to look to NAFTA as a model of an honest effort to promote reciprocal benefits and economic development.[103]

---

[99]Cf., John O'Shea 'Giving money to corrupt Third World leaders not the answer,' *Irish Times*, 12 August 2000; O'Shea concludes, 'That corruption is the single biggest obstacle to sustainable aid for the poor in the developing world is beyond argument'.

[100]Recall here my opening remarks about the indivisibility of liberal democracy; 'integration' of a developing country into the world market is, today, a process requiring concomitant democratization.

[101]This was argued cogently by the director of Oxfam Ireland, 'Oxfam campaigns for fairer trade,' *Irish Times*, 12 April 2002, at the launch of a campaign calling, *inter alia*, on the EU to cut its farm subsidies. The *Irish Times* (needless to say?) buried its brief report on the launch at the bottom of an inside page; contrast this with the half-page spread given the item by Brendan Keenan 'Free trade can be best aid for poor,' *Irish Independent*, 18 April 2002.

[102]*Irish Times*, 11 March 1997.

[103]You would think that the Irish, of all people, would recognize this inexorable logic concerning the how and why of economic development; all they

Despite this, the late Erskine Childers, in perhaps his last newspaper column,[104] claimed that the core obstacle to Third World economic development was the 'refusal' of the industrial powers to negotiate, within the UN, global macro-economic strategy. As an example of splenetic woolly-headedness, his 'argument' couldn't be bettered. The truth is that, for decades, the ability of UN bodies to effect Third World economic development was vitiated by the unremitting campaign to legislate the NIEO – for decades, the UN was hijacked by a self-serving and hypocritical alliance of the developing countries (negotiating as the 'Group of 77') and the Soviet-bloc into one vapid macro-economic negotiation after another over one nonsensical economic scheme after another. The NIEO, in brief, was quite simply central-planning (Soviet-style) on a global

---

need do is look around themselves. When I first arrived in Dublin in 1988, Ireland's national accounts were in crisis and the country was on the verge of being taken into receivership by the IMF. Less than a decade later, Ireland had become the 'Celtic Tiger' with a booming economy. How? There were, obviously, no new natural resources and the Irish work-force was just as well-educated and productive in 1988 as in 1998. Ireland did receive substantial 'ODA' (in the form of EC structural funds, etc), but the bottom-line cause was investment – primarily, foreign direct investment but also domestic (the commonsensical finding of all experts including UNIDO in its *Industrial Development Report 2002/2003*; see 'Republic ranks third in UN global competitiveness table,' *Irish Times*, 10 August 2002). Productive investment generates a confident business climate which generates increased investment. Profits re-invested create increased profits which, as a by-product, generate increased state tax revenues resulting in – depending on the democratic choices made – increased spending on social programs. An old joke, told to me numerous times by different Irish men and women, was that Ireland would be a banana republic except that its weather was too awful. This was an attempt to explain the persistent strain of reflexive anti-Americanism in the Irish public debate on international affairs as a consequence of its small country status, the bogus post-colonialist mind-set adopted by its intelligentsia, and its then relative economic backwardness.

[104]*Irish Times*, 1 July 1995.

scale; and its schemes were shamelessly designed to induce massive and automatic transfers of resources (mostly money) from the developed countries to the *governments* of the developing countries. That the developed-country 'donors' would have no say whatsoever in the use of the money by developing-country governments was an essential element in the NIEO. In the terms of one of the NIEO's founding documents, the Charter of Economic Rights and Duties of States, the developing countries had rights and the developed countries duties. This was, in those years, the level of 'logic' at which the so-called 'North-South Dialogue' operated.[105]

The period of this NIEO dominance of the economic-development debate within the UN – indeed, the NIEO constituted a cancer spreading its rancorous demands throughout the system, even in such tangential specialized-agencies as the Universal Postal Union – was marked in particular by a seemingly endless series of global meetings. As one after another of these gatherings, usually in a Third World capital, failed to reach even polite agreement, the standard accusation of the G-77 countries was that the developed countries lacked the 'political will' to agree to their demands. The reality, of course, was precisely the reverse: we in the developed countries had great political will and determination to resist the G-77 demands as, quite simply, economically-wrongheaded.

Our objections were, indeed, substantive and not just to the specifics of various schemes but as regards the very basics of how economies operate. In flat repudiation of the foundational G-77 declarations, we did 'not perceive the operations of the present international economic system as inequitable, nor its origins as

---

[105]See my review, 'Why the poor are with us always,' *Sunday Independent*, 15 October 2000.

illegitimate'.[106] We rejected the fundamental bias of the G-77 approach as statist and dirigiste. We rejected their indictment of the developed countries as responsible, in the past, present and future, for the underdevelopment of the Third World. We rejected the accusations of neo-colonialism. And we rejected the underlying operational ideology of the G-77's demands: their claims that there existed an absolute state sovereignty on the part of the developing countries over their development in all its phases and requirements, no matter how extra-territorial this might prove to be – the operational thrust of the G-77's claims portending a concomitant obligation on our countries to allow our own domestic policies to be regulated by international negotiations in which the G-77 countries would have majority decision-making powers. Thus, while the proposed global negotiating-bodies would have oversight – indeed, directive and coercive powers – over the economic policies of the developed countries, the domestic behavior of the developing countries would be solely their own business. They would run their affairs and they would run ours.

Nevertheless, despite this unbridgeable gulf on substantive issues, what prevented most of these meetings from reaching even minor agreements – and at most such global meetings there were, on the table, some practicable proposals which could have assisted economic development – was the political obstinacy and incompetence of the Third World negotiators. They were incapable of either organizing or conducting negotiations in a manner which would have permitted useful agreements to be reached. Rather, their sole negotiating stance was accusatory rhetoric. The Third General Conference of the UN Industrial

---

[106]Donald J. Puchala, ed. *Issues Before the 35th General Assembly of the United Nations 1980-1981* (New York, 1980), p. 73.

Development Organization (UNIDO-III) was a case-in-point. This global gathering was held in New Delhi in January-February 1980. It ended in a flat confrontation between the G-77 and the Western industrialized countries (Group B). The final resolution of the conference – the so-called 'New Delhi Declaration and Plan of Action' – was adopted by a vote of 83 to 22 (the Holy See abstained). Group B voted solidly against the resolution.[107] Even such stalwart opponents of confrontational situations as Austria, the Netherlands, the Nordics and Australia – the 'like-minded states' – voted 'No'. It could all have been foreseen. As I will detail, there was, in those years, a growing sense of global confrontation – UNCTAD-V at Manila, only six months previously, had ended in the same apocalyptic manner – but the immediate cause of the failure of this UNIDO conference lay in its operational specifics, in particular the manner in which the G-77 prepared and conducted it. UNIDO-III proved a case-study of the real constraints to economic negotiations in a UN global conference.

For UNIDO, the NIEO nightmare proper began with its Second General Conference which was held in Lima, Peru in March 1975. Along with the Sixth Special Session of the UN in 1974 and its resolution calling for the bringing into being of the NIEO and the subsequent adoption by the General Assembly of the Charter of Economic Rights and Duties of States (CERDS), UNIDO-II administered another shock to the economic sensibilities of the Western industrialized countries (which, in addition to Western Europe, included the United States, Canada, Japan, Australia, and New Zealand). Both the atmospherics and the substance of UNIDO-II were acrimonious. The draft general resolution tabled by the G-77 (the product of a G-77 ministerial

---

[107]UNIDO ID/Conf. 4/22, pp. 55-56.

meeting in Algiers) sought to introduce into UNIDO all the dirigiste concepts of the NIEO and the condemnatory assertions of the CERDS. This caught the Group B countries by surprise. Rather naively as it turned out, we had not anticipated such an attempted radicalization of the work-program of an organization which, up to then, had been devoted to practical industrialization projects in the Third World. In the end, however, only the United States voted against the Lima Declaration and Plan of Action as a whole (though Belgium, Canada, West Germany, Italy, Japan, and the United Kingdom abstained). The United States felt that an unambiguous expression of the fundamental differences it had with the G-77 would be more beneficial to future discussions than a false consensus.[108] This publicly-expressed view did not appease the G-77 who contended that their willingness through long hours to negotiate away so much of the contentious language of their original document should have been rewarded by consensus agreement. Many G-77 representatives stated for the record that they had been led to believe that this was to be the result and, consequently, they felt 'betrayed' by the call for voting not only on separate paragraphs but on the resolution as a whole. They seemed to believe that the rejection by the Western countries of the ideological assertions in their document was simply a smoke-screen, and they genuinely seemed not to realize that the West truly did believe that the bulk of the G-77 proposals in their 'Plan of Action' – particularly the most prominent of them such as the indexation of the prices of the imports and the exports of developing countries – constituted, quite simply, economic nonsense.[109] This lack of perception was not entirely the fault of the G-77 representatives. Our language of bluntness

---

[108]U.S. Department of State UNEC D-785/76, Rev. 1, pp. 1-8.

[109]Lincoln Gordon *Growth Policies and the International Order* (New York, 1979), p. 154.

on specific proposals was reserved for national position papers; it emerged in public utterances discreetly veiled behind obeisances to the mechanisms of a free market – an unpromising pattern for the future.[110]

At the first of the year, 1976, the UNIDO secretariat was itself extensively reorganized by its Executive Director to bring it into organizational line with the priorities mandated at Lima. Its various technical assistance divisions (that is, those which actually planned and executed industrial development projects in the developing countries) were consolidated into one division, thus effectively marginalizing what had, up to then, been UNIDO's *raison d'être*. New divisions and sections were created to mirror Lima's special objectives such as the transfer of technology and special assistance to the least developed countries. An International Center for Industrial Studies was established to serve as the 'brain' to map out the industrial component of the NIEO; its scenarios and global models aimed at achieving Lima's 'target': that the share of the developing countries in total world industrial production should be increased to at least 25 percent by the year 2000.[111]

On the part of the member states, attention was focused largely on two of Lima's primary objectives: the conversion of UNIDO into a specialized agency and the establishment of a

---

[110]This diplomatic avoidance of frankness caused even astute scholars to stumble into imagining that there can be serious 'negotiations' in the absence of any meeting-of-minds on the nature of the *quid*; cf., John Gerard Ruggie 'On the Creation of a New International Economic Order,' *International Organization* 30 (1976), p. 327: '...the proceedings of the Seventh Special Session indicate that although there is still no agreement between the rich and poor countries on the substance of fundamental issues, there now exists an explicit commitment to negotiate'.

[111]Para. 28 of the Lima Declaration and Plan of Action on Industrial Development and Co-operation (Vienna: UNIDO, 1975).

'system of industrial consultations'. The former proved achievable, the latter the very ideological devil itself. Five intergovernmental negotiating sessions on a constitution were held in Vienna followed by a plenipotentiary conference in New York in February 1978 which failed and another in Vienna in April 1979 which succeeded. The resulting document was largely satisfactory to all sides – the developing countries would have their agency with its own budget and administration separate from the UN secretariat in New York, and Group B (and on this issue, the Soviet-bloc countries – Group D – as well) would have the ability to control the budgetary process.

The establishment of a system of consultations took a different turn. As envisioned by the developing countries at Lima, such a system would involve the international negotiation of the 'redeployment of certain productive capacities existing in developed countries' to developing countries.[112] In plain terms, this meant that the countries of the world would, first, agree, via intergovernmental negotiations, on each country's fair share of production in any given industrial sector and would, then, direct the physical transfer of industrial plants from developed countries to any developing country lacking the requisite industrial production-capacity to meet its allotted share. In the vision of the G-77, this literally meant that steel plants, for instance, would be dismantled in the United States or West Germany and relocated in Brazil or India and that this would all be paid for by the affected developed country. At Lima, Group B had attempted to attack this proposal by indirection – by distinguishing between 'consultations' and 'negotiations' and by putting linguistic distance between the 'system of consultations' and the concept of 'redeployment' (purposely left undefined).

---

[112]*Ibid.*, para. 61 (d).

The first effort by the UNIDO secretariat to produce a work-program for the system of consultations, at the 1976 spring session of the Industrial Development Board (UNIDO's intergovernmental governing body), was flatly rejected by Group B. It envisioned a hierarchically-organized system of government representatives culminating in a ministerial-level commission charged with ratifying the negotiated division of international industrial production. As a compromise, the G-77 obtained, on a two-year trial basis, a new unit within the secretariat entitled the Negotiations Section and, for its part, Group B succeeded in circumventing the establishment of set rules-of-procedure so that the actual consultation meetings on given industrial sectors (such as fertilizer production) would be open not just to government representatives but to all interested parties (which specifically included industry representatives) and so that decisions would be taken by consensus (which, as throughout the UN system, meant the lack of overt opposition to a given proposal). This effectively limited the conclusions of any given consultation meeting to recommendations to the industry concerned. In such ways were the battles fought between the G-77's vision of a global economy run by central-planning and Group B's defense of a market economy.

Things did not improve with the secretariat's proposals for a draft agenda for UNIDO-III, first presented at the 1978 spring session of the IDB. Group B wanted a succinct, neutrally-worded agenda that would, by avoiding prejudicial language, allow the negotiations to focus on specific operational proposals. The secretariat's draft, in contrast, spoke of 'strengthening' proposals which had been rejected at Lima by Group B countries. The draft was also unnecessarily complex. What followed then in the IDB was truly surrealistic. I give it, in some detail, to illustrate the sort of mind-boggling 'debate' that was all too standard in those times.

After some fifty hours of negotiation, the chairman was able to announce at the last evening session of the IDB that agreement had been reached on all the items but one. On that sub-item, the G-77 and Group D supported one reading; Group B another. Both had been, as was (and is) the practice, left in brackets. Though the complexity of the agenda had been left largely untouched (and, indeed, in some items even added to), Group B was satisfied that the prejudicial language had, for all practical purposes, been eliminated. None of us, however, was particularly happy. At best, the draft agenda had been neutralized. But it had not been shaped into the sort of guide to practical action that agendas ought to be. It was another case of our operational philosophy of those years: 'winning is not losing'.

After a lengthy debate on what to do with the bracketed sub-items, the Group D spokesman – the Soviet ambassador – in what seemed an effort to inject a touch of humor into the strained atmosphere, proposed that the brackets be removed from the Group D/G-77 text and retained around the Group B text. In the midst of the ensuing laughter, the G-77 spokesman insisted that that had been a formal proposal and called for a vote. The vote was taken and, given the structure of membership on the IDB, passed over the unanimous objection of Group B. The G-77 spokesman than mused aloud – 'so there would be no misunderstandings' – that since the G-77/Group D text had just been approved, the Group B text had logically been stricken from the provisional agenda. The Group B spokesman countered that the logic was impeccable but irrelevant since the vote had not been to approve or disapprove a given text but had been on a specific proposal to remove brackets from one text and retain them around another. Group B insisted on the text of the provisional agenda being transmitted to the General Assembly in that form. The president of the IDB, which by rotation happened to be a Group B ambassador, ruled in favor of Group B's interpretation. The G-77 spokesman called for a vote on the president's ruling. The president ruled the motion out-of-order. Three hours later, after much rancour, exasperation, and name-calling on the margins, the matter was so resolved, and the provisional agenda was sent on to New York with Group B's text still in brackets. Such was the way that well-paid ambassadors and their staffs spent their evenings and nights in the Hofburg Palace conference hall in those days. I myself spent so much time looking at the ceiling, as I leaned back and rested my head on the back of my chair, that I could have qualified as an expert on baroque decorations.[113]

We all then began preparations for New Delhi. The Seventh Special Session of the UN General Assembly had called for a 'joint study...undertaken by all Governments under the auspices of UNIDO, in consultation with the Secretary General of UNCTAD, making full use of the knowledge, experience and capacity existing in the UN system of methods and mechanisms for diversified financial and technical co-operation which are geared to the special and changing requirements of international industrial co-operation, as well as of a general set of guidelines for bilateral industrial co-operation'.[114] Although at first unconnected with UNIDO-III and later proposed for consideration under an agenda item at the conference, it was commonly accepted by mid-1978 that the 'Joint Study' would be UNIDO-III's major thematic guide and would be supported by a special edition of the *Industrial Development Survey* (one of the

---

[113]The G-77 ambassador who provoked and sustained this bit of procedural farce subsequently became UNIDO's Director General!!

[114]Res. 3362(S-VII)1975

UN's major statistical productions) focusing on a review of progress made in implementation of Lima.

Largely dormant since it was first called for, the 'Joint Study' was moved to the top of the list by the Executive Director who detailed the deputy director of the joint World Bank/UNIDO industrial investment promotion office to head up a special 'Joint Study Group'. In confirmation of his commitment to the study, the Executive Director bestowed upon the group its own budget authority. Initial contacts with the 'Joint Study Group' by Group B were promising. As a World Bank official on temporary assignment to UNIDO, the Group's director seemed to us to be directing its efforts very much along World Bank lines, defining the goal of the study to be the elimination of absolute poverty and avoiding such contentious (for Group B) proposals as the meeting of specific quantified targets. Contact was largely lost, however, as the Group's director proceeded to hold the work of the Group tightly within it, isolated not only from the member governments but also from other UN agencies and even from other members of the UNIDO secretariat. However, periodic meetings with the director – my boss and I took him to lunch more than once – in which we urged him to concentrate on the development of specific projects falling within UNIDO's competence and not to be lost in global considerations did produce reassuring noises. The first draft,[115] ready in the spring of 1979, was, consequently, a substantial surprise.

Nearly three hundred pages in length, the study covered every imaginable aspect of industrialization (except domestic policy changes within the developing countries themselves) and called for the establishment of dozens of new institutions, such as TRIC,

---

[115]*Industrialization for the Year 2000: New Dimensions* (Vienna: UNIDO, 1979).

CLIC, and REGINA (a Tribunal for Resolution of Industrial Conflict, a Contractual Liability Insurance Consortium, and Regional Guarantees for Industry). Submitted first to a meeting of 'eminent persons,' the study was uniformly savaged – by those from Group B countries for being unrealistic and blurring the bounds of UNIDO's competence, by Group D for ignoring the experience of the Socialist countries, and by developing-country experts for being so overly ambitious as to be impractical. The Executive Director defended the study on the grounds that it was the secretariat's task to identify the 'gaps' which existed in the international industrial system and to propose means to fill those gaps. It would be up to the Conference to choose which proposals were to be implemented and which body was to implement them. A subsequent meeting of representatives of the concerned UN agencies, convened by UNIDO, was equally dismissive and was equally dismissed by the Executive Director. The final version of the 'Joint Study'[116] proved, in the event, to be lengthier than the first draft and contained some eight proposals for global action ranging from an International Industrial Finance Agency and a Global Fund for the Stimulation of Industry to a Manufacturing Trade Target.

By the late summer of 1979, focus within the groups had swung away from the secretariat to their own internal preparations. A disturbing factor for Group B was that, while preparing directly for UNIDO-III, we also had to deal with G-77 proposals on industrialization in other UN fora, particularly in New York in the Committee of the Whole – the projected oversight body of North-South negotiations – and in the General Assembly. As always, the G-77 used every opportunity to pursue a 'commitment in principle' on the part of the Western countries

---

[116]*Industry 2000: New Perspectives* (Vienna: UNIDO, 1979).

to the G-77's underlying dirigiste philosophy. The attack, which never let up, was both incremental and cumulative. Even a seemingly banal recognition by us of the 'importance' of industrialization in the development process portended a consequent commitment by us to a basic change in the pattern of world industrial production which, in turn, portended a rejection by our countries of a primary reliance on market forces to produce these changes. Rather, as the G-77 would have it, we would pursue polices which would produce the necessary 'restructuring' and provide, as well, concessional financing. It was contentious and essentially theological in that it dealt, in hairsplitting niceties, not in substance but in beliefs.

We turned to the OECD secretariat for help. A North-South group of member state representatives was established to direct the work required. Using the various proposals and recommendations of the 'Joint Study' as a focus, we asked the OECD secretariat to study the implications of these proposals for industry-government relations in the OECD countries. Throughout the fall of 1979, a series of meetings was held in Paris, papers submitted and refined, areas to be covered broadened. From the beginning, difficulties were foreseen. Although UNIDO recognized that the majority of the people in the Third World lived in rural areas, there was little in the 'Joint Study' regarding agro-based industries. There was, as well, a tendency to treat industry in isolation from the social and economic realities of any given country. Development strategies were categorized solely by their degree of dependence on the North; the widely varying resources of the individual developing-countries were ignored. As a result, the industrialization process emerged as a purely mechanical one, governed solely by plans and programs and governmental decisions. People didn't seem to be involved.

In capitals, most member countries of Group B had formed inter-agency coordinating committees at the sub-ministerial level to prepare for UNIDO-III. All were busy producing their own position papers, covering the various proposals, the enduring themes of the North-South Dialogue, the known G-77 activities, and positive measures which might be proposed. In addition, Group B in Vienna formed a group of deputies which attempted to sort out additional papers which were emerging from the UNIDO secretariat and to produce analyses of them by drawing upon direct knowledge of the personalities and other influencing factors in the secretariat. The agenda which had cost us so much time and anger had proved to be little more than indicative. It certainly restrained no one in the secretariat from pushing their own pet proposals. The briefing books for the member countries of Group B would be massive.

All of these multifarious efforts, moreover, proceeded under the constant constraint of lack of knowledge of G-77 intentions. There were some encouraging signs. Despite some rhetoric, none of the regional G-77 meetings had invoked ritual accusations of bad faith on the part of the North and none had made exorbitant demands for financial transfers. Our hopeful attitude was strengthened by the behavior of the G-77 at the 34th Session of the General Assembly that fall. Though their draft resolution on UNIDO-III, submitted by India in the Second Committee, contained sufficient difficulties to provoke long negotiations before a consensus text could be developed, the draft broke no new ground and the difficulties were over old battles: they wanted unconditional and obligatory transfers; we said no taxation without representation. In the end, the concerned paragraphs in the G-77 draft were modified to meet our concerns. The sole disquieting factor was the insistence of the G-77 that the United Nations both service and fund the upcoming G-77 ministerial. This violated UN procedures and principles, particularly the 'universality' principle that all UN meetings must, at least in principle, be open to all UN member states. The G-77 pushed it through on a vote of 84 to 7, with 25 abstentions. Though we hardly realized it at the time, it would prove to be a far more accurate indicator than any document of the intransigent determination of the G-77 to have their own way – regardless of legality and regardless of the impact their precipitate actions would have on the realities of international cooperation.

The G-77 ministerial to prepare for UNIDO-III was, after several false starts, finally held in Havana in mid-December. Originally scheduled to be held in October in Brazil, the meeting had slid forward due to internal G-77 difficulties. Though Group B was not pleased when the Latin American regional group entrusted UNIDO's Executive Director with the task of locating a venue for their ministerial, we did not formally object, feeling that overlooking this transgression of propriety by the head of a UN agency was justified by the need for the G-77 to meet so that their intentions could be put on paper. Those who had been at UNIDO-II in Lima remembered how all Group B's preparations had simply been 'thrown out the window' because the G-77 demands – which were not tabled until the opening of the conference itself – differed so radically from normal expectations. The choice of Havana, however, was less than pleasing. Just a few months earlier the summit of the Non-Aligned Movement (the political counterpart to the G-77) had been held in Havana, and memories were still fresh of Cuban manipulation of conference facilities and procedures and the Cuban call for the endorsement of the Soviet Union as the 'natural friend' of the developing countries.

Following the Christmas holidays, the G-77 representatives returned to Vienna. I remember running into my Romanian counterpart in the new UN building in Vienna and reminding him that UNIDO-III itself would open on 21 January and we still did not have copies of their draft declaration. He assured me that the UNIDO secretariat which was responsible for editing and publishing the document would soon have it ready and that, in any case, I shouldn't worry. In his words, I 'would be pleased' when I saw it. It was 'moderate and practical and action-oriented'. I expressed, politely, my doubts. I was in the UN building that day because I had been telephoned by a senior member of UNIDO's editorial staff who thought I should, privately and confidentially, be given a copy of the draft. I was there to pick it up. The staff-member passed it to me not out of any sympathy for the Western countries but out of deep concern for the future of an agency he had dedicated his career to.

The draft proved to be 95 paragraphs long, mostly in English but with some paragraphs in Spanish or French. And, as had been feared, it was basically simply a grab-bag of every developing-country's pet desires and was replete with inconsistencies and polemical paragraphs. There had been no apparent attempt to produce a document which could serve as the basis for negotiations. As an example of incompetency on a global scale, it could not be bettered. Some sample paragraphs:[117]

- Aware that the vast majority of the developing countries have been forced into poverty by alien occupation, racial discrimination including apartheid and Zionism, colonialism and neo-colonialism and that it is the duty of the international community, particularly the developed countries, to help them

---

[117]The following paragraphs are quoted from a photocopy of the draft text of the 'Havana Declaration;' no changes have been made in the text except to correct obvious typographical errors.

emerge from underdevelopment, occupation and subjugation.

- The Ministers viewed with profound dissatisfaction the fact that despite recommendations and commitments at various fora, most developed countries have not yet evinced the political will necessary for the successful conclusion of negotiations leading to a fundamental restructuring of the international economic system envisaged in the New International Economic Order.

- The Ministers welcomed also the recent victory of the people of Iran and assert their right to have full control of their economy and natural resources.

The polemical tone and accusatory language could be negotiated away, as they generally were. Even before negotiations began, internal inconsistencies and infelicities could largely be eliminated by editing by the UNIDO secretariat, though experience had demonstrated that the G-77 could be surprisingly, and disturbingly, stubborn in resisting efforts to coordinate and unify the policy prescriptions of their draft resolutions. The condemnation of a 'basic needs strategy' as a divisive tactic in one paragraph and the endorsement of it as a fundamental aim in another would not necessarily bother them. Consequently, Group B focused, in the little time remaining, on the most troublesome operational proposals.[118] These we identified as a commitment for

---

[118]Our initial reaction to these proposals was to simply refuse to discuss them; as a tactic, the standard reference to 'late receipt of pertinent documents' was trotted out. In the end, it seemed too tepid a maneuver in light of the magnitude of the conference about to take place in New Delhi.

the attainment of the 'Lima target' and its disaggregation into regional and sub-regional targets; a commitment by the governments of the industrialized countries to 'intervene actively' to effect redeployment of industry from developed to developing countries; a commitment to increase ODA to a target percentage of GNP and to increase the percentage of ODA going specifically to industrialization; the conversion of the 'system of consultations' into a formal negotiating forum for implementing redeployment objectives; and, most disturbingly, a commitment to a massive transfer of resources to a 'Global Fund' to aid industrialization (originally a proposal by Fidel Castro, it called for a transfer of $300 billion to the developing countries in the decade, 1980-90).[119]

Two thousand delegates from 133 countries, including two heads of state and seventy-nine ministers, participated in the three-week conference.[120] The general debate, which ran throughout the course of the conference, involved some 142 speakers and stood in some contrast to the course of the negotiations being carried on simultaneously in two, and then three, committees. Relatively few G-77 speakers gave blanket endorsement to the 'Havana Declaration' or to the G-77 draft plan of action. Virtually all did lead with by-now ritual condemnations of various international *bêtes noires*, such as perceived increases in trade barriers to developing-country exports, and virtually all called for increased and concessional technology transfers and increased and concessional financial transfers (though most did not specifically support the proposal for a Global Fund). However, most of them also recognized the need for domestic

---

[119]The startling nature of the 'Havana Declaration' can be judged by Group B's belief, as late as 8 January, that no proposal for major new funding would surface from the G-77 ministerial meeting.

[120]The official report is UNIDO ID/CONF.4/22 (dated 11 April 1980).

efforts, particularly in developing links between industrial development and other sectors such as agriculture and the necessity of responding to the basic needs of their peoples. There was, then, a good deal of rationality in the general debate.

In contrast, discussion in the negotiating committees was openly adversarial. Two committees had been foreseen by the resolution authorizing UNIDO-III, and agenda items had been distributed between them by the final preparatory session of the IDB in November 1979. However, both committees were stalled due to the demand by the G-77 that their draft 'Plan of Action' (adapted, mostly verbatim, from the 'Havana Declaration') be adopted as the *de facto* agenda. Group B insisted that the agenda as approved by the General Assembly be followed, arguing that our preparation for the conference had been made on the basis of this agenda which had resulted from long and arduous negotiation in the IDB (remember the rancorous 'debate' into the early hours in the spring of 1978?). After a prolonged procedural wrangle, the *modus operandi* reached was that the debate would proceed on the principle of forbearance.

On each item, debate would be opened by the secretariat with a background statement drawn from the proposals and recommendations of the 'Joint Study'. On certain items, such as the development and transfer of technology, additional background papers had been prepared by concerned sections of the secretariat which had been frozen out of the preparation of the 'Joint Study,' and the proposals and recommendations contained in these background papers would be introduced as well. The G-77 spokesman would then read from the pertinent paragraphs of their draft 'Declaration and Plan of Action,' and the Group B and Group D spokesmen would speak to the actual agenda item. After working in this fashion through the agenda, both committees converted themselves into informal working groups to negotiate on the basis of the G-77 draft. As the second week ended, it had become evident that the two working groups would not be able to cope with both the 'Declaration' and the 'Plan of Action' simply because of the sheer volume of text – a total of seventy pages. Consequently, following some Group D resistance, a third working group was formed to deal with the 'Declaration'.

Though progress was made towards agreement on some of the operational proposals of lesser significance, positions on the major issues, both principles and operational proposals, remained entrenched. In the working group on the 'Declaration,' Group B submitted a re-draft of the G-77 text, deleting political and anti-Western content. This was rejected, virtually *in toto*, by the G-77, though such efforts had regularly been successful in the past. This time, the G-77 refused, as well, to accept previously agreed language from such resolutions as those of UNCTAD-V or the UN General Assembly or even from the Lima Declaration, arguing that these were all in the past and they were looking to the future. In the two working groups on the 'Plan of Action,' a similar stand-off occurred on the key proposals. On industrial technology, for example, the G-77 refused to recognize the proprietary nature of most technology and continued to insist that developed-country governments arrange for its transfer on undefined 'concessionary terms,' without any consideration of the legal limits to such actions; and on energy, efforts by Group B to introduce concerns about energy supply were coldly received (remember that this was the heyday of OPEC). The keystone of the G-77 'Plan of Action,' though, was the creation of the $300 billion Global Fund for the stimulation of industry. They insisted that for the conference to be successful a 'commitment in principle' on the 'parameters, purposes and principles' of the fund must be reached.

With three days remaining in the conference and no agreement in sight, the president formed a 'presidential contact group' limited to three heads of delegation from each group, plus one expert adviser for each group who would change according to the subject of negotiation. The group met, around the clock, for the next two and a half days. At the first meeting, the president presented his 'compromise' text. Negotiation proceeded on a paragraph-by-paragraph read-through of this text. If any group proposed an amendment to the text, the amendment would have to be accepted by all the groups, otherwise the 'compromise' text would stand. From our point of view, the president's text was, needless to say, hardly a 'compromise'. The preambular paragraphs in its 'Declaration' were virtually verbatim from the 'Havana Declaration' as it had been presented, after being edited into proper format, to the conference. The sole significant change was the deletion of the references to Zionism. The section on industrial financing also dropped specific reference to Fidel Castro's proposal and any mention of an overall target, but set the annual level at $15 billion and maintained a 'decisive role' for the developing countries in the management of the fund. After hours of debate, Group B decided to abstain on the document as a whole and ask for a paragraph-by-paragraph vote. Our intention was to vote on some twenty paragraphs out of the 315 paragraphs of the text. When the president was informed of this, he urged that his text be adopted by consensus with Group B covering its concerns through explanations-of-vote. We refused and the president withdrew his 'compromise' text. The G-77 then presented its original draft text as the 'New Delhi Declaration and Plan of Action' and it was adopted by the vote already described.

Obviously, the basic cause of this total failure was substantive. In polite terms, it can be described as the Group B position of reform versus the G-77 position of restructuring. In real world terms, it was a confrontation between those of us who wanted to effect improvements in the way UNIDO could assist industrialization efforts in the Third World and the G-77 ideologues who professed a view of international economic relations which, quite simply, was unworkable – indeed, if their 'system' had ever been implemented, it would have proved as destructive of the global economy as it was of the economies of the Soviet Union and the other Communist-ruled countries. Simply put, an economic system which relies not on incentives but coercion implodes, sooner or later.

It is only partly a mystery how the individually-moderate and constructive attitudes of the developing countries could be transmuted into the polemical, radical and economically-mindless document of the 'Havana Declaration'. Any member-state in good standing in the G-77 was evidently able to have included in this document whatever it wanted. No one seemed to have attempted to control it; and, yet, the integrity of the document as a whole was maintained at New Delhi by the steady pressure of the G-77 leadership. Though the moderates, such as Kenya, Nigeria, Chad, Bangladesh, the ASEAN countries, might exhibit a continuing undercurrent of dissatisfaction with their leadership, they never publicly challenged them. Though India might seek a moderating role and be visibly distressed at the outcome of the conference, Indian diplomats never attempted to moderate significantly the radical and insulting proposals of their group. Instead, at the ending of the conference, the president, who was the Indian foreign minister, publicly placed the blame for the failure 'squarely in one quarter' – the rich nations.

The obdurate stance of the G-77 provoked speculation that the radicals – the Cubans, Algerians, Mexicans (with ex-President Echeverría as delegation head), the Nicaraguans, Iranians, and Romanians – were pushing for a UNIDO-III blow-up, as part of their long-term North-South strategy and with no consideration whatsoever for UNIDO as an institution. Specifically, it seemed that some of these extremists believed that the forced adoption of a highly slanted and polemical text would give them 'leverage' over Group B in the upcoming global negotiations scheduled to begin early in 1981 – we would be constrained, they believed, to be more 'forthcoming' in light of this failure.[121]

These considerations of substance and of global 'strategy' aside, the more immediate reason for the failure in New Delhi was procedural – the total absence of any negotiating mechanism capable of getting a handle on a text as lengthy and diffuse as the draft presented to us by the G-77: 'The Havana Declaration...restates the whole Group of 77 position on the present state of the world, if anything in looser and more strident terms than before. There is little attempt to put forward meaningful proposals for negotiations with the developed countries, still less of a recognition of the need for the developing countries themselves to adopt more sensible policies'.[122] Certainly, there was no recognition whatsoever of the fundamental need of countries, entering on a global negotiation, to come prepared. In the minds of the G-77, there was, evidently, no problem at all in all of us Group B delegates just showing up and agreeing – 'in principle' – to whatever they chose to put forward. A less business-like approach is not imaginable. But, then, the G-77 diplomatic representatives contemned

---

[121] A caustic overview of the entire NIEO negotiating process from a Western point-of-view is Robert K. Olson 'North-South: Negotiating Survival,' *Foreign Service Journal* November 1980, pp. 27ff., especially p. 29: 'Illusion 5: That UNCTAD or any other Third World dominated conferences on the NIEO are negotiations; they are not.... These 'negotiations' are more of an international court where Group B countries are judged and ordered into line....'

[122] A.F. Ewing 'UNIDO III,' *Journal of World Trade Law* May-June 1980, p. 252.

businessmen. At the end, the senior aide to the Indian president of the conference actually complained to us that the conference's failure was wholly due to Group B's failure to come prepared to negotiate a beginning for the Global Fund.[123] The G-77 simply refused to acknowledge that a proposal of such magnitude cannot be agreed to off-hand but requires a staffing-out process which can mean months, if not years. It would be unkind to suggest that this is due to the decidedly-different and more personally-direct nature of the decision-making process in most of their countries. But, at the least, it is certainly a case of wilful blindness.[124]

Regardless, the G-77, throughout the remainder of the blessedly-brief reign of the NIEO, continued to push for agreements to proposals which were based on economic concepts which market-economy countries could never accept. It seems now that it must all truly have been a rather confused nightmare. Like dealing with Soviet economists, you found yourself engaged in debates with no bearing on economic realities and using terms which had no life outside the pages of UN documents. I certainly enjoyed my time in Vienna. If you cannot enjoy being a diplomat in Vienna, then you're not suited for the business (nor for life itself). In my own case, I was particularly fortunate. It was my second tour-of-duty and, as a junior officer, I could not have had a better posting. As the deputy permanent representative to UNIDO, I was the number two in the U.S. Mission to that organization (as I used to tell people, I was the number two in a two-man mission). And, though we were an independent diplomatic mission, we had an office suite in the American embassy on Boltzmanngasse, a lovely eighteenth-century baroque palace which we had acquired after World War II. At some

---

[123]U.S. Department of State UNEC D-313/80, p. 25.

[124]Robert L. Rothstein *The Weak in the World of the Strong* (New York, 1977), pp. 365-68.

previous time, it had housed the Austrian diplomatic and consular academy. Over the main entrance, supported by granite putti, were the shields of Austria and Hungary with the motto, 'Inseparabiliter et indivisibiliter'. As a prophecy, it provoked chuckles but, for me, it was, as well, a condign (and daily) reminder of the utter lack of relationship of the nature of the work I was compelled to pursue with the actual world of economic development.

Four

Economics 2: Soviet Realities and East-West Economic Cooperation

It soon became commonplace to hear the post-Soviet Russian economy described in despairing terms.[125] Standardly, it was claimed that Yeltsin insiders, exploiting their entrenched positions in the old Soviet bureaucracy, had allied themselves with corrupt business magnates to seize control of the country's industry, diverting IMF loans into their own pockets on the way, and had thus caused economic and political 'reform' measures to result in universal impoverishment, rather than ushering in the intended prosperity. An 'enriched corrupt kleptocracy' amid general penury encapsulated this conventional wisdom.

Certainly, the pervasive corruption was all too real, but the facts on the ground suggested a rather different reality concerning the general level of economic well-being and, while not underestimating the seriousness of Russia's problems, we need call up but a few of these facts to belie this depiction of an economy, and a country, on the verge of dissolution. In 1989, when the Berlin wall came down, the Soviet Union ranked 77th in the world in personal consumption and Soviet citizens spent between 40 and 68 hours a month in queues. A decade later, the queues were gone, the shelves in the shops were full, and not only was Russia self-sufficient in grain – for the first time in forty years – but was actually exporting millions of tons. However creakingly, then, the economy was coming round.

---

[125]An earlier version of this essay was presented, on 10 January 1995, at the Centre for European Economic and Public Affairs, directed by Dr Richard Sinnott, at University College Dublin.

So why such a discrepancy between image and reality? At the superficial level, it is simply one more tiresome example of the prevailing tendency in the media to judge situations in absolute terms, to see in frozen-image snapshots, and to measure 'progress' against an abstract standard of perfection. We witness this journalistic paradigm in operation every time the United States is involved in a war – if, for instance, civilians are accidentally killed, the U.S. stands convicted in the media of war crimes as heinous as those of the tyrant it is seeking to deter. Within this judgmental framework, then, it was self-evident that post-Communist Russia, because it had not yet achieved a stable liberal democracy and a fully-functioning free-enterprise economy, was, therefore, a failure.

But, underpinning this general cognitive myopia, has been a reportorial failing specific to Russia: an ahistorical amnesia concerning the realities of the Soviet economy. Most everyone seems to have forgotten what it was like. It is not commonly acknowledged, for instance, that not only has corruption been endemic in Russia for centuries, but – more to the present point – it reached its apogee under Communist rule. By eliminating all legal and personal restraints – including press freedom and judicial independence – and by concentrating all power in the hands of state bureaucrats, Soviet totalitarianism achieved a steady-state of enrichment through bribery and outright theft, while the economy stagnated. This Soviet centrally-planned economy was to a market economy as anti-matter to matter. It was not just that the institutional mechanisms were bogus – the distribution, trading, statistical, and information systems, for instance, were either parodies of their market counterparts or were simply non-existent – it was also that this command economy extirpated all the personal characteristics and incentives which drive the free-enterprise system: personal initiative, personal responsibility, honesty, even common sense. It will take decades of democratic politics and press freedom and the rule of law and the operation of the market to construct, as though anew, a Russian society at home with freedom and opportunity.[126]

To call up an historian's cliché: if we are to understand where we are going, it is helpful to know where we've come from. My own experience with Soviet realities came in the area of international trade. Indeed, I spent four years in the trenches of the Cold War. I can't claim they were uncomfortable since this particular front line was in Geneva, but it was hand-to-hand ideological combat with representatives of the Soviet-bloc countries. These were the four years, 1981-85, I served as the principal officer at the U.S. Mission in Geneva dealing with the Economic Commission for Europe. The ECE was the first of the UN's regional economic commissions, established within a few years of the UN itself. Its first Executive Director was Gunnar Myrdal, and Eugene Rostow served as his senior economic adviser. I committed the *faux pas*, when I learned of this history not so very long after my arrival, of commenting to the then-current senior adviser, 'There were giants here in those days'.

By the time of my arrival, in the summer of 1981, the ECE had long become an East-West negotiating forum.[127] The western

---

[126]Perhaps the most essential liberal-democratic reform required in all the former Communist countries is a system of legally-enforceable property rights; see Hernando de Soto *The Mystery of Capital* (London, 2000), *passim*. For an overall assessment, see Anders Åslund *Building Capitalism: the Transformation of the Former Soviet Bloc* (Cambridge, 2003). Anders was a diplomatic colleague during my first years in Geneva; since then he has become the most noted of analysts of the economic transformation of the successor states of the Soviet Union.

[127]As sufficient indication of its politicized nature, the Executive Director was always a neutral (that is, from a member-state not a member of either NATO or

countries – all of Western Europe together with Canada and the United States – were grouped as the Western Caucus, and the Soviet-bloc countries – or, as they were officially termed, the Eastern European Socialist countries – were the Eastern Caucus. Not that these groupings had any official standing. In origin, the ECE's mandate had been pan-European economic re-construction and cooperation. This vision immediately fell victim to Stalin's clanging-down of the steel curtain: his rejection of Marshall Plan aid for the countries where the Red Army was encamped[128] and the adventurist brinkmanship of the Berlin blockade. Three-plus decades on from those dark days, the ECE could be justly proud of a solid record of achievement, particularly in the promotion of standardization aimed at facilitating international trade. The TIR carnet was a prime example. This allowed a transport vehicle to be sealed and to then roll across several frontiers with only its custom documents having to be inspected, rather than the contents of the vehicle being unloaded for inspection at each border-crossing. However, other areas of its work-program – such as environmental protection, statistics, and business promotion – were, to say the least, less advanced. Indeed, how retarded we didn't truly realize in those years. We didn't, for instance, understand at all how extensive and, indeed, systemic environmental degradation was in the Soviet-bloc countries.[129] Instead, we were regularly lectured by their delegates on how these countries were world-leaders in this area. What we did

---

the Warsaw Pact), his deputy a Soviet, and the senior adviser, who was the third-ranking official, an American.

[128]This also put paid to our preferred option of having the Marshall Plan operate through the ECE; see George F. Kennan *Memoirs 1925-1950* (Boston, 1967), pp. 338-41.

[129]Cf., David Landes *The Wealth and Poverty of Nations* (New York, 1998), pp. 496-98.

understand in those days, however, was that the failure to progress was, in every case, due to the intransigence of the Soviet Union and its satraps.

This was, of course, an understanding which, at the best of times, was kept under wraps. In official exchanges, we all participated in the charade that the Soviet-bloc countries were cooperating in the promotion of whatever was on the agenda. This wasn't due to any lack of willingness to confront the realities of Soviet economic pretense. It was a hard-headed recognition that this was the only way to get any cooperation at all out of them. Any publicly-stated objection to their way of 'doing business' was met with the charge that this constituted 'slandering Socialism as an economic system' and if it was not withdrawn then the Eastern Caucus countries would withdraw altogether until it was. It's difficult to credit, today, how suffocated the exchanges were. Nevertheless, it was something you learned to live with. What I never truly adjusted to, though, were discussions within the Western Caucus itself when this same pretense – that we were dealing with serious economics on the Eastern side – was maintained. The single worst offender in those years were the Austrians. To them, the Soviet Union was forthcoming and the U.S. was the one digging in its heels and blocking agreement and progress. It was looking-glass stuff.

Years later, I read of Saul Bellow's surprise, on arriving in Paris in 1948, at discovering the apparent general ignorance among the French intelligentsia of the history of the Soviet Union. When reading such as Sartre, who would, in fine Marxist style, speak of an 'oppressive bourgeois ideology' while turning a wilfully blind eye to the crimes of Stalin, Bellow could only conclude that Sartre and his fellow-travelers were not simply displaying an extraordinary naiveté under the guise of European sophistication and intellectual superiority – as arrogantly self-assumed as it was unjustified – but were, in fact, cynically 'positioning themselves for a Russian victory'. Over subsequent decades, Bellow found that the continuators of this Sartrean stance of literature as radicalized-political engagement were particularly adept at what he termed the 'equivalence game' – that is, if you attempted to explain particular failings in a liberal democratic society, you stood convicted of crimes against humanity itself. Or, as Bellow paraphrased Günter Grass' attack on him: 'You have spoken well of the American system because you are an apologist for it and a stooge; you are not concerned about the poor, and you are a racist to boot'.[130]

The particularly infuriating aspect of this stance was that it was based not on facts but on ideological conviction. Liberal democracy in the West, and in the United States in particular, was judged systemically evil because of observable wrongs (such as the brutal history of racial discrimination in the U.S.) while quantifiably far worse evils in Communist countries (such as the murders of tens of millions) were dismissed as aberrations or written off entirely as propaganda fabricated by anti-Communists or, most dismayingly, justified as necessary 'sanitary' measures on the path to the workers' paradise. There are, today, still those who take this stance, though they are now rightly treated as wholly marginal and living in an ideological fantasy-land. They have found themselves on the wrong side of history, as the internal contradictions of Communism caused its implosion. History has proven them to be the pathetically-deluded fools they always were.[131] One ironic consequence of this utter demolition of their 'arguments' is that it is difficult to truly recall today how pervasively they dominated, for nearly three decades from the

---

[130]Saul Bellow *It All Adds Up* (New York, 1994), pp. 106-11.

[131]Cf., Robert Conquest *Reflections on a Ravaged Century* (London, 1999), pp. 115-84; and my review, *Sunday Independent*, 27 February 2000.

early 1960s, the political debate, not just in France where political debate, like philosophy, is no more than intellectual gamesmanship, but even in politically-sensible countries like the United States or Great Britain. We know they did do so, but we resist crediting our memories out of the absurdity of it all. How could the radical left have so succeeded in portraying their delusions as reality?

I witnessed their success first-hand. I was an undergraduate at the University of California at Berkeley. When I began as a freshman in the fall of 1962, patriotism was still a virtue and both the student body and the faculty would have – not unquestioningly but, nevertheless, resolutely – believed that America's Founding Fathers had, in the Declaration of Independence and the Constitution, created a system of governance which promoted stability, legal equality, and justice. Certainly, there were wrongs and these were recognized – this was, after all, the height of the era of the fight for civil rights – but it was held that the American system provided the means within itself to correct these wrongs. Underpinning this shared vision was a comparative understanding of the past. People, then, understood that things were better than they had been; they kept the past in mind when contemplating the present. After all, the parents of the students then as well as the majority of the faculty had gone through both the Great Depression and World War II. In particular, we were under no delusions about the nature of Communism. Whatever the apologists for it might claim, we Americans could witness for ourselves the suppression of worker demonstrations and revolts in East Germany and Poland and Hungary; indeed, the American labor movement had suffered first-hand from attempts at Communist subversion. There was also the small matter of the bitter war fought against Communism in Korea. We could see facts as facts. I remember standing in a crowded television room in the Student Union in October of that year listening to President Kennedy announcing to the nation the discovery of offensive ballistic-missiles in Cuba and his consequent decision to impose a naval quarantine on the island. One student began to boo; he was hustled out of the room. Support for the president's statements and for his position was all-but-total.[132]

In the mid-1960s, I spent my own three years in the U.S. Army. When I returned to Berkeley in 1968, all had changed.[133] In my absence, it was as though there had been a seismic shift in fundamental assumptions and beliefs, and 'Amerika' now stood guilty of evil at home and of evil abroad. This wasn't just the attitude of the radical few. If the faculty and student body were polled, there would have been consensus agreement that the United States was an aggressively imperialistic nation which was without doubt the superpower at fault in the Cold War. This 'judgment' would have been considered a truism and, as a conceptual tool, it permeated treatment of American foreign policy in the media and in intellectual debate, particularly in academia. A whole pack of platitudes were devised to bolster this fundamental belief: the prime one, perhaps, being that Soviet post-war policy was purely defensive and reactive. The imposition of Stalinist-regimes in Eastern Europe was now seen as justified by the Soviet Union's need for a defensive buffer-zone; after all, didn't we invade Russia in 1918 and didn't we drop the atomic bomb on Hiroshima solely as a warning to the

---

[132]Cf., my review, 'Kennedy's ideals in the years of the Cold War,' *Sunday Independent*, 25 February 2001.

[133]See my article, 'Revolutionary Berkeley, then and now,' *Sunday Independent*, 9 August 1998.

Soviet Union?[134] You questioned such 'truisms' at the risk of being ridiculed as naive. Among the well-educated, the abdication of intellectual integrity was wholesale; this *trahison des clercs* was perhaps only paralleled in our time by the shift, in the 1930s, from a wholly-justified belief in Germany's basic responsibility for the war to a self-flagellatory stance of guilt over what was now considered the shameful, punitive treatment of the defeated Germany.[135]

How to account for this? Even having witnessed it first-hand, I am still at a loss to account for how this perversion of reality became the prevailing view, but its origins are evident – in the sustained attack on the integrity of American statesmanship generated by the school of revisionist American historians of the Cold War. Most of this school's major names were self-identified Marxist historians – that is, they believed that Marx had, indeed, discovered the iron laws of historical evolution (the very mechanics by which history operated) and they gathered their material and wrote their analyses in accordance with Marx's deterministic vision.[136] For them, all that happened and would happen was clear and understandable provided you viewed it in Marx's 'scientific' framework. For serious historians, such as George F. Kennan, these historians' treatment of source material was slippery and unscrupulous to the point of dishonesty.[137] But,

---

[134]On this, perhaps still the most succinct and measured presentation of the arguments and the facts is Arthur Schlesinger, Jr. 'Origins of the Cold War,' *Foreign Affairs* 46 (1967), pp. 22-52.

[135]See George Orwell 'As I Please 18,' *Tribune*, 31 March 1944 (reprinted in *Essays*, New York: Everyman's Library, 2002, pp. 575-78).

[136]Cf., my review of Walter LaFeber's *Michael Jordan and the New Global Capitalism* in the *Sunday Independent*, 3 October 1999.

[137]Many of their views and conclusions were simply equivalent to Communist propaganda; see George F. Kennan *Democracy and the Student Left* (New York,

then, Kennan, after all, had merely witnessed first-hand the treacherous nature of Stalin's regime and diplomacy. What was that to lay against ideological conviction?

As I say, so pervasive was this condemnatory view of American foreign policy in our intellectual life – its operating assumptions held total sway in the pages of our quality general-circulation periodicals such as the *New York Review of Books*, the *Atlantic Monthly*, and *Harper's* – that it was a surprise to me to discover, when I entered the American diplomatic service in the summer of 1973, that the State Department operated wholly uninfluenced by it. No one there paid any attention whatsoever to the revisionist view and its propagators. If anyone read Noam Chomsky, it was for amusement. Never was there such a gulf of perception between academe and the professionals. For my own part, having concentrated on early medieval history as both an undergraduate and a graduate student, I recognized my need to go on a forced diet of reading in American history and I purchased two dozen or so recent works. Among them were books by revisionists like Gabriel Kolko and David Horowitz. I too found them amusing (Horowitz's *The Free World Colossus* was a particular gem). More seriously and profitably, I read all the books by Richard Hofstadter that were available in paperback.[138]

1968), pp. 137-40; and David Mayers *George Kennan and the Dilemmas of US Foreign Policy* (New York, 1988), pp. 286-88.

[138]So insidious had been the creeping dominance of the Cold War revisionist historians, that even Richard Hofstadter, as late as 1969, had not foreseen that they, and not those he termed the 'consensus historians,' would seize the moral high-ground in American academia. Indeed, he actually projected a revisionist historical swing back to a starting-point based on the American verities that America was different and better; see his *The Progressive Historians* (New York, 1970), pp. 437-66. It may just be that he had such contempt for the Marxist historians' shabby abuse of historical sources and arguments that he didn't

I don't remember now if I ever asked my fellow brand-new Foreign Service officers if they had read Hofstadter, but he could have served as our particular mentor. We too shared his cynicism about American politicians and we also shared his belief in the essential goodness of the American character, as shaped by our history and taught in our schools. We saw not conflict but congruence between our American principles and the policies we would be asked to help implement. Certainly, many of us did not share in the general admiration of Henry Kissinger. I thought his approach sinister and a deviation from traditional American diplomacy (his view of diplomacy was not just academic but Germanic, and his apotheosization as 'Super K' was a creation of the media and the Eastern establishment, not the result of approbation by the professional diplomats who worked under him).

When I arrived in Geneva in 1981, Kissinger, fortunately, was no longer in power. Those of us dealing with the Soviets were concerned to repair the damage done to American integrity by his so-called policy of détente in which he had envisaged the encouragement of 'organic' linkages between the Soviet Union and its client-states in Eastern Europe. We went back to encouraging democracy and economic liberalization. Not that there was fertile ground for such encouragement in the ECE in my time there. Rather, we were in a Stalinist-type freeze, as we reacted to the imposition, on the demand of the Soviet Union, of a military dictatorship in Poland. This mini-freeze lasted through most of my tour of duty in Geneva. Early on, I was approached by my Polish counterpart, Jan Bielawski, who said that he wanted to discuss with me ways that we could improve the working

consider them to have merited historiographical consideration; certainly, their works are lacking from his bibliography.

relationships between our two governments. I had to tell him that I was sorry, but that my government didn't want improved relations with his government as it was then constituted. What we wanted was for them to lift the oppression of the Solidarity labor movement and of other pro-democracy elements in Poland. Nevertheless, Jan and I became good friends – to the extent that, at one point, he told me the following Polish joke: General Jaruzelski is in a quandary about what to do about all the unrest. Nobody in Poland is able to give him any effective advice, so he goes on a pilgrimage to Moscow and kneels next to Lenin's body and beseeches Lenin to tell him what to do. Lenin's body rises up to proclaim, 'Use the classic Marxist response. Arm the workers.' Jan was a realist.

He was also an exception. With the further exception of the Hungarians (who were, already, well on their way to surpassing even their own brand of 'goulash Communism'), the other Soviet-bloc representatives all acted as though they believed what they said. I recall one lunch, a large group of us working-level diplomats at the restaurant table, when I overheard the Soviet diplomat claiming that the Red Army had never occupied a country which it had not then evacuated unless invited to stay. When I queried this, I was assured by the Bulgarian that it was so. The Austrian concurred. The same looking-glass irreality prevailed in the official meetings of the ECE. There we were told by Soviet economists, who religiously invoked their scientific methodology, that there was no inflation in the Soviet Union, there was no unemployment in the Soviet Union, and all the economic problems that might exist in the Soviet Union were imported from the West. In the environmental protection committee, the only measures the Eastern Caucus representatives would permit on the agenda were those dealing with 'transboundary' pollution problems; no consideration was permitted of their internal environmental standards. Indeed, no information was forthcoming from them. The ECE had over a dozen standing committees covering all conceivable industrial and economic sectors, from steel to energy trade. Each turned out an annual statistical report. Given the high quality of the statisticians and economists working in the ECE's secretariat, these would be reports of great value, except that the Soviet-bloc countries regularly failed to comply with the reporting requirements and the ECE, as an intergovernmental body, could only report those statistics officially received from governments. One hopes that the members of the secretariat staff were squirreling away in their office files whatever statistics they were able to obtain unofficially.

Why did we put up with it? Simply because it was the only game in town. No one at that time could have foreseen that, by the end of that very decade, Communist rule would simply disappear. We all presumed a long future to our efforts to deal with – in the official boiler-plate phrase – countries of 'differing economic and social systems'. For a variety of reasons, it was far preferable to push on with our incremental successes in inducing a modicum of rationality in East-West economic relations than to simply write them off as incompatible. Certainly, trade had a moderating influence, politically, however negligible it seemed at times. And there was the straightforward objective of profit for our businesses – whenever, that is, they managed to get a toehold on the glacier-face of Soviet bureaucracy.

Indeed, trade manifested all the myriad other-world aspects of dealing with the Soviet command-economy. It wasn't just that you had to face up to a resistant bureaucracy. It was all bureaucracy. There were no businessmen on their side, and, from our side, our businessmen were not allowed contact with their industrialists. There were no visits to shop-floors except on

Potemkin-village tours run by the bureaucracy. Marketing simply wasn't part of the interaction. You dealt with the designated central government official, period. I remember the astonishment when the Soviet delegate to the annual Development of Trade Committee meeting announced that he had brought with him for distribution (one copy to each delegation) the first-ever guide for businessmen to the Soviet Union. In the thick booklet, there was lots of information on sights to see; there were no telephone numbers of individual industrial concerns. When an Austrian delegate – a businessman serving as an expert adviser – pointed this out, obliquely hinting that the guide seemed more an obstacle-to-trade than a help, he was slapped down, immediately, by the Austrian diplomat heading his delegation who apologized for this 'inadvertent' insult.

This was the world of state-trading companies. And of counter-trade. Which was, for some reason I now no longer remember, officially referred to in the ECE as 'compensation trade'. In most cases, it amounted simply to barter deals. If a company wanted to do business with the Soviet Union, it had to sign a contract requiring it, for instance, to purchase from Soviet concerns goods equal in value to the goods it sold to the Soviet Union. From the Soviet side, this had two immediate benefits; it obviated the need for the Soviets to pay in hard currency and it enabled them to export their goods without the need to market them (in effect, the Western company was coerced into becoming a marketing agent for Soviet goods). In practice, Western companies had developed the negotiating expertise to whittle the Soviet demands down to a percentage of the value of the goods which they supplied – businessmen will be businessmen. Personally, I thought that nothing could be more revealing of the rudimentary nature of Soviet economic thinking – international trade as barter deals between governments.

And nothing was more revealing of the 'unreal' character of our work in the ECE. The field of battle was one of their devising, and, for us, it amounted to constant resistance to their objective of compelling us to create, on our side, a mirror image of their 'trading' system. As with the theological debates which dominated the North-South dialogue, our efforts in the ECE were directed more at deflecting bad economics than of supporting positive measures. Not that there weren't moments. Once during the annual governing-body meeting of the ECE, my ambassador and I were having a corridor conversation with the East German ambassador who was acting as the chief negotiator for the Eastern Caucus. He had initiated the conversation, wishing to complain about our restrictions on technology trade. Specifically, he was abusing COCOM (this was a relatively informal committee, established under the NATO aegis, which sought to coordinate the export policies of member-states regarding security-sensitive goods such as computers).[139] His abuse was ritual; the Soviet-bloc countries (who were, after all, COCOM's targets) had long demonized the body. Feeling mischievous, I pointed out that the U.S. government had a program which regularly provided expert assistance to developing countries to enable them to take full advantage of our GSP scheme to promote their exports of manufactured goods into the U.S. Perhaps, I suggested, we could agree in the ECE on a similar scheme to provide advice to the Eastern European countries on how to conform to COCOM restrictions. The East German ambassador actually smiled.

While all these areas – trade, the environment, statistics, transport – required close attention on my part, my primary concern, for the first three years of my time in Geneva, was the

---

[139]On this and other trade terms, see John J. Harter *The Language of Trade* (Washington, D.C.: USIA, 1983).

Senior Advisers on Energy. We had long been concerned about East-West energy trade. Many western countries were increasingly looking to Eastern Europe as a source of energy supply. For political and security reasons, we thought this a basically bad idea. Nevertheless, the Germans and others pressed ahead with the huge gas-pipeline project with the Soviet Union. In the ECE, these same countries wished to promote increased cooperation in this area. In principle, we did not oppose cooperation, provided that it *was* cooperation (that is, a genuinely two-way exchange of information and benefits). The Soviets had different ideas. There were obvious benefits for them in East-West energy trade – hard currency and access to technology being two – but, to outward appearances, these seemed to run a poor second in the Soviet mind to propaganda. In 1975, East and West had signed the Helsinki Final Act. This embodied political, human rights, and economic commitments by all the signatories. The economic commitments were in the section of the agreement known as Basket II. As their particular follow-up to Basket II, the Soviets had proposed high-level meetings (HLM's) in environmental protection, energy trade, and transport. These were known as the 'Brezhnev Proposals' and became enshrined in the work-program of the ECE. The HLM on the environment was held in 1979. Its major achievement was an agreement to curb long-range transboundary air pollution (as already noted, the Soviet-bloc countries were only willing to negotiate concerning pollution which crossed international borders; their internal production of pollution was nobody else's business). The next item was energy trade, and the Senior Advisers on Energy was established on an *ad hoc* basis to prepare for its HLM.

We weren't happy about this. We agreed that the HLM on the environment had resulted in an agreement which was, at least, an incremental step towards getting the Soviet-bloc countries to face up to their environmental problems (the devastating extent of which, as I've already noted, was not even guessed at by any of us at that time), but we queried whether this was worth giving the Soviets such a propaganda coup. In our analysis, the Soviets had two primary objectives. The first was to trumpet the HLM's as evidence of their 'commitment' to Helsinki (while they ignored their obligations under the human rights articles). The other was to use the HLM's as wedges to split the Western Europeans from the U.S. – in the Russian language version of ECE documents, the HLM's were termed 'All-European Congresses'. In our reading, they considered any economic benefits to themselves as entirely secondary.

Our arguments did not make much headway within the Western Caucus until the Soviets, in December 1981, compelled the imposition of martial law in Poland. Now, there was general agreement within our caucus that there could no longer be 'business as usual'. This didn't mean that our European friends agreed on a freezing of economic cooperation with the Soviet Union. They were still compelled by their long-standing desire to avoid friction. In this, they weren't just being weak sisters. As they constantly reminded us, the ECE, even during the darkest days of the Cold War, had nurtured the flickering light of the possibility of cooperation. But they did recognize the need for a meaningful response to such a fundamental violation of the Helsinki Final Act (as well as the UN Charter etc etc), and, given our focus on energy trade, this was the chosen target. Language promoting the Brezhnev Proposals was stripped from the agenda and the resolutions of the governing body, and projects supporting the HLM on energy were eliminated from the ECE's work-program. Not that all was sweetness and light on our side. In internal Western Caucus discussions, particularly those held as the time for the annual governing body came nearer, the Nordics and the Neutrals[140] constantly attempted to whittle away at the firmness of our position. The particular bone of contention was the Senior Advisers on Energy (SAE). It had a three-part mandate. In addition to preparing for an HLM, it was charged with promoting exchanges of information on energy trade and with developing a work-program in this general area. We – the U.S. – were accused of blocking practical cooperation in this area due to our opposition to the HLM. Some of what was said, particularly by the Austrian ambassador, came close to accusing us of bad faith. The truth was the reverse; it was the Soviet Union which was using the blocking of the HLM as justification for its not engaging in practical cooperation in this area, cooperation which it had never had any intention of providing. For them, the HLM was pure propaganda and the SAE was its delivery vehicle.

Then came Gorbachev. And a general desire to ease the stand-off. Though we didn't realize it at the time, this partial thaw was the beginning of the melt-down of Communism in Eastern Europe. We responded by indicating to the Western Caucus in the lead-up to the annual governing body in the spring of 1984 that we would no longer object to the scheduling of a session of the Senior Advisers on Energy provided, solely, that it did not proceed with planning an HLM. This was welcomed, and the French ambassador, as the president of the EC, diplomatically indicated this to the other side. He stressed that this was part of a Western approach which sought to emphasize the positive developments in East-West relations. Additionally, the Western Caucus would refrain from political attacks during the governing body (that is, no more condemnations of the Soviet-compelled crackdown in Poland) in order to promote an atmosphere

---

[140]A succinct designation of my own devising for those member-states of the Western Caucus who might as well have been described as Soviet apologists.

conducive to doing business. He sought, and believed he had received, assurances from the Soviets that their side would behave likewise. We were disabused in the first plenary session. Their rhetoric was hostile and unrelenting. At the first meeting of the negotiating contact group, the French ambassador blasted the Soviets and their allies for breaking the clear understandings between the caucuses that such behavior was out. They attempted to justify what they had said: it was all dialectical logic and Marxist terminology; 'imperialism,' for instance, simply meant 'market economics'. The Irish ambassador drily remarked that calling an Irishman an imperialist was just not on. The French ambassador took their recalcitrance as a personal rebuff and insult. The upshot was that, despite no country having any substantive objection to scheduling the Senior Advisers on Energy and despite our having dropped our political opposition to it, the decision to do so was never allowed on the table by the French ambassador.

I considered this more than an ironic turn-of-events, after all the antagonism I had faced over the issue for the best part of three years. More delicious irony was in store. After several months, the Executive Director of the ECE began making noises indicating that he believed that, since no country objected to the scheduling of the Senior Advisers on Energy, he intended to proceed to do so. He was encouraged to this view by West Germany which had long been a prime mover in this area. However, for some reason none of us ever discovered, the Swiss were incensed by it all. They insisted that to agree, outside the framework of the annual governing body, to convene such a meeting would be not just to reward the Soviets for their bad behavior at the plenary but – of more long term concern – to vitiate the negotiating authority of the governing body. All this put us Americans in an invidious position. We could hardly go back on our new position without damaging our own policy of conciliation. But we could hardly say, as the West Germans were pressing the Western Caucus chairman to have us say, that all was now fine with us. The Swiss, always our invaluable and tough-as-nails ally (except on acid rain), would feel abandoned, and Western Caucus unity would be damaged (not a minor concern for us, since we had more often than I cared to remember relied on caucus unity as the bottom-line argument why our minority position should prevail – and for 'minority,' you could more often than not read 'minority of one').[141]

In a corridor chat with my Swiss counterpart, I suggested that perhaps a way out would be for the Western Caucus to agree to meet informally with the Eastern Caucus, as well as with the Executive Director, and agree on terms for the next session of the Senior Advisers on Energy, on the understanding that any agreement reached would both need to be and would be ratified by the next governing body. This satisfied those who wanted movement on the issue (as well as wanting it removed as a contentious item from the agenda of the governing body) and also satisfied the legitimate need to maintain inviolate the authority of the governing body. At the meeting of the Western Caucus called to discuss this problem, the Swiss presented this as their proposal. I was happy to support them fully. The French ambassador broke

---

[141]The simple reason for our awkward insistence on maintaining our position in the face of at-times unanimous opposition from 'friends' is that we take seriously and literally the obligations contained in a UN resolution; we are not prepared, as far too many of our Western colleagues are, to play the hypocritical shell-game of signing up rhetorically to resolutions we have no intention of observing in fact. Contrary to the mean-spirited assertions of such as Garret FitzGerald 'It's time Ireland took positive role in European foreign policy,' *Irish Times*, 4 April 1998, this does not amount to our having a 'dismissive attitude' to the UN and to international law; the obvious truth is, rather, that we take a perhaps too-rigorous view of what it means to give our word to an agreement.

EC ranks to flatly support the Swiss contention that the decision itself could only take place at the plenary. Others spoke up in support of informal negotiations as well. It was so agreed. And, thus, after three years of fighting a bitter rearguard resistance to the Senior Advisers on Energy and all its works, I ended up as its savior and the mid-wife of its rebirth. Out of such stuff were diplomatic successes constructed. At least in those years. Across the board, you felt in a sort of parallel world where words had been deprived of their normal meanings. No inflation in the Soviet Union, no unemployment in the Soviet Union, and all this supported by 'scientific' analysis. I may not have witnessed myself the wanton cruelty of Stalin's regime but I saw, in abundance, the Soviets' disregard for the truth, their conspiratorial secrecy, and their assertions of infallibility.

When my tour in Geneva was up, I was transferred to The Hague. There I was no longer dealing with economic issues but political. Still, I found at play the same prevailing dissociation of belief and behavior from facts.[142] It was the time of the great

---

[142]I have already noted at the beginning of this chapter the abundant evidence, exhibited by our Cold War revisionist historians, of this tendency in our own time towards cognitive dissonance. Noam Chomsky can serve as the classic example. Those who are competent to make such a judgment assert that Chomsky's contributions to linguistics are on a par with those of Einstein to physics. He is, then, a person of towering intelligence. This makes his stance on politics and international relations genuinely mystifying. How can such an intelligent man be so perversely wrong-headed? You feel that the only explanation has to be ulterior – a psychological need for notoriety, perhaps (cf., Isaiah Berlin *Against the Current*, London, 1997, p. 281). Some on the left blame censorship for the disappearance over the last two to three decades of Chomsky (whom they term a 'noted dissident') from the mainstream press, even from such left-leaning periodicals as the *New York Review of Books*. The truth of course, is that Chomsky finally wandered so far out of the realm of rationality in pursuit of his own deviate agenda that no reputable editor, concerned with objectivity and factual accuracy, would touch him, despite his continuing drawing-power. Chomsky, as does

agitation against the deployment of Cruise missiles. In the Netherlands, we witnessed demonstrations numbering in the tens, if not hundreds, of thousands. Some of the participants were simply cynical; they didn't want to become nuclear targets. Many, perhaps most, however, were driven by conviction – they truly believed that they had nothing to fear from the peace-loving Soviet Union. I remember being asked by the international

---

everyone, has the right to his own beliefs, however bizarre and unjustifiable, but he does not have the right to his own facts. For anyone unfamiliar with the methodology of Chomsky's polemics, I would direct them to an early classic, 'Objectivity and Liberal Scholarship,' *American Power and the New Mandarins* (Penguin, 1969), in which Chomsky linked his analysis of the fate of the 'popular revolution' within the Spanish Civil War with the American vs Communist conflict in Vietnam in order to discredit what he saw as the systemic bias of left-liberal intellectuals against 'social revolution'. What this article actually reveals is Chomsky's wilfully-naive belief in exemplary behavior by those radical leftists whom he considers sufficiently in tune with 'popular mass movements' – for instance, he claims that the Chinese rural collectivization was based on 'persuasion and mutual aid' rather 'than on force and terror' (p. 113, n. 56). Pity about the 30 million who died in this man-made famine. This radical naiveté of Chomsky's (combined with a carping disdain for the very possibility of good faith on the part of American efforts) effects his ideologically-bent cognitive world in which everything true Marxists do (particularly those of anarchist or libertarian Socialist predilections) is good because they have done it, while everything we (the West, the Americans, the 'Imperialists') do is correspondingly sinister. Today, the only ones who still credit Chomsky are immature university undergraduates and those who inhabit the same otherworldly realm of self-indulgent ignorance and woolly-headed thinking. Indeed, Chomsky's 'thinking' on international politics bears the same relationship to the actual world of inter-state relations as New Age religion does to philosophy. In practical terms, he is to the left what a John Birch polemicist is to the right. We should also note, in conclusion, that Chomsky's combining genius in one field with wilful idiocy in others is not unique. As H.L. Mencken *Thirty-five Years of Newspaper Work* (Baltimore, 1994), p. 38, commented of an acquaintance, a world-class surgeon who was also a bible-thumping fundamentalist, 'From him I learned the useful lesson that a man may be really distinguished in a difficult field of human endeavor, and yet remain, in all other respects, a complete jackass....'

representative of the FNV, the largest of the Dutch labor federations, what 'proof' I had that the Soviet Union intended or would ever intend to use its newly-installed SS-20 intermediate-range ballistic missiles. Logically, I replied that intentions were impossible to prove (until, of course, after the fact) but that capabilities were countable. The SS-20s were real and countable as was their deployment in Eastern Europe. As were the tens of thousands of tanks and the Soviet divisions stationed in those countries. As were the forward-based materiel dumps. The whole configuration of the Soviet military forces in Eastern Europe was not defensive, but offensive.[143] My interlocutor wanted nothing to do with logic or with numbers or with military realities. He preferred wishful thinking. It was a widely-shared preference in those days.[144]

---

[143]All facts which, in the post-Soviet era, have been publicly confirmed by senior Russian military officers.

[144]Cf., my review, 'Days of subversion,' *Sunday Independent*, 31 December 1995.

Five

Politics 1: The U.S., Ireland and the first Gulf War

Although I was a senior officer at the American embassy in Dublin throughout the first Gulf War – indeed, I was the *chargé d'affaires* when Saddam invaded Kuwait – I will have relatively little to say about the performance of the Irish government during that crisis. To some degree, I am inhibited by diplomatic privilege. But, perhaps more telling is that Ireland, as a country, absented itself from the conflict and there is, accordingly, little to be said. So, this chapter is, rather, a look, from an American perspective, at public Ireland at that time.[145] How it was, that is, that that Gulf War was perceived and presented by the Irish political class – the media and the politicians and all those who both concern themselves with such affairs and whose views are felt to matter – and what we Americans made of it all.

The Gulf War broke out on 2 August 1990 as Saddam Hussein's military overran Kuwait. He declared Kuwait part of Iraq. On 3 August, the UN Security Council voted 14-0 to condemn the invasion. On 6 August, the Security Council ordered sanctions against Iraq. On 7 August, President Bush announced the sending of U.S. troops to protect Saudi Arabia, and some fifty American, British, French, and Soviet warships converged on the Gulf to enforce the sanctions. On 10 August, twelve of the twenty Arab League states voted to send troops to assist the U.S. in defending Saudi Arabia. This, in very capsule format, was the first week of the Gulf War.

---

[145]An earlier version of this paper was delivered, on 13 January 2001, to the Irish Association for American Studies at University College Dublin.

I do not intend to proceed in such a detailed fashion for the entire war. I note these events simply to set the stage and as a reminder of how virtually universal was the condemnation of Saddam Hussein's action among both Arab and non-Arab countries. Many myths rapidly developed about this war, myths which are re-flogged whenever there is a flare-up of tensions in the Gulf. One was that this was a war driven by Western interests. As indicated simply by my capsule summary, this was clearly not so. Another which is regularly stated as simple fact was that the American ambassador in Iraq had given Saddam Hussein the 'green light' to go ahead with the invasion.[146] It is tiresome to have to deal with such unthinking assertions but, unfortunately, these factoids seem to have a life of their own. The truth, of course, is that the American ambassador, called precipitously to a meeting with Saddam, reiterated the U.S. policy-line that we took no position on the border dispute between Iraq and Kuwait and expected this dispute to be settled by negotiations between the parties. Why did our ambassador not deliver a strong warning against taking hostile action? Simply because no one – I repeat, no one – anticipated that Saddam would be so mad as to invade another Arab country. Let me quote the opening sentence of the lead *Irish Times* article on 3 August: 'Iraq's invasion...of Kuwait...surprised everyone in this region – Iraqis, Kuwaitis, Saudis, Arab and Muslim...western and eastern diplomats and the Israelis'. This article was by Michael Jansen, not a journalist – as we shall see in some detail later – disposed to reporting events which could be taken as favorable to an American interpretation; indeed, I would imagine that she later much regretted reporting so

---

[146]For example, Vincent Browne 'Coverage of sex circus squeezes out the real news,' *Irish Times*, 28 January 1998.

objectively, given as she is to spinning facts into conspiracy-
theories.

It was during this initial period of two to three weeks, that we
at the embassy were most concerned about the attitude of the Irish
government. Let me make this very clear. We were not, in any
way, concerned about the official position which the government
would take. We were sanguine that the Irish government, as with
all other member-states of the EC, would support the UN
resolutions on the war. Support for the UN Charter had, after all,
been one of the specific policy positions on which Ireland had
entered the UN in 1955.[147] Beyond that, we did not expect the
Irish to actually provide material support. We had long learned
the local limitations. What we were concerned about however
was a certain Irish governmental inclination towards
pusillanimity in the face of public disquiet. Over the previous two
years (that is, the period after my arrival in Dublin), there had
been a number of international issues on which the government
did not seem willing to vigorously defend its own position in
public. I could, for instance, attend parliamentary question time
for the Taoiseach or the foreign minister in the Dáil and hear
statements which we in the embassy could have written, they so
mirrored our own understanding of the issue concerned. But,
outside the Dáil, it seemed that if any given handful of people
were vociferous enough, the government started ducking for
cover.

A prime example of this was the public furore over Cambodia
in the autumn of 1989.[148] The occasion was the resolution in the

---

[147]Cf., Joseph Morrison Skelly *Irish Diplomacy at the United Nations. 1945-
1965* (Dublin, 1997), pp. 37-39; and my review, 'High-minded Interventions,'
Irish Review 22 (1998), pp. 123-24.

[148]What follows treats of the Irish government's role re this issue; for that of
the Irish public, see chapter 2 above.

UN which set down the basic conditions for a political solution in that sad country. The original sponsors, who negotiated the language of the resolution, were Cambodia's regional neighbors, the member-states of the Association of Southeast Asian Nations (ASEAN). It was co-sponsored by some seventy-five other nations, and it was eventually passed by a vote of 124-17-12. The resolution called for the withdrawal of all foreign military forces, for free elections under UN supervision, and for no return to the 'universally-condemned policies and practices of the past'. However, because the resolution did not specifically condemn the Khmer Rouge but referred to their evil only in this back-handed way, the resolution was condemned in Ireland by all the opposition parties. The United States came in for particular vilification. One senator accused the Irish government of 'lick spitting to United States imperialism'.[149] Large-scale demonstrations were held in front of the American embassy. Editorials condemned us for cynical complicity in genocide.[150] The Irish government was fully aware that none of this was rational. It knew – if for no other reason than because its diplomats at the UN were first-rate and assiduous and knew well who the actors were – that the U.S. was, at best, a marginal player in this affair in New York. It also knew that when the Irish ambassador delivered Ireland's 'explanation-of-vote' – which carefully pointed out that Ireland's vote in favor of the resolution could not, in any way, be construed as support for the Khmer

---

[149]See the official report of Seanad Éireann, Vol. 123, No. 5 for 16 November 1989, col. 489.

[150]This odious travesty was all-but-duplicated, a decade later, by the *Irish Times* in its editorial on the 'Death of Pol Pot' (17 April 1998), in which it referred to the 'cynicism of Cambodia's international partners' and claimed the 'Khmer Rouge coalition enjoyed wider international support from the United States and European powers at the United Nations'.

Rouge – that the sentiments expressed were identical with those expressed in the American 'explanation-of-vote' (indeed, ours expressed not just condemnation of the Khmer Rouge but also our adamant opposition to any return to power by them). And the Irish government also knew that our $24 million dollars in 'non-lethal' aid which went to Prince Sihanouk was directed to Cambodian refugees along the Thai border, with those refugees within Cambodia itself being excluded since these camps were controlled by the Khmer Rouge.[151] Nevertheless, the Irish government was not willing to stand up to this public flak. Rather, they chose to use the Irish presidency of the EC, which began just a few weeks later in January 1990, to push the EC into adopting the policy of an 'empty seat' at the UN for Cambodia. We know, because the ASEAN participants told us so, that when this policy-shift was announced to them at the EC-ASEAN summit they were appalled. On such a sensitive issue for their region, they were being unilaterally told that the Europeans knew better. Well, the ASEAN diplomats knew as well as we did that the shift was not taken for policy reasons.

It was with this sense of concern that I, as *chargé d'affaires*, kept my eagle eye on Iveagh House. What I feared appeared on the front-page of the *Irish Times* on 14 August under the headline, 'Dublin views US tactics as contrary to UN stance'. Ascribed to a spokesman for the Department of Foreign Affairs, the article began, 'The Government is withholding support from the United States military build-up and naval blockade in the Gulf, on the grounds that it does not accord with the United Nations resolution arising out of the invasion of Kuwait. '[152] We at the embassy were, of course, fully aware of Irish neutrality and

---

[151]See the *Irish Times* coverage, 15-17 November 1989.

[152]Front page, though below the fold, 14 August 1990.

the complications this policy posed for the Irish government in a military conflict. But let's recall what was involved on the 14th of August, less than two full weeks after the invasion. It was not yet a question of a military strike against Iraq; it was a question of defending Saudi Arabia and of enforcing UN-imposed sanctions against Iraq. Additionally, no one had any intention of asking Ireland for any direct assistance. The piece struck me as gratuitous and as pandering to the vociferous nutters who we in the embassy felt dominated the public foreign policy debate in Ireland.

I first confirmed, with the spokesman in Iveagh House, that the article was accurate and I then advised him that my report on it would not make happy reading in Washington. I believe I may have said something about American congressmen being briefed as well.[153] In any case, it was the last such leak. For the next few months, the Irish government was faced, as so many countries were, with maneuvering rhetorically between firm support for the UN resolutions on the crisis and concern for the Irish citizens who were being held hostage by Iraq. The government held firm. And, fortunately, the Irish citizens were finally let leave. Many of them, while they were in hiding, had used our beleaguered embassy in Kuwait to keep in contact with family or friends in Ireland. Their messages were passed, in confidence, by us to Iveagh House. It would be nice to be able to say that we received thanks from the Irish government once the Irish citizens

---

[153]The Irish embassy in Washington had long engaged in by-passing the State Department and conducting, quite successfully, the substance of U.S.-Irish relations with the Congress; for an early example, see Troy D. Davis *Dublin's American Policy: Irish-American Diplomatic Relations, 1945-1952* (Washington, D.C., 1998), p. 207 (see also my review, *Irish Historical Studies* 31, 1999, pp. 583-84).

concerned had got to safety.[154] I suppose we Americans must be satisfied that, in the debate on the Gulf War in the Dáil on 18 January, the government repeated its position of support for the UN resolutions and its intention to fulfill its obligations under the UN Charter and that Foreign Minister Collins specifically stated that there could 'be no question of invoking neutrality' in regard to supporting these resolutions.[155] It may, nevertheless, have helped if such a declaration had been made much sooner. Indeed, before the Dáil debate, it had been left to the deputy to the ambassador at the American embassy to point out publicly that Ireland was not in fact neutral in this crisis. It might also have been nice if, on the same occasion of a brief interview with the *Irish Times*, this American diplomat had not felt obliged to point out that Ireland was the only member-state of the EC which was not making either a military or a financial contribution to the coalition effort[156] – a point underlined, however inadvertently, by the Taoiseach in the Dáil debate when he announced with what seemed to be some satisfaction that the U.S. military transports which were being allowed to transit Shannon were paying 'full commercial rates' (I might here note, parenthetically, that Luxembourg offered not just to waive landing fees for our aircraft but to refuel them without charge).

Why this pusillanimity on the part of the government? Why, for that matter, was the Irish Labour Party the only serious socialist or social democratic party in Europe to actually oppose the coalition in the war? We have now reached the real concern of

---

[154]While we didn't, the British did receive public thanks in the Dáil for providing the same assistance; see Joe Carroll 'Gulf War fails to do serious damage to Irish-American relations,' *Irish Times*, 18 March 1991.

[155]'Decision to allow refueling facilities at Shannon overwhelmingly endorsed,' *Irish Times*, 19 January 1991.

[156]'Irish stance on Gulf "not neutral,"' *Irish Times*, 12 January 1991.

this book, for I believe that the answer lies in the area of public perceptions and, specifically, in the damage done to Irish perceptions of American foreign policy by decades of misinformation and distortion by a wide variety of public commentary. Since at least the early 1980s, many foreign commentators have noted, often with considerable surprise, the anti-American bias in much Irish public commentary.[157] As I explored at length in the Introduction, the causes of this phenomenon – which finds its common expression in overt contempt for American actions and motivations – are as varied as they are nebulous of proof. Some are, in themselves, benign: elements of small-country resentment, of self-justification for Ireland's own powerlessness to effect significant results on the international scene, of self-fulfilling 'folk-memories' of Ireland's colonial past, and even a residue of the counter-cultural anti-Western mind-set dating from the university years of those now in positions of influence. Malign causes – notably, true-belief in varieties of Marxist ideology – are now as nearly absent in Ireland as they are elsewhere in the Western world. But, whatever the motivating mixture, Irish commentators – uniformly enraptured by the patently false (but all-too-common) conceptual premise that American foreign policy has always been 'the decisive mover of events everywhere in the world'[158] – have persistently sought to portray the United States as playing a sinister role in its interventions on the global scene. In its self-righteous leftist bias,[159] this pervasive compulsion[160] constitutes

---

[157]For examples, see my article, 'Irish Attitudes towards USA Foreign Policy,' *Studies* 82 (1993), pp. 265-75.

[158]For the longevity of this bogus premise, see George F. Kennan *American Diplomacy* (Expanded ed., Chicago, 1984), pp. 165-66.

[159]Eunan O'Halpin *Defending Ireland* (Oxford, 1999), pp. 346-48 (and my review, *Irish Historical Studies* 32, 2000, pp. 293-96). I should cite a specific

precisely the same sort of abdication of critical integrity as evidenced, for instance, in the right-wing claims by the China Lobby in the United States that China was 'lost' because of a

---

example in support of my contention that a self-righteous leftist mind-set has pervaded Irish consideration of American foreign policy. In the first of Seamus Heaney's Oxford lectures (*The Redress of Poetry*, Oxford, 1995, p. 3), he states, 'If you are an American poet at the height of the Vietnam War, the official expectation will be for you to wave the flag rhetorically. [But] to see the South-East Asian expedition as an imperial betrayal...is to add a complication where the general desire is for a simplification'. My point, here, is not that this is a ridiculously-erroneous view of the Vietnam War, but that, regardless of how you view or viewed that war, this is a wholly inaccurate rendition of the public perception of the war *at the time*. Indeed, this is leftist myth-making of a heroic degree where poets – I imagine, Mr Heaney had intellectuals in general in mind – who opposed the war are depicted as acting on their individual consciences, fully prepared to sacrifice what might be their own best interests from a material point-of-view. Nothing could be further from the reality of the time. It would, in fact, have been extraordinarily courageous, then, for an intellectual to have supported the American government's position (cf., John Updike 'On Not Being a Dove,' *Self-Consciousness*, New York, 1989, for his account of his treatment for simply questioning the assumption by intellectuals of a self-ordained rectitude in judging the war). Nothing was easier – or, indeed, more rewarding – than going with the flow of self-righteous condemnation. Not that this was anything new, even at that time; making anti-Communism appear as something intellectually risible has been, indeed, a noted success of the left in the post-war world – an altogether peculiar phenomenon in light of Communism's track record of brutal and repressive governments in all regions of the world, a truism as valid for the behavior of the North Vietnamese as for that of Stalin. For a consideration of this tendency, throughout the last century, for Western artists and intellectuals to 'huddle together under a left-leaning shelter,' see D.M. Thomas *Alexander Solzhenitsyn* (London, 1998), pp. 55-58.

[160]See Kevin Myers 'An Irishman's Diary,' *Irish Times*, 23 February 2001, for a perplexed consideration of the determination of the Irish media to give disproportionate coverage to 'the opinions of every anti-NATO, anti-American, anti-British fringe group'.

world-wide Communist conspiracy of which President Truman was a conscious agent.[161]

How, then, did this mind-set play out in Ireland during the Gulf War? Here, I will be mostly concerned with the public statements of politicians and the coverage in the *Irish Times*. The editorial line of the *Irish Times*, as presented in its leading articles, was straightforward and closely paralleled the preoccupations of the Irish government. There was a concern for neutrality and its implications. There was an overriding concern for the UN and for preserving its authority. Obviously, none of this bothered us at the American embassy. This moderation in its leading articles was, however, belied by tendencies within its news reporting which sought, not to report objectively on the war, but to belittle and defame the United States. The main protagonists here were Sean Cronin in Washington, Leonard Doyle at the United Nations in New York, Michael Jansen somewhere in the Middle East, Robert Fisk in the battle zone, and Paul Gillespie in Dublin. While some accusations were simply petty,[162] the following list might be considered the main desiderata of problematic *Irish Times* coverage:

---

[161]The mental world of such determinist observers bears close resemblance, as a belief-system, to the constructs of mythology. Thus, their 'history' is, at the unimpeachable level of enshrined dogma, made up of versions of various historical events which have, in fact, been demonstrated by real historians to be false and in most cases were absurd to begin with (e.g., that the CIA overthrew Mossadegh and Arbenz). Their causative factors are supra-natural agents whose ability to mold events is exaggerated beyond rational credence (e.g., the operating assumption noted in the text that the U.S. is the globally all-powerful determinant of events). And, psychologically, they exhibit the same need to be comforted – where the actual facts are incompatible with their ideologically pre-determined needs – by taking refuge in the creation of alternative worlds (e.g., a Cold War world where the Soviet Union is the 'progressive' power).

[162]One which peppered its reporting throughout was that the war was all about oil supplies, insinuating, mostly, that our concern was to ensure cheap oil and

- that the UN role was a sham, the UN being under the control of the United States;
- that the West had armed Iraq and was therefore acting hypocritically;
- that the war was, regardless of how it was dressed up, a war of the West against Arabs and the West would, consequently, incur the enduring enmity of the Arab world;
- that the United States was engaged in a massive campaign of deceit manifested by its censorship of the news coverage of the war;
- and that the United States was pursuing a hidden agenda which exceeded the UN mandate of liberating Kuwait.[163]

The contributions by Cronin and Doyle were particularly evident in the early months of the crisis. Both sought to portray the U.S. as hypocritical, bullying and incompetent. I don't believe that anyone in Ireland paid much attention to what they said so I won't spend much time on them. But here are a few examples. On 19 October, Doyle began an article on the latest happenings at the UN in New York by referring to the U.S.'s 'muddle headed

---

petrol and always presented with the air of having revealed a dirty secret. In the meanwhile, the grown-ups got on with the difficult tasks of dealing with economic and political realities (for which, see President Bush's commonsensical explication as set out above in the Introduction).

[163]This was also a major thesis in RTE's coverage, particularly that of 'Morning Ireland,' Irish radio's leading current-affairs program, which found no difficulty in shifting, without the blink of a metaphorical eye, from this accusation of our 'hidden agenda' to the post-war accusation – once President Bush had called a halt to the fighting as soon as the UN mandate had been accomplished by the expulsion of the Iraqi army from Kuwait – that we were now adhering to the 'tacit compromise' of keeping Saddam Hussein in power.

diplomacy'. On 20 October – the following day – he stated that
the U.S. had 'wrested the diplomatic initiative' and was now
'dictating' UN action. Never let inconsistency interfere with a
good smear. To turn to Cronin, his particular technique was to
attempt to trivialize American motives. On 27 October, for
instance, he claimed that the U.S. was attempting to 'demonize'
Saddam Hussein,[164] an accusation which has become a standard
'analytical' tool of self-righteous leftists to characterize
America's attitude towards its adversaries. In the early stages of
the Gulf War, this accusation was used to support the argument
that the United States had 'coerced' Saudi Arabia into joining in
the coalition against Saddam. Despite the overwhelming evidence
that the Iraqis were in what is termed a 'strategic pause' – that is,
the re-grouping of its military forces preparatory to further
aggression – the 'demonizing' argument claimed that Saddam's
intentions towards Saudi Arabia and the other Persian Gulf states
were entirely benign[165] and that it was only the American
depiction of Saddam as driven by irrational dreams of glorious
conquests – as well as American economic arm-twisting (or
outright bribery) – which brought Saudi Arabia (and, by
extension, the other dozen or so regional participants) into the
coalition against Iraq.

As late as 2 February 1991, Cronin's contribution to
understanding the reasons for the Gulf War was a longish pseudo-
historical survey of interventions by the U.S. over the centuries

---

[164]'For US, the Palestinian dead are anonymous,' *Irish Times*, 27 October
1990.

[165]For the record, there were nine Iraqi divisions perched on the Saudi border,
comprising 130,000 soldiers, 1200 tanks, and 800 artillery, facing a total Saudi
army of 66,000 men. General Schwarzkopf's estimation was that the Iraqis could
have overrun the Saudi oil region in a week; H. Norman Schwarzkopf *The
Autobiography: It Doesn't Take a Hero* (London, 1992), pp. 300-13.

attempting to discredit the American leadership role.[166] It is so riddled with historical errors and false assumptions that it would be interesting to look at it in detail as a classic example of how ideologically-driven polemicists – whether of the left or the right – create their own 'facts' and then manipulate them into a sort of parallel world 'reality' more comforting to their deviate agendas. But this would lead us as far afield from the Gulf War as Cronin's meanderings in fact were. I will, instead, make one general observation and then refer to just one of Cronin's factual errors as indicative of the whole.

The basic flaw in this sort of scatter-gun condemnation is its lack of historical contextualization or, specifically, periodization. You cannot, in making a valid historical argument, simply indifferently transpose events from one historical period to another. Understandings of acceptable inter-state relations do change. Before World War II, for instance, colonialism and imperialism were generally accepted as norms, even desirable norms, of international behavior. I do not mean that there were not highly vocal and persuasive advocates against such conduct but they were in the distinct minority and their views were not reflected in such internationally-negotiated and approved arrangements as the Versailles Peace Treaty and the establishment of League of Nations mandates. All this has changed. Today, only a mad man would argue for a return to colonialism or for the present-day merits of imperialism.

Now for the factual error, chosen to stand for the whole: Cronin claims that in 1965 there was an American 'expedition to the Dominican Republic to prevent the legal government from taking power'. I suppose we shouldn't be too hard on Cronin for

---

[166]'A history of a country set on leading the world,' *Irish Times*, 2 February 1991.

getting it all so wrong since this version of events has become a central tenet in the cosmology of self-righteous leftism.[167] However, what actually happened was rather different. In 1963, the legal government headed by Juan Bosch was ousted by a military junta. Two years later, elements of this junta fell out and a civil war threatened. U.S. Marines and then paratroopers were landed to keep the warring parties apart. Within a week the Organization of American States voted to set up an Inter-American peace force. It was headed by a lieutenant general from Brazil and included military contingents from a half-dozen Western Hemisphere countries. The American forces came under its command. The OAS negotiated, first, a truce and, then, a constitutional settlement which led, a year later, to the election of a new constitutional government. Damn these pesky facts.

This excursion has taken us rather far from the realities of the Gulf War but perhaps it has accomplished a most useful service in providing a perspective on just how misleading some of the *Irish Times* reporters could be – whether disingenuously or mischievously or deliberately. Attached to this same article by Cronin, for instance, there was a cartoon by Martyn Turner in which an Uncle Sam figure and a John Bull figure are shown 'inside an Iraqi minefield,' each finding their own landmines at use. This was a leading theme in *Irish Times'* editorials: the claim that the U.S. was responsible for Saddam Hussein's military power.[168] There was no factual evidence for such an argument –

---

[167]As I also noted, in detail, in chapter 2 above.

[168]An editorial on 27 August 1990, for instance, claimed that during Iraq's war with Iran 'most of the Western world supported Iraq, in one way or another' (note the weasel-wording), while their editorial on 5 January 1991 ratcheted the charge up to the flat claim that Saddam Hussein's forces were 'armed mainly by the countries of the West' The leader-writers of the *Irish Times* had clearly not read their own newspaper: Colonel E.D. Doyle 'War is likely to be decided on the ground,' *Irish Times*, 16 January 1991, detailed the armament possessed by the

the simple facts are that the U.S. did not, in any way at any time, supply Saddam Hussein either directly or indirectly with any military materiel or technology or assistance whatsoever. That Martyn Turner knew better was demonstrated by another cartoon of his but a week earlier in which Saddam Hussein is depicted dressed up like a Formula 1 race-car driver festooned with sponsors' badges from his arms suppliers in which the Soviet Union, rightly, features prominently and Germany is tagged with supplying chemicals and France missiles.[169] This particular

Iraqis, spelling out in bullet-paragraphs the make and capabilities of their aircraft, missiles, artillery, and main-battle tanks, and stating flatly, 'Most of the weapons and equipment are Soviet manufactured;' accompanying this lengthy article there were even two graphics with tabulated lists of the types of aircraft in the air forces in the region. Despite these demonstrable and widely-known facts, this accusation that it was the West – indeed, specifically the U.S. – which provided Saddam with his weapons has not only continued to be made, but is regularly asserted in just that blunt a manner; see, for two typical examples, David Andrews, 'Our UN role should be to end the arms trade,' *Irish Times*, 2 December 2000, who claims that 'it was the West which armed Saddam Hussein and enabled his military advance into Kuwait in 1990;' and Patsy McGarry, '"Aarland" finds a warm welcome,' *Irish Times*, 6 January 2001, who bluntly states 'it was the British and Americans who supplied the arms which enabled Saddam Hussein wage the Iran-Iraq war'.

[169]In this Turner cartoon of 26 January 1991, Saddam also wears a tag citing the CIA as 'The Intelligence People'. Presumably this is a reference to the factoid that the U.S. supplied satellite intelligence to the Iraqis during their war with Iran. I know of no evidence in support of this, though it has become a standard assertion which is treated as a truism. For instance, Mark Pythian *Arming Iraq: How the U.S. and Britain Secretly Built Saddam's War Machine* (Boston, 1997), pp. 34 and 39-42, claims that Reagan actually signed a national security directive ordering this intelligence-sharing with the Iraqis; but, typically, he provides no repeat no evidence, citing solely books similar to his and articles in the *New York Times* by Seymour Hersh (re Hersh's reliability, see my review, 'Seymour Hersh and the hoaxers,' *Sunday Independent*, 8 February 1998). Pythian even claims that this activity was kept secret from the House and Senate intelligence committees. The truth seems to be that this factoid was a creation of a BBC correspondent who 'felt' that the Iraqi success in rolling back the Iranian counter-offensive just had to be due to some factor beyond their own capabilities and who concocted an absurd

cartoon accompanies another Sean Cronin article in which he declares that the Gulf War 'is not about human or national rights'.[170] How does Cronin reach that conclusion? It's because Turkey is still occupying northern Cyprus. The connection? Go figure.

Actually it's no more far-fetched than the argument that there was a linkage between the Arab-Israeli conflict and the Gulf War. Again, this is an issue on which it is necessary to be very clear.[171] American rejection of the linkage being pushed by Saddam Hussein was not based on any depreciation of the seriousness of the issue and of the need to reach a resolution of the conflict between Israel and the Palestinians. More than any other people outside those of the region itself, we Americans are conscious of the need, there, for justice and peace and security. We rejected the linkage because of the simple reality that Saddam Hussein did not invade Kuwait due to any concern whatsoever on his part for the Palestinians. Additionally, even if the Israelis and Palestinians had miraculously come to a sudden resolution of their conflict, Saddam Hussein would not have withdrawn from Kuwait. The two issues were not linked. Nevertheless, the fourth of the four

---

theory concerning the Exocet strike of the USS Stark. Similarly, Pythian claims that the U.S. authorized Arab allies such as Jordan to tranship U.S. military equipment to Iraq and authorized sale of dual-use technology and equipment 'knowing' it would be used for military purposes. Needless to say, he provides no evidence; rather, he relies on weasal-worded rhetoric and repetitive, even circular, arguments. Surely, if any of his assertions were true, the UN inspectors would have uncovered evidence. For the record, Saddam's main armament were Soviet T-72 tanks, South African 155-mm heavy artillery, Chinese and Soviet multiple rocket launchers, Chinese Silkworm and French Exocet anti-ship missiles, Soviet Mig-29 and Su-24 and French Mirage warplanes.

[170]'Anti-war rally will test strength of peace movement,' *Irish Times*, 26 January 1991.

[171]What follows draws on my presentation, on 25 January 1991, to the Irish United Nations Association in Buswell's Hotel, Dublin.

challenges which President Bush saw that region facing in the post-war period – in his formal declaration of the U.S.'s war aims – was the 'search for a just peace and a real reconciliation' in the Arab-Israeli conflict.[172] This tracked closely with the sentiments expressed by the Irish foreign minister to the UN General Assembly in September 1990. After an eloquent condemnation of Iraq's aggression as striking at the very foundations of the system of international order and justice, he stated that 'we must not forget the other great source of tension in the Middle East: the Arab-Israeli conflict' and that we 'must resume the peace process with a view to a comprehensive settlement...'[173]

Despite these truths, the 'linkage' featured as a motif throughout the coverage by many reporters but if one is to be singled out as its champion it would be Michael Jansen. Jansen is a specialist in quasi-mystical evocations of the 'hearts and minds' of the Arabs. Her articles are peppered with 'the Arabs' or 'the Arab view' or 'the Arab attitude' or 'Arab anger'. Uniformly she wrote, and still writes, as though the views she pushes are representative of Arabs in general. In truth, they are no more

---

[172]The first three challenges foreseen by President Bush were an effective regional security structure so that national sovereignty and security in the Gulf region could be maintained without the presence of foreign troops; regional arms control, including both conventional weapons and weapons of mass destruction; and economic reconstruction and recovery. Despite this clarity, reporters, particularly Paul Gillespie and Robert Fisk of the *Irish Times,* repeatedly claimed that there were no allied plans for the post-war period (for example, Paul Gillespie 'A skilful piece of political intercourse,' *Irish Times*, 16 February 1991; and Robert Fisk 'Far more than the mere settling of accounts,' *Irish Times*, 16 January 1991).

[173]'Collins stresses UN's role in Gulf crisis,' *Irish Times*, 27 September 1990. In his address, Foreign Minister Collins also provided a succinct definition of what President Bush would describe as a 'new world order' – that is, 'a truly post-war world where the institutions of international order, established after World War II, could function as intended'.

representative than would be the views of someone like Noam Chomsky in the United States. Jansen's views are simply the Middle East variant of self-righteous leftism and, if I may myself generalize, during the Gulf War differed little from Saddam Hussein's propaganda. This was *the* major complaint we had against the *Irish Times* throughout the war. We were vociferous in letting them know that we felt that this sort of reporting was unacceptable – to the degree that, after the war was over, we had a meeting with editorial representatives of the newspaper and were astonished to be informed by them that they had made a deliberate decision to present – as they put it – a 'balance between the Western and the Arab views of the war'. Never mind interpreting their responsibility to their readers as one of balance rather than objectivity, it was the identification of 'Arab' with Saddam Hussein that struck us as, quite simply, amateurish.

But that's just what they did.[174] Jansen's articles were first identified as reporting on the 'Gulf Crisis,' but they soon became labeled as reporting on 'The Arab View'. In Jansen's 'analysis,' a U.S. victory would alienate Muslims from Morocco to Pakistan. The U.S. was assembling a 'pile-driver to crush a walnut' and Saddam Hussein was depicted as a 'lone Iraqi warrior armed with an elderly fowling piece' facing a massive high-tech arsenal (for the record, Saddam's army was the fourth largest in the world, ranking behind only those of the USSR, China, and Vietnam, and comprised 900,000 soldiers in sixty-three divisions). The U.S. intended to push on to Baghdad, according to 'Arab' analysts.[175]

---

[174]Ironically, in a leading article on 22 August 1990, the *Irish Times* chastised Foreign Minister Collins for seeking to convey to the Iraqis the impression that the Irish position on the conflict was one of 'balance'.

[175]'Losing the 'hearts and minds' of the Arab World,' *Irish Times*, 12 January 1991; 'Arab morale raised by Iraqi missile attack on Israel,' *Irish Times*, 19 January 1991; 'Winning hearts and minds of the 'Umma'', *Irish Times*, 2

It would be unfair, of course, to single out Jansen for this sort of reporting. Robert Fisk would have to share the honors. The main difference is where Jansen was strident, Fisk was sneering. His standard line during the Gulf conflict was set out in one of the first of his pieces run at that time by the *Irish Times*. It concerned a press conference by Prince Khaled, the Saudi commanding general, at which he introduced an American major general who would be attached to his staff. A reporter would have identified the American as a liaison officer; Fisk sneers at him as a sort of handler or spin-doctor, claiming that he inserted into General Khaled's press statement the line that in Saudi Arabia 'US troops [were] standing up for what is just and right in the world' and identifying this as the 'only embarrassing paragraph' in the statement.[176] Nothing like setting out your bias at the very start.

But isn't Fisk an award-winning war correspondent vastly experienced in the Middle East? You could never tell it by his articles during the Gulf War. Fisk's considered strategic analysis was that Kuwait would become an American protectorate with at least two divisions garrisoning the country and that Iraq would become a Western mandate.[177] He also stated that an Iraqi defeat would cause an explosion of 'Arab' anger (that 'Arab' again) and would mean an end to 'Arab' power (I can't help but keep wondering where, to mention just two Arab powers, Egypt and Syria have gone to in Fisk's parallel world). His tactical analysis was that, unlike the British who would invade Iraq alongside the

---

February 1991; and 'Coalition overkill may sour relations with Arab world,' *Irish Times*, 28 February 1991 are representative of Jansen's 'reportage' which was deplorable throughout.

   [176]'Saudi general gets a US major-domo,' *Irish Times*, 29 August 1990.

   [177]'US action may generate uncontrollable fall-out,' *Irish Times*, 29 September 1990 and 'Far more than the mere settling of accounts,' *Irish Times*, 16 January 1991.

U.S., the French would 'respond differently' (I guess they forgot
to inform the French 6th Light Armored Division of that) and that
Arab forces would play only a 'cosmetic role'[178] (and someone
also forgot to so inform the Saudi armored divisions which led
the attack into Kuwait City along with the Kuwaiti 6th Brigade
and the two Egyptian armored divisions which followed in
support). But, then, Fisk's brand of reporting seems to improve in
the telling. At the time, he sought, in numerous articles, to depict
the U.S. ground forces as virtually an undisciplined rabble,
lacking maps, lacking night-vision binoculars, even lacking
rifles.[179] In a speech at University College Dublin on 11 March
1997, Fisk actually repeated some of these claims as examples of
his truth-seeking no matter how unpalatable it might be. His most
startling claim – if I was hearing him correctly – was that he had
reported during the war that American carrier pilots would watch
pornographic films to psych themselves up for their air raids.
What Fisk actually reported at the time, however, was a claim to
have heard, at second or third-hand, that a news report that carrier
pilots watched pornographic films 'to relax' had been
censored.[180] This isn't just a question of memory; it is also a
question of basic competency. War reporters are supposed to
have some understanding of the mechanics of war. What do you
make of a war reporter who, as Fisk did, would write that allied
pilots had observed 'Iraqi planes flying on a non-combat status

---

[178]'General Disorder could turn out to be the overall commander,' *Irish
Times*, 8 December 1990.

[179]'Tales of the unexpected at the battle front,' *Irish Times*, 23 January 1991.

[180]'Skirmishes in Gulf, but most of the media have surrendered,' *Irish Times*,
6 February 1991. Throughout the war, Fisk complained of censorship. Apparently,
he believed that reporters had the right to wander willy-nilly around a battle zone
where an army was preparing a major offensive. Since the war, he has continued
this idiocy on all occasions. In this UCD lecture, he repeated it once again.

around them over Iraq'?[181] But, then, in Fisk's view this was a war of 'Western' armies, the armies of 'Christendom,' the 'Christian' armies against Muslims, and it was a war in which Saddam's battle-hardened soldiers would inflict 'massive casualties'.[182]

The damning thing here is that Fisk is actually capable of seeing what's in front of his eyes. His reports on 26, 27, and 28 February as he followed the coalition forces into Kuwait City were as accurate as the fog of war ever permits. He wrote of the effectiveness of the rout inflicted on the Iraqi forces and of the destruction that the Iraqis had perpetrated on the city while they had held it and of their brutality towards the Kuwaitis. 'One sensed,' he wrote, 'that something very wicked, at times evil, had visited this city.'[183] To be frank, I was astonished at the time. Particularly when I read him reporting a U.S. Marine as saying that the only reason the advance wasn't going faster was because 'we want to make them surrender rather than kill them' or that the Western commanders were 'sending US Marines into the city alongside the Kuwaitis to prevent any attempts to stage a bloody revenge on civilians who may have been accused of collaborating with the Iraqis'.[184] This positive objectivity, however, soon proved too much for Fisk. In short order, he was, reportedly,

---

[181]'A 'bodyguard of lies' provides desert shield,' *Irish Times*, 19 January 1991.

[182]'West waits as Arabs bear burden of bombing,' *Irish Times*, 24 January 1991.

[183]'The Liberation of Kuwait City,' *Irish Times*, 28 February 1991.

[184]'Not a soul in sight, a dead land greets allies,' *Irish Times*, 26 February 1991; and 'Kuwait City revels in liberation,' *Irish Times*, 27 February 1991. It was, of course, too much to expect that Fisk would remind us how he had been predicting that the Palestinians in Kuwait city could expect to be massacred with the allies essentially ignoring it all; 'Scorched earth and burning questions as jolly generals boast of victory,' *Irish Times*, 15 January 1991.

accusing the allies of having committed an 'atrocity' in having buried Iraqi soldiers alive during the war.[185] Indeed, some Iraqi soldiers certainly met that fate, but hardly in the manner Fisk was said to project. We need to recall, first of all, the defenses which Saddam had his occupying army put into place. The most ambitious part of his defense arrangements was the 'Saddam line,' a 175-mile long fortification in depth of the Kuwaiti-Saudi border. Its principal features were a wide and deep trench, often filled with crude oil, with the excavated sand piled up on the outward side to form a towering berm as the first line of defense. Behind this, Iraqi engineers built in cement bunkers for dug-in tanks, artillery, and infantry.[186] When the land war was launched, those Iraqi soldiers manning the 'Saddam line' who were firing on the coalition forces and who refused to surrender were buried in their fortified bunkers as the armored excavators and bulldozer tanks punched their way through the berms and other fortifications so that the armored columns could push on into Kuwait. Hardly an atrocity, then, but it has proven to be one of the more enduring myths of the war, even featuring some years later in a television documentary made by Maggie O'Kane.[187]

---

[185]See Emily O'Reilly 'Why are we moral cowards on foreign policy?' *Irish Press*, 30 November 1991, in which she cites this claim of an atrocity by Robert Fisk at a conference in Belfast 'some months ago'.

[186]See the graphic, 'Iraq's Front-line defences,' *Irish Times*, 2 February 1991 and, especially, Colonel E.D. Doyle's accompanying article, '"Break-in battles": land and sea assaults'.

[187]And, as with the myth that the U.S. armed Saddam, this myth continues to be repeated; see, for two typical examples, Denis Halliday, 'Continuing UN sanctions against Iraq only serve US ambition to control Middle East,' *Irish Times*, 11 August 2000; and Harry Browne, 'Radio Review,' *Irish Times*,13 January 2001 (who as his authority cites, approvingly, John Pilger!). If he is the *fons et origo* of this slur, Fisk cannot plead innocence or ignorance; he began his report on 26 February (' Not a soul in sight, a dead land greets allies,' *Irish Times*) with a graphic description of crossing the 'infamous berms...half-filled with black

One myth which I haven't considered yet in detail enjoyed a very brief lifetime; indeed, it flourished only while the war lasted. That was, of course, the myth that the U.S., sometimes said to be backed by the UK, was pursuing a hidden agenda of seeking to exceed the UN mandate and destroy Saddam Hussein. At the *Irish Times*, the main exponent of this myth was Paul Gillespie. Gillespie specializes in think-pieces, and his thinking on the Gulf War was that the U.S. was determined to eliminate Saddam Hussein.[188] He even argued that this 'escalation' was the price to be paid for Israeli restraint in the face of Saddam's Scuds.[189] His argument rested on what he termed the 'ambiguities' of the UN mandate which allowed the U.S. to interpret it to suit its own foreign policy. Of course, he rather undermined himself when he quoted, at length, that great political thinker, Gore Vidal,[190] in support of his thesis that the U.S. was indulging in 'imperial overstretch'.[191] And, of course, this particular myth simply evaporated when President Bush called an end to the war once it had achieved the UN mandate of expelling the Iraqis from

---

sludge...[where] the allied armies were supposed to have been incinerated....' This compulsion to concoct justifications for wilful wrongheadedness caused Eoghan Harris 'Great leaders see more clearly when it comes to spotting evil,' *Sunday Times*, 13 June 1999, to coin the verb 'to fisk,' which he defined as 'to not face the facts for as long as possible and, when found out, to divert the public from your mistake by spinning shiny stories'. See also David Pryce-Jones 'The dangers of Fisking,' The Spectator.co.uk, 15 November 2003.

[188]'Bush extends mandate to demilitarising Saddam regime,' *Irish Times*, 19 January 1991.

[189]'When escalation may be the price for Israeli restraint,' *Irish Times*, 26 January 1991; Gillespie begins this analysis with a quotation from a French newspaper editor which he characterizes as a 'shrewd evaluation' – it predicts that the outcome of the war would be the 'eclipse of the PLO'. Shrewd, indeed.

[190]Cf., my review of Vidal's *Palimpsest: A Memoir*, 'Gore's gossip,' *Sunday Independent*, 26 November 1995.

[191]'US accused of 'imperial overstretch'', *Irish Times*, 9 February 1991.

Kuwait. But, then, it was immediately replaced by the myth that the U.S. had always intended to keep Saddam Hussein in power.[192] This is now the received wisdom at the *Irish Times*.[193] (I suppose that it is, unfortunately, necessary to point out that the subsequent war in Iraq and its occupation by American-led coalition forces do not come into play in this analysis. What we are concerned with, here, are American motivations and intentions at the time of the first Gulf War and how commentators, such as Fisk and Gillespie and Jansen, were determined to claim that they were other than officially stated, to misrepresent them – past the point of ludicrous inconsistency in their assertions – in order to portray the U.S. as acting sinisterly. In 1990, President Bush the father said we were going to war to oust Saddam's forces from Kuwait, and that is just what we did.

---

[192]A further pervasively-repeated myth which I haven't yet mentioned is that President Bush encouraged the Kurds and the Shiites to rise in revolt against Saddam's rule. Indeed, along with the myth that the U.S. sought all along to keep Saddam in power, this has proved the most enduring of generally-believed myths about this war, most who claim it repeating it as simple fact; see as typical now Eamon Delaney *Accidental Tourist*, p. 173 (Delaney was an Irish diplomat at the UN in New York at the time). The truth is otherwise. What Bush actually said (in response to a reporter's question, a week or so before the launching of the ground war) was that, if Saddam was the 'obstacle' (the reporter's word) to the withdrawal of the Iraqi forces from Kuwait, then the 'Iraqi military and the Iraqi people should take matters into their own hands' (see my review 'The dilemma of the Kurds,' *Sunday Independent*, 14 March 1999). At the time, this was seen for what in truth it was: an unambiguous call for a coup (see as typical then the leader in the *Sunday Independent*, 17 February 1991). That these two myths – the retention of Saddam in power and the urging of revolts against him – are mutually contradictory and yet are pushed in all apparent seriousness by the same pundits (see my article, 'When in doubt, blame the Americans,' *Sunday Independent*, 22 November 1998) aptly illustrates the inherent illogicality of true-believing anti-Americans. Somehow, we're always to blame.

[193]Cf., Michael Jansen 'Arabs fear what will happen after US launches its firepower on Iraq again,' *Irish Times*, 17 February 1998.

In 2003, President Bush the son said that we were going to war to oust Saddam himself, and again we did just what we said.)

I don't want to leave the impression that there was nothing of value in the Irish media coverage of the Gulf War. The reporting, especially at times of particular activity, was intensive and, if I may single out one who wrote frequently – though at this point he might well consider this to be the kiss of death – we in the American embassy breathed a sigh of relief whenever we saw that that day's issue of the *Irish Times* carried a feature article by Colonel E.D. Doyle. We knew that what we would get would be straightforward and expert military analysis.

What, then, about the politicians and other leading voices? Overall, their response was a rational one – that is, the Irish political class based their consideration of the war on demonstrable facts and drew their conclusions in a fair-minded and logical fashion.[194] As a consequence, they supported the war effort.[195] Opposition was largely confined to the fringe – CND,

---

[194]Indeed, many of them publicly voiced the same disquiet over the media coverage as we in the American embassy did; see for examples, 'RTE to discuss Deasy's criticism,' *Irish Press*, 4 March 1991; and 'FG slams RTE war coverage,' *Irish Press*, 5 March 1991.

[195]The vote in the Dáil on 18 January 1991 in support of the UN resolutions was 122-23 (see the official report of Dáil Éireann, Vol. 404, No. 3, for 18 January 1991, cols. 765-772); one notable absentee was David Andrews (who, some years later, actually became foreign minister). His own favorite myth at the time ('Pressure mustn't get in the way,' *Irish Independent*, 17 December 1990) was that sanctions would certainly have worked and that, therefore, the U.S. was engaging in 'hypocrisy' and 'indecent haste' in moving to force (see my article 'Why Andrews doesn't cut the US mustard, *Sunday Independent*, 11 October 1998); perhaps Andrews should have read Robert Fisk in the *Irish Times* on 29 September 1990: 'Anyone who still thinks that Saddam Hussein will evacuate Kuwait under the pressure of UN sanctions does not understand the Iraqi leader.' But, then, present-day realities may not be Andrews' forte; as late as 9 December 2000 ('Committee will urge Iraq to co-operate with the UN,' *Irish Times*), he was arguing, *contra* the UN sanctions imposed on Iraq, that 'Kuwait was an integral

the Greens, the Workers' Party, Eamonn McCann's rag-tag grouplet (the last surviving true-believing Marxists in Ireland). As I have mentioned, the Irish Labour Party officially opposed the war but of its public representatives only Michael D. Higgins was notably active in opposition, joining for instance in opposition marches and rallies with the other fringe types. In Dáil debate, he delivered a speech remarkable even for him. In the first half of it, though his heated rhetoric rather vaporized whatever logic there may have been in his theatrical tirade, he would seem to have roundly condemned all of us in the West for intervening in a regional conflict, and in the second half to have roundly condemned all of us for not having imposed democracy on the region.[196] The churches made considerably more sense. They prayed for peace and debated the conditions for a 'just war'.[197] When the war came – which the Irish government termed 'unavoidable' in light of Iraqi intransigence[198] – church leaders,

---

part of Iraq for about 3,000 years....' What a stunning assertion – present-day aggression justified by Babylonian territorial claims! In contrast, the Irish people had no trouble seeing Saddam's aggression for what it was; a *Sunday Independent*/IMS poll conducted shortly after the ending of the war showed that 67 percent supported the use of force – even among members of the Irish Labour Party support was at 59 percent – with only 19 percent actually opposed (*Sunday Independent*, 10 March 1991).

[196]See the official report of Dáil Éireann, Vol. 401, No. 9, for 29 August 1990, cols. 2323-2341.

[197]For examples, see Andy Pollak 'Churches seek peaceful solution in Gulf conflict,' *Irish Times*, 30 November 1990. Of interest is an op-ed piece, written at the time of a subsequent Gulf crisis, in which an Irish theologian found that the Irish 'failure to support the UN offensive against Iraq in January 1991 was not moral;' see Seamus Murphy, SJ, 'Rite and Reason,' *Irish Times*, 17 February 1998.

[198]'Goverment statement,' *Irish Times*, 18 January 1991.

including Cardinal Daly and Archbishop Eames, expressed regret and prayed that it would end with a minimum of deaths.[199]

It would seem that this time God was listening. Coalition losses were just slightly over a hundred dead, wounded or missing-in-action. Iraqi casualties were also light, surprisingly in view of the utter rout inflicted on them (out of the 42 Iraqi divisions involved in defense of its invasion, 27 were destroyed and 6 put out-of-action). Total casualty figures may never be known, but in one of the most-widely publicized incidents of the war – the destruction of the Iraqi army column retreating from Kuwait City to Basra – we do know the figures because we occupied that battlefield and we buried the dead. You will hear figures of 40,000 killed in that airstrike, particularly from the ideologically-bent. The actual figure was under 400.

Aeschylus claimed that, in war, truth is the first casualty.[200] In the Gulf War, at least, the executioners of the truth weren't the allied military commanders.[201]

---

[199]In general, they also expressed their condemnation of the Iraqi invasion, Andy Pollak, 'Church leaders pray for minimum deaths in war,' *Irish Times*, 18 January 1991.

[200]This was a quotation John F. Kennedy treasured, copying it into a commonplace book just after the end of World War II; see Arthur M. Schlesinger, Jr *A Thousand Days* (Boston, 1965), p. 105.

[201]Though it might have been more politic to have made the following comment at the opening of this chapter, I should say that I have no doubt that many of those who opposed the war at the time and who continue to oppose the coalition's use of force, including some whom I have named in this book, were and remain people of integrity whose views are held with great sincerity. I close by simply noting that, likewise, those who, in the decade following the first Gulf War, most voceriferously condemned the continuance of the sanctions regime imposed by the UN to compel Saddam's compliance with the commitments he made to obtain the ceasefire agreement (specifically, the destruction of his atomic, chemical and biological weapons) were, in general, the same people who argued prior to the launching of the coalition attack on Saddam's occupying military that force was unjustified on the basis that sanctions would, if given time, compel

Saddam's retreat from Kuwait. (The realities of the sanctions-regime, post-war, are considered in detail below in the Epilogue.) Postscript: Not surprisingly, the same self-justifying posturing was common in Ireland in the lead-up to Gulf War Two; see the final section of this book.

Six

Politics 2: The U.S., Ireland and Northern Ireland

In the *Tempest* (I, ii, 402-4), Ariel sings of a drowned man: 'Nothing of him that doth fade/But doth suffer a sea-change/Into something rich and strange.' He might well have been describing the overt involvement of the Clinton administration in the Northern Ireland conflict: first drowned in scorn and ridicule and even vituperation, it is now ranked by Irish observers as Clinton's finest foreign policy achievement – something 'rich and strange,' indeed.[202]

When the idea of such a pro-active role for the United States was first floated, I was on the eve of my departure from Dublin, after having served as the First Secretary for Political Affairs at the American embassy for four years, 1988-92. As I recall, the idea of an American 'peace envoy' was publicly proposed by Cardinal Law of Boston and taken on board by Bill Clinton, then still but a candidate for president, in the way that Democratic presidential candidates are wont to do. Certainly, when we were asked by the State Department to comment on the proposal – as were, as well, our embassy in London and our consulate general in Belfast – we replied that in the view of the Irish it was a classic non-starter. It would be rejected so vehemently by the Unionists and the British government as outrageous interference in their affairs that both Dublin and the SDLP had to consider it as harmful. I believe the cable I wrote setting out these views was my last in Dublin. But I remember reading in the newspapers,

---

[202]An earlier version of this essay was delivered, on 25 March 1998, to the Irish Association for Cultural, Economic and Social Relations at the Mansion House, Dublin.

some months later, that Albert Reynolds in his first call on the new president counseled Clinton precisely along these lines.

Of course, the idea didn't go away (though it perforce progressed in various stealthy guises). And, despite the continuous venting of spleen on the part of various Tories and nearly all the Unionists – being told to mind our own business was the mildest of their comments – the United States did become a 'player' in the Northern Ireland conflict. Eventually, President Clinton visited Belfast and Derry and Dublin, and visits to the White House became part of the consultation circuit for Northern Ireland politicians – indeed, in the last few years of his administration, more Northern Ireland politicians, from all the parties, saw the inside of the White House than the inside of 10 Downing Street.

This trajectory of public perceptions of our involvement in Northern Ireland – from ridicule at our arrogance and/or our naiveté to praise for our good-faith efforts and honest professionalism – is a familiar one to me as a professional American diplomat. Indeed, in terms of Irish *bien pensant* perceptions of American diplomatic endeavors, it traces a classic path. As I have amply noted, there has been, over the last two decades or so, much criticism in Ireland of American foreign policy, particularly in areas like Central America and Cambodia. While not revisiting those episodes in this chapter, it would, nevertheless, be useful to point out that our involvement in Northern Ireland could well serve as a paradigm of how our foreign policy operates (in the real world, not in fantasy-land). We have been, for instance, much criticized, even condemned, for some of the people we have found ourselves having to deal with in various parts of the world. A 'certain tolerance for death squads' is how one former Taoiseach tends to put it. That charge, in itself, is baseless; there has been no tolerance on our part for such squalid behavior. But that the charge can be so casually made reflects the readiness in Ireland, as in other like-minded European countries, to pass condescending moral judgments on what we have found it necessary to do. May I point out, then, that over the last many years now there has been a virtual parade of terrorists from Northern Ireland visiting my country, indeed, being invited to the White House. Except for the marginalized few who rather shrilly assert that President Clinton signed on as an ally of the IRA,[203] the consensus view by commentators is that this policy initiated by President Clinton and carried on by President Bush has been courageous and positive. Certainly, again except by those who are pursuing their own deviate agendas, the moral correctness of the motivations for this policy has been unquestioned. Our good faith is not in doubt. Let us also recall, once again, that the immediate origins of President Clinton's interest in Northern Ireland were to be found in his campaign for election in 1992 – that is, his exploitation of America's ethnic politics. Much of what he signed on to, in order not to alienate Irish American support, was rather naive but it laid a basis of knowledge.[204] He knew what the issues were even if he

---

[203]This has been Conor Cruise O'Brien's standard charge, e.g., *On the Eve of the Millennium* (New York, 1994), p. 40. See also Raymond Seitz *Over Here* (London, 1998), pp. 285-93; and my review, 'The anger of Ray Seitz,' *Sunday Independent*, 8 March 1998.

[204]Let us scotch, right off, the truly-obtuse assertion, repeated *ad nauseam* by Irish commentators, that the 'real' reason for Clinton's involvement in Northern Ireland was to win the Irish American vote. At the very least, even the wilfully ignorant ought to recognize that, outside of South Boston, there is no ethnic Irish American voting-bloc in the U.S. and there hasn't been for decades. The only Irish Americans who care so passionately about what happens in the 'ould sod' that it would determine their vote in any U.S. election are romantically-diehard supporters of the IRA. Otherwise, an American of Irish descent, like any other American, will decide his vote on the basis of American issues. See George Mitchell's judgment as quoted by Joe Carroll in his 'Letter from America,' *Irish*

did not yet have a grasp of their ramifications. Without that process of education, without that acquired frame of reference, John Hume and Albert Reynolds and the others would have found the task of interesting this president in an issue of only peripheral concern to U.S. interests truly against the odds. Please keep this in mind the next time you see someone blithely dismissing the concerns of the exiled Cuban community.[205] Finally, on this excursus, what is the leverage which the U.S. brings to efforts to resolve the Northern Ireland conflict? Yes, that's right – it's U.S. business investment. American multi-nationals with demands on hiring and firing and marketing – and bringing jobs to communities where there have been none for decades. Keep that in mind the next time some pundit pens another diatribe on neo-

---

Times, 30 September 2000. See further on the role played by Irish America in n. 215 below.

[205]In this regard, there is a further parallel which would be instructive to all those Irish who conceive of Fidel Castro primarily as some sort of patriot who freed Cuba from being a client-state of the U.S. The prime evidence they put forth to support this characterization is, inevitably, the Platt Amendment which imposed certain provisions on the constitution of the newly-independent Cuba, one of which permitted the U.S. to intervene should it be necessary to preserve Cuban independence or peace and order. It had a most unfortunate consequence: instead of the Cubans working out their own differences, discontented factions regularly rose against the government of the day precisely to bring about U.S. intervention. What judgment, then, should be made about the repeated calls by Irish politicians, following the Good Friday Agreement of 1998, for the White House to get directly involved in resolving the resulting deadlock over arms decommissioning? George Mitchell characterized this 'client-state' attitude precisely: 'It is not helpful that people keep suggesting that I come back because it can create recalcitrance on the part of the participants. If they think negotiations are not really going to begin on each issue until I or someone else comes in from the outside, they're much less likely to be forthcoming and to be willing to compromise among themselves. I think that attitude has to change' (quoted from Joe Carroll 'The longest year in the life of a peacemaker,' *Irish Times*, 3 April 1999).

liberalism or accuses U.S. foreign policy of being in the thrall of 'big business'. Keep also in mind the bottom-line objective of this American policy towards Northern Ireland, with all of the dealing with terrorists and the appeasing of ethnic 'voting blocs' and the promoting of American business interests – it's called the bolstering of democracy.

Now, back to Northern Ireland. It would be best to begin by clearing away some conceptual undergrowth that has long obscured the realities of American considerations of the Northern Ireland conflict, starting with the prevailing judgment in Ireland that, in the past, the U.S. adhered to a pro British line on the issue. This is nonsense. Nevertheless, it is a judgment which has been repeated so often and for so long that it is treated as self-evident. It is mouthed by pundits and by politicians and even by Taoisigh.[206] Most, I imagine, have never even considered the possibility that there might not be any validity to the charge. After all, as Garret FitzGerald remarks in his memoirs, the 'State Department was traditionally strongly Anglophile'.[207] To be brutally frank, this is embarrassingly parochial. It is discouraging that even Irish political leaders such as Dr FitzGerald with vast experience on the international scene are unable to transcend narrow national concerns and envision inter-state relationships on a global basis. A misconception no matter how widely held or how often repeated by however many people is still a

---

[206]On a visit to Dublin in May 1994, I was introduced to former Taoiseach Charles Haughey at a promotional function in The Commons restaurant. He was in good form. On hearing that I was from the American diplomatic service, he growled that Whitehall had been running the State Department for years. 'Fair's fair,' I replied, 'Iveagh House has taken over the American Embassy.' But that's another story (see my article, 'Kennedy Smith is not our business,' *Sunday Independent*, 16 February 1997).

[207]*All In A Life* (Dublin, 1991), p. 348.

misconception. Of course, there is an imbalance of critical mass between our relationship with Ireland and our relationship with Great Britain.[208] On the political side, relations between the U.S. and Ireland are essentially a one-item agenda – the conflict in Northern Ireland. You can begin to get some sense of its current singular prominence if you recall that, within the context of the relationship between our two countries, Northern Ireland was, until relatively recently, far outstripped in both public concern and official attention by such a burning social-cum-economic issue as American visas for Irish emigrants. In contrast, on the political agenda of U.S.-British relations, Northern Ireland would, at least up through the recent past, have normally found it difficult to break into the top ten. That list would be headed by such pressing preoccupations as international terrorism, nuclear disarmament, the future of NATO, the progress, or lack of progress, of democratic liberalization in the successor states of the former Soviet Union, and the Middle East. There is also an imbalance in reciprocity. We and the British have long been each other's staunchest ally. The 'special relationship' is not just rhetoric. Here, there still seems a belief that there is such a thing as a free lunch.[209] Nevertheless, the simple truth is that in a world full of crucial problems the Northern Ireland conflict, for long decades, did not rate as an international problem for us. Its dreary steeples never rose above the international horizon. Not unreasonably, it was seen as a problem which the two sovereign countries concerned could well be expected to work out between themselves. That the U.S. had traditionally enjoyed friendly relations with both of the countries involved in the conflict re-

---

[208]See my article 'Honest broker's balancing act,' *Sunday Independent*, 3 December 1995.

[209]On this question of a lack of reciprocity in the U.S.-Irish relationship, see my concluding remarks in the Epilogue below.

inforced our determination to stay out of it.[210] Our policy could best be described as abstentionist neutrality. In this, it was similar to our policy on Gibraltar. But, even when the issue of Gibraltar's status became a live problem with Spain's accession to NATO, I don't remember Spaniards accusing us of toeing the British line because we continued to stand firmly on the sideline.

A second misconception to be cleared away is that U.S. policy changed to a definite pro-Irish position with President Clinton's decision to grant Gerry Adams a visa. No. American policy did change from our longstanding abstentionist neutrality, but that change had occurred under President Carter.[211] He pledged that the U.S. would provide positive support for joint efforts by the British and Irish governments to promote peace and reconciliation in Northern Ireland. This was a fundamental shift from abstention to involvement. Carter pledged financial support for any agreement that might emerge. This policy was continued under Presidents Reagan and Bush. And it was continued under President Clinton. What actually changed, then, in 1994 was not the attitude in Washington but the situation on the ground in Northern Ireland.

---

[210]Already in 1951, President Truman had informed Irish Foreign Minister Sean MacBride that the U.S. could not helpfully intervene on partition because it 'was an issue between two countries with which the United States was equally friendly' (quoted from Troy D. Davis *Dublin's American Policy: Irish-American Diplomatic Relations, 1945-1952*, Washington, D.C., 1998, p. 208; see also my review, *Irish Historical Studies* 31, 1999, pp. 583-84).

[211]For reasonably-accurate accountings of the evolution of U.S. policy on Northern Ireland, see Adrian Guelke 'The American Connection,' *Northern Ireland: The International Perspective* (Dublin, 1988), pp. 128-52; and John Dumbrell 'The United States and the Northern Irish conflict 1969-94: from indifference to intervention,' *Irish Studies in International Affairs* 6 (1995), pp. 107-25.

When I arrived in Dublin in the summer of 1988, the Northern Ireland scene was dominated by megaphone diplomacy and the politics of the latest atrocity. The first six months of 1989 in particular seemed marked by one demonstration of British 'insensitivity' after another, driving Garret FitzGerald at one point to ask outloud if anyone in the British government talked to anyone else. In the meanwhile, I dutifully filed reports to Washington, trying to explain it all. Most of my reports were timed to the regularly-recurring meetings of the Intergovernmental Conference of the Anglo-Irish Agreement. As I recall them now, there was much in them on the Agreement as a 'mechanism' for practical improvements in the life of the Nationalist community in the North. Regular concerns were super-grass trials, the Diplock courts, a code of conduct for the RUC, the policing of funerals. Talks for a political solution in Northern Ireland was an aspiration for the far distant future. Even talks about talks were not on the horizon. All this coming to me from the Irish side, of course. I became, in particular, quite an adept on the question of extradition – extradition, that is, of Republican suspects to the UK. The 1987 Extradition (Amendment) Act and its accompanying Extradition (ECST) Act became old acquaintances. Not to speak of the 1976 Criminal Law Jurisdiction Act. For the most part, I had little difficulty explaining to my government why the Irish side – whether it was the government or the courts – was acting as it did. For instance, when the Irish attorney general ruled against the extradition of Father Paddy Ryan – though, as he pointed out, there was sufficient cause under the prevailing extradition laws to do so – Americans had no difficulty understanding the concept of prejudicial statements irredeemably affecting the right to a fair trial, nor had we forgotten that Ireland was a sovereign country where the rule of law was observed whatever intemperate politicizing some other country's head of government might indulge in.

Not that it was all an easy ride for me explaining it all. There was the Supreme Court decision in March 1990, setting free two Maze escapers, which raised more than a few eyebrows in Washington. On the surface, it seemed that the whole neuralgic issue of the political-offense exception to extradition had been revived. It took me some considerable effort to explain that this was not the case (or so we hoped) and that, in particular, the decision was based on the specific circumstances of the 1983 escape (or, rather, on the maltreatment of the prisoners which followed) and did not, thus, constitute a general attack on the British system of justice as some British politicians seemed to be claiming. Of course, there was the rather politically-awkward subsidiary finding by one of the justices that the motivation of the two escapers appearing before the court was identical to the policy of the Irish government – that is, to achieve the unity of the Irish state. If I remember correctly, at that point I simply sent a copy of the judgment to the State Department. These theological brouhahas aside, we had no difficulty understanding that, for the Irish, the bottom-line was the unyielding administration of impartial justice. Without justice being done and being seen to be done, the Nationalist community in the North would never trust any government to the degree necessary for its support for the IRA to fade away. On this, we could easily agree with the Irish, and should the British approach us over some failed extradition request we could play the concerned and informed observer – just as we could should the Irish express concern to us over British resistance on security issues in the North.

What is amazing to me now is how little attention I paid in that period to Sinn Fein. I spent much time explaining to

Washington the varying positions on Northern Ireland of the political parties in the Republic and I also attempted to add, to the analysis coming from our consulate general in Belfast, what I could usefully say about the positions of the constitutional parties in the North. But we didn't talk to Sinn Fein. They were the dark side of the moon. Still, I did try to understand the phenomenon which went under the embracing name of the 'Republican Movement' and to explain it to Washington. What I learned was, from the perspective of American interests, not encouraging. In September 1988, not so very long after I first arrived in Dublin, it was publicly revealed that John Hume and Gerry Adams had been conducting a series of meetings, a 'dialogue' aimed, at least on Hume's side, at eliminating violence as a Nationalist weapon. The dialogue failed. I must say that reading the transcripts of their exchanges while I sat at my desk in the American embassy was not just discouraging; it felt like entering an altogether different and disquieting world. In particular, the language used by Adams was alien. People simply did not use that language on the streets of Dublin, not as the last decade of the twentieth century approached. It was like going to a meeting of the Socialist International to find speakers reverting to the workers-to-the-barricades rhetoric of the 1930s. Even before reading the transcripts of the failed dialogue, I had already experienced that sense of temporal and spatial dislocation which Sinn Fein projected. Sometime early on in my posting at the embassy, there had been, on a Saturday, a protest march from Parnell Square to the British embassy in Ballsbridge. I went to watch it. Gerry Adams and other Sinn Fein leaders were in the front marching behind the banner proclaiming the cause of their protest, holding the banner at waist-height. Most of those marching behind them were various youth groups from the North, all dressed in para-military style. As it happens, there was to be a rock concert that evening at the RDS – 'Simple Minds,' if I'm remembering correctly – and local teen-agers were already there in large numbers. As the marchers passed, the local teen-agers laughed; some jeered. It was easy to see why. The Northern teen-agers, strutting past in military fashion, looked not so much shabby as tacky and ridiculous. Wholly out-of-date. As were Adams' arguments and his rhetoric and, insofar as these accurately reflected his thinking, his grasp of present-day reality.

In this regard, I might skewer another misconception. It is virtually an article-of-faith among many that 'British pressure' led to our long-standing refusal to issue Adams a visa to visit the United States. Sometimes, British intelligence is identified as the source of our identification of Adams as a terrorist. Again, this is nonsense. We in the American embassy in Dublin did not talk to Sinn Fein because the Irish government did not talk to them and because we agreed with the democratically elected Irish government that Sinn Fein was not a democratic organization. We did not ring up the British embassy for our marching orders. And we also did not have to go to anybody's intelligence files to learn the realities of Sinn Fein. They were readily available in published sources in any bookstore in Dublin. And when we wrote a visa-opinion on Gerry Adams recommending denial, all we needed to go to was our own file of press clippings and read his own statements which unequivocally and even arrogantly supported the right of the IRA to pursue their objectives through violence – the 'armed struggle' in Sinn Fein/IRA-speak. It was to these sources that I went when I wrote such an opinion on one occasion. And we were also able to go to Adams' own books; he has been, after all, a prolific author. Much of my reading then comes back to mind as I listen to Adams and McGuinness and other Sinn Fein leaders in these years since the lifting of the live-broadcasting ban. As we are all all-too-aware, they have

constantly repeated, almost as a mantra, that they do not speak for
the IRA, that the IRA and Sinn Fein are separate organizations,
and that they represent Sinn Fein and speak only for Sinn Fein.
This is greeted by most commentators as, at best, disingenuous or
as a necessary legal fiction (given the illegal status of the IRA).
Some have publicly termed it a 'charade'. After all, the 'past'
IRA activism of Gerry Adams and many of the other Sinn Fein
leaders has been, as I have already noted, publicly documented in
numerous publications. To take just one instance, Tim Pat
Coogan in his narrative account of the troubles in Northern
Ireland, published after the lifting of the broadcasting ban, flatly
stated that Martin McGuinness had served as IRA chief-of-staff,
being succeeded in that position, in 1979, by Gerry Adams.[212]
The service of both on the IRA Army Council was sometimes
claimed to be current.[213]

The analysis which I sent to Washington at that time was,
then, very much at one with the generally-held analysis. Like two
sides of a coin, Sinn Fein and the IRA were a unity however
different their public faces might seem. Indeed, I found it more
useful, in my attempts to grasp their relationship and their
significance in the Northern Ireland conflict if I thought of them
in different terms – that is, if I used for purposes of analysis a

---

[212]*The Troubles* (London, 1995), p. 215.

[213]Following on McGuinness' admission, in May 2001, to the Bloody Sunday
tribunal that he had been the IRA's second-in-command in Derry at the time, such
claims of on-going membership in the Army Council received new impetus; see,
for example, Paul Tanney 'Move against McGuinness fails,' *Irish Times*, 9 May
2001; and *idem*, 'Adams denies he is senior IRA figure,' *Irish Times*, 10 May
2001. By the time the IRA moved to decommissioning, assertions that both
Adams and McGuinness were among the seven Army Council members became
commonplace; see, as typical, Liam Clarke 'Dying days of the 30-year war,'
Sunday Times, 28 October 2001.

mental construct with different labels.[214] Thus, Sinn Fein/IRA as an entity became Physical Force Republicanism, with Sinn Fein as the Political Wing and the IRA as the Military Wing. Considered in this ideologically-rendered incarnation, Physical Force Republicanism was seen to have deep roots in the centuries of Irish struggle for independence. This all must sound rather naive to the Irish. But one has to bear in mind that my job was to convey political and historical realities to policy-makers in Washington with little, if any, knowledge of Irish history. Intuitive recognition of these realities is the very stuff of political discourse in this country but, outside this island, they are alien concepts – concepts from a political world that, in the United States, disappeared in the nineteenth century. To remind myself of this conceptual dichotomy, I would, periodically, re-read the Easter Proclamation of 1916.

What, then, did Physical Force Republicanism want? This was proclaimed more straightforwardly during the years when I was at the Dublin embassy than it is now. As I have already noted, Gerry Adams has been a prolific author, and a number of his books, of those published before the lifting of the broadcasting ban, were political tracts, giving his vision of what a united Ireland ought to be. There were also the published records of Sinn Fein conferences. There was also *An Phoblacht*. On this issue, these sources then spoke with one voice: the united Ireland of Physical Force Republicanism would be a socialist republic. What was specifically envisaged at that time was a centralized state with a command economy, a state motivated by an exclusivist hyper-nationalism. In political science terms, this bore more than a passing resemblance to fascism. May I add, yet once

[214]See my article, 'Dispatches from the frontline of peace,' *Sunday Independent*, 3 March 1996.

again, that we didn't need to go to the British to figure this one
out. In addition to pointing out that the democratic credentials of
Physical Force Republicanism were, thus, highly questionable
and that their electoral support was risible in the South and
relatively minuscule in the North, it was, however, also crucial
for me to point out to Washington that this particular
manifestation of the Republican Movement represented a force in
the dynamic of the Irish conflict with the British that commanded
unquenchable support from its true-believers and wide acceptance
of its basic legitimacy by Irish nationalists in general.

Thus, as is readily evident, the analysis which I sent to
Washington was all very fundamental – even superficial in that
the truly vital operational questions were not even raised.
Questions such as whether or not the Political Wing leaders had
the authority to compel the hard-men of the Military Wing to give
up violence or the even more fundamental question of whether
they wanted peace or victory. These questions were not raised in
my reports to Washington because the need to do so, on our side,
had not yet arisen. The questions did not directly affect American
interests. Nor did we ask what was to be done about it all. During
and preceding my time at the American embassy, we did not ask
these questions because we were not actors in the tragedy. Rather,
my attempts to understand the problem and to explain it to
Washington were directed at the pressing need we Americans had
– that of addressing our own domestic problems consequent upon
the spill-over of the violence in Northern Ireland. It was, and
remains, proper for Irish Americans, like all Irish, to honor those
who fought for the independence of Ireland, just as we Americans
honor those who fought in our own bloody War of Independence
against Britain. But we needed to make it very clear that we did
not consider Physical Force Republicanism to be legitimate. The
Anglo-Irish War took place in a different historical era. Modes of

international behavior which were considered wholly acceptable then are totally rejected as illegitimate today. As I have noted a number of times already, colonialism and imperialism, for instance, were then considered not only the norm, but even desirable. Today, only the morally obtuse would make such a claim. And, through the period of my time at the American embassy, our own national interest in the Northern Ireland conflict, defined narrowly, consisted solely of eliminating the IRA as a factor in international terrorism. For decades, the U.S. federal government agency with the lead on Northern Ireland had been, effectively, the FBI. Beyond eliminating the criminally corrosive effect of the IRA on Irish Americans and their linkages with terrorist-states such as Libya, any further American official involvement in the Northern Ireland conflict was strictly humanitarian. This is hardly unique. Nor does it mean that the commitment was somehow less. Most of our involvements with international crises have been driven by humanitarian concerns. Inter-state relationships are not just, or even primarily, a question of international law. Just as human beings relate to each other primarily and mostly outside the dictates of the law – that is, for reasons of love or compassion or hate or curiosity – so with nations.

In our view – that is, the view from the domestic American perspective – the core tragedy of 1968-69 in Northern Ireland was that the conflicts gave re-birth to Physical Force Republicanism, rather than proceeding on the path of non-violent civil disobedience. For us, at the time, it was irony of the bitterest sort that 1968 also witnessed the murder of Martin Luther King, Jr. In line with this observation, it would also be useful to keep in mind President Clinton's own personal history – a child of the American South whose dedication to civil rights for all Americans cannot be questioned; a governor of a state which witnessed, during his childhood, the earliest battles of the fight for civil rights for black Americans; a student at Oxford in the first years of the Troubles in the north of this island. Does this personal history explain the president's readiness to get involved? Yes, I would believe that it goes a long way. But the actual reason – the consequential bottom-line – why President Clinton made the operative decision to get involved was because he became convinced the U.S. could make a difference. To repeat: by 1994 the situation on the ground had changed. The initiative for a peace process, first launched by then-Northern Ireland Secretary Peter Brooke, had, for all its hiccups and back-tracking and shows of Unionist obduracy, served, at the very least, to demonstrate to the two governments that they could work together and, within limits, could trust each other. And the Hume-Adams dialogue which had so rhetorically failed in 1988, had now, on a second attempt, succeeded. Or, at least, John Hume believed it had, and, as Conor O'Clery's account of it all details, John Hume convinced President Clinton's staff that he had convinced Adams to go for peace.[215] Just to drive a basic concept

---

[215]*The Greening of the White House* (Dublin, 1996), pp. 80-81. Another common fallacy among commentators, both Irish and American, is not so much to overstate as to mis-state the role played by Irish America in bringing about active American involvement in the Northern Ireland peace process. Some actually claim that it was the core group of influential Irish Americans – politicians like Senators Kennedy and Dodd, businessmen like Chuck Feeney and Bill Flynn, activists like the late Paul O'Dwyer and Niall O'Dowd – who convinced President Clinton that Adams and his colleagues were ready to go for peace (see, for one example, Paul Arthur *Special Relationships*, Belfast, 2001, pp. 157-59). Not so – it was John Hume. But Irish America did play crucial roles. For starters, political Irish America provided the legitimizing cover for Clinton to grant Adams his visa; it is inconceivable that Clinton could have done so if Senator Kennedy, with his hard-earned credentials of opposition to Republican violence and of support for peaceful methods, had publicly opposed his doing so. More fundamentally, it was Irish America, and particularly corporate Irish America, which finally woke

home: President Clinton, in trusting John Hume's judgment and in, consequently, opting for overt American involvement in the Northern Ireland conflict by approving a visa for Gerry Adams, was not being pro-British or pro-Irish. He was not taking sides. He was, rather, acting very much in defense of American interests – he was pro-peace (as had been Presidents Carter, Reagan, and Bush before him and President George W. Bush after him).[216]

Adams and company up to present-day realities by bluntly informing them of the home-truths of economics – both inward investment and fund-raising in the U.S. Irish America frog-marched Sinn Fein to the negotiating table; John Hume persuaded the president.

[216] A tangential point here is the claim by any number of pundits that President Clinton felt free to take the 'pro-Irish' decision of granting Adams a visa because, with the ending of the Cold War, our reliance on the United Kingdom had been significantly diminished (see, for one example, John Doyle 'The Northern Ireland peace agreement as internationalised governance,' *Irish Studies in International Affairs* 10, 1999, pp. 209-11). And, in a near-mirror reflection of that bit of 'analysis,' some pundits then began arguing that, with the rapprochement in U.S.-British relations due to the personal and political friendship of Clinton and Blair, the Irish were in danger of seeing their nascent influence with the White House fade away. Both were nonsense. Clinton took the decision he did because he found it to be very much in American interests to do so; the state of our relationship with either Ireland or the United Kingdom did not, and will not, have any consequential affect on American decisions towards the peace process in Northern Ireland. (The *Irish Times* persisted in this misjudgment in its editorial on the departure of Ambassador Jean Kennedy Smith, 4 July 1998.) Finally, so far as the Cold War goes, the real effects of its ending would appear to be twofold. First, the British government no longer saw Northern Ireland as integral to UK defense (see Eunan O'Halpin 'Northern Ireland: the Troubled Peace Process,' *Irish Studies in International Affairs* 12, 2000, p. 246). And, secondly, it put paid to the IRA's supply of armament – indeed, the drying-up of their ready access to Soviet-bloc weaponry and particularly Czech-made Semtex (through Libya) may prove to have been the decisive cause of their giving up on their 'long war' strategy; additionally, Soviet-bloc and Libyan embassies were no longer there to serve as IRA bolt-holes.

Still, Clinton's decision to go for the visa was bold. Since Carter's decision to adopt a position of positive neutrality, our nightmare had been one of being maneuvered into taking sides. But President Clinton made his judgment call and issued a visa to Adams. And a second visa. And a visa to Joe Cahill. And so on. Was all this a triumph of Irish diplomacy? Very much so, but not in the sense of getting one over on the British. And not in the sense, as the standard interpretation of the pundits would have it, of freezing out of the picture the Anglophile State Department ('Brits with American accents,' as one unnamed half-wit labeled American diplomats) and moving the control of Northern Ireland affairs to the National Security Council. The decision on Adams' visa was elevated to presidential level because both – and, I repeat, both – the British and Irish governments insisted on its vital importance to them. And, once it had become a question of presidential decision-making, the NSC staff, as the secretariat of the office of the president, took charge.[217] This is how the

---

[217]There are, additionally, both personal and institutional dimensions to the key role played by the NSC staff in convincing the president to go with John Hume's judgment. Quite simply, neither the Dublin or London embassy nor the State Department were in a position to make consequential assessments of Hume's political credibility. Though always ready to talk, at length, with anyone – I once spent several hours late one night talking one-on-one with him in an Irish bar in Brussels – Hume had spent decades effectively cultivating U.S. government support through the Congress. He did so, first I imagine, because he felt more at home with fellow members of the legislative branch and, secondly, because, given the geo-political irrelevancy of Ireland to the U.S., the only reliable avenue of influence was through Irish American members of Congress. Here, it must be noted that Nancy Soderberg, the key NSC staffer throughout Clinton's involvement in the Northern Ireland peace process, had long served on Senator Kennedy's staff and had learned to trust Hume implicitly. (Anecdotally, I might add on the question of Ireland's global 'irrelevancy' to the U.S. that, in my four years of relatively-voluminous political reporting from Dublin, only once was an item considered of sufficient import to be excerpted in the State Department for inclusion in the Secretary of State's morning reading.)

American bureaucracy works. And let us recall, in this context of presidential decision-making, that President Reagan has been credited with helping, perhaps even decisively, to convince Margaret Thatcher to move forward with the Anglo-Irish Agreement. Last time I looked, no one had accused Reagan of turning his back on his old friend Margaret to tilt pro-Irish.

What I am saying is that there was much less to this supposed row over Adams' visa than met the eye and ear. And I am also saying that viewing it in terms of a battle for American support between the British and the Irish is not helpful, for those who do so will draw the wrong conclusions about how to move forward. Perhaps an analogy would help make clear how misleading a Brit-vs-Irish focus can be. During that period of jockeying in Washington, an editorial writer on a Sunday business newspaper in Dublin opined that a particular visit by then-junior minister Michael Ancram had been a disaster for the British. Ancram was accused of not recognizing that for Americans the 'bearing of arms' was constitutionally sacred and that, consequently, trying to sell the Clinton administration on the decommissioning of weapons would be like trying to sell pork to Muslims. As a misreading of the American political scene, this couldn't be topped. The reality was, of course, that everyone Ancram would have talked with at that time, from the State Department to the White House, would have been convinced advocates of gun control. Whatever the wider political implications might be, decommissioning itself would have immediate appeal to those Americans. Indeed, the major problem of 'decommissioning' for President Clinton proved to be, as various televised press conferences demonstrated, his remembering to use these precious codewords, rather than such plain English as 'turning in your guns'. What I am saying is, if you want to understand why the Americans do things, then you must try to see the situation as

Americans see it. Not as the British do. Nor as the Irish do.
President Clinton made it very clear, repeatedly, that the role he
saw for the U.S. was that of an honest broker – not in the sense of
a broker who mediates a conflict but, rather, one who encourages
all sides to a conflict to keep open minds. One of the traditional
roles of an honest broker in international conflicts is to take risks
for peace which the parties to the conflict, for domestic or other
reasons, cannot take. Political coverage is often a domestic
necessity. It's no coincidence that it was in Washington that then-
Northern Ireland Secretary Mayhew finally met with Gerry
Adams. There was more than an element of good cop/bad cop in
all the shadowboxing at that time – more than just a hint of tacit
cooperation.

It was, after all, natural that the role of playing good cop with
Sinn Fein should fall to us Americans.[218] For all the talk of a
majority of Irish Americans being of Ulster Protestant descent, it
is the big-city Irish Catholics who generate the ethos of Irish
America. And for all the success of Sean Donlon and subsequent
Irish ambassadors in projecting onto American consciousness the
reality of the IRA and their supporters, the 'national cause'
remains deeply embedded in the Irish American psyche. If, as
many have argued, there is no alternative to dealing with Sinn
Fein (the Political Wing of Physical Force Republicanism), then
the key, obviously, is to co-opt Adams and his colleagues into
democratic politics and to keep them so co-opted, to embed them
so root-and-branch into the democratic peace process, that there
can be no turning back to support for violence – if for no other
reason than that a prolonged state of non-war, however edgy, will
cause the combat effectiveness of a non-active IRA to simply

---

[218]Cf., David Owen 'The Internationalization of the Peace Process in
Northern Ireland,' *The Recorder* 15 (2002), pp. 56-70, particularly pp. 60-65.

atrophy (as it had in the 1960s). You can't achieve this by treating Gerry Adams as a terrorist. This doesn't mean you forget about his past; it does mean that you trust him, in the present, as the democratic leader you need him to be.[219] Otherwise, what an appalling vista would open up.

So, the key question for Washington remains, Do Adams and his colleagues really intend to work a political solution within Northern Ireland? This isn't a question of trusting Adams' sincerity. Rather, as in any diplomatic situation, it is a question of whether or not Adams and the others are sufficiently intelligent to recognize realities and see where their best interests lie. The Americans' judgment that Adams is capable of this has been tested, repeatedly. One testing instance came in a national newspaper interview, during his visit to the U.S. in the summer of 1997, when Adams claimed, 'There is no organic link between Sinn Fein and the IRA. Sometimes you read that the IRA is the military wing of Sinn Fein. We don't have a military wing.... We are an independent political party...'[220] This would have set alarm bells a-clanging in Washington – alarm bells which would already have been ringing loudly since the Canary Wharf atrocity. Fudging the issue is one thing but such a flat declaration would have raised the scary prospect that Adams actually believed what he said. This would be specifically alarming to Washington because it would suggest that Adams' 'realities' weren't of this world – but, rather, of the sort of other-worldly nationalism of noble freedom fighters which Irish Americans have been so justly

---

[219]See Garret FitzGerald 'Two issues that could cast shadows on peace process,' *Irish Times*, 17 July 1999, for a penetrating analysis of the 'constructive ambiguities' which are necessary to working the peace process, particularly in regard to the relationship of Sinn Fein and the IRA and the IRA membership of virtually all of the Sinn Fein leadership.

[220]*USA Today*, 4 September 1997.

accused of inhabiting; a world, outside of time and actual history, where the IRA exists as the eternal embodiment of the Irish nation and possesses, in an almost-mystical sense, ultimate authority over the fate of that nation. In this scenario, Sinn Fein would be at the negotiating table, not because of any democratic credentials, but as the representatives of a guerrilla army in the field. Just like in any colonial war.

This is a sinister scenario. On the other hand, I recall the origins of the Troubles. For two years during that early period, I was at university in England. I remember that there was great sympathetic understanding of the IRA on the part of Americans, and I am not just speaking of Irish Americans. The IRA was seen as the defenders of Catholic communities. At that time, the ordinary American would have considered Gerry Adams a hero. But, then, the IRA went on to pursue a campaign of atrocities. The no-warning bombings of wholly innocent people. The torture and execution of suspected informers. Today, the ordinary American would consider the IRA as a contemptible gang of murderers with no conceivable justification for its continued existence. So, how could Americans today see Gerry Adams or any other leader of Sinn Fein who came out of the leadership of the IRA as anything but devious and sinister – coming as they do from this legacy of mindless violence? Emotionally, it is difficult to the point of being impossible. Rationally, it is arguable. A young man like Adams, brought up in the Republican ideology and co-opted into violence by the violence visited upon his community by the then-existing state, could well have come to believe that the only way to reconcile the Republican Movement to a political solution in Northern Ireland was through the Movement itself. While others such as John Hume sought valiantly to wean Northern nationalists away from the physical force tradition, Adams could – at least, conceivably – have sought to bring that tradition to negotiation. He could not control the hard-men, but perhaps he could keep them onside.[221] There *are* reasons, other than hypocrisy, for refusing to 'condemn' IRA atrocities.[222] Certainly, there are analysts in Washington who argue strongly that Adams is a man dedicated both to the nationalist community and to peace and that he genuinely believes that the only path to peace in Northern Ireland – the only way to commit the Republican Movement to peaceful democratic politics – is through the Movement itself.

Having said all this, it is worth repeating, one last time, that this does not mean that the White House necessarily recognizes any legitimacy accruing to this manifestation of the 'Republican Movement'. In the view of Washington, the IRA, as a guerrilla force committing terrorist acts within two constitutional democracies, has no legitimacy whatsoever; and the

---

[221]The key operational question in all this is how much authority the Sinn Fein leadership can exert over the IRA commanders, if indeed they can exert any. Given the 'active service unit' and brigade command-structure of the IRA, which confers great autonomy of authority on the individual commanders, as well as the IRA's internal constitutional dictates governing the relative authority of its Army Council and its Convention (not to speak of such deeper-lying sources of legitimacy of authority for Physical Force Republicanism as the near-mystical belief in the legitimist Second Dáil), the consensus among those analysts closest to the mind-set of Republicans would be that, at best, Adams and the others can only be persuaders of their IRA colleagues; they cannot command them. (The decision-making structure of the IRA is well-documented; for a succinct and straightforward explication, see Ed Moloney 'Who has the power in the Provos?' *Sunday Tribune*, 20 February 2000.)

[222]It may well be that Adams understood early on that there was no possibility of an IRA military victory (he was, after all, a member of the IRA delegation which negotiated with Northern Ireland Secretary William Whitelaw in July 1972). However, if he did, this would not have been an understanding shared either by the IRA rank-and-file or by the broad tranche of Adams' fellow IRA commanders. Guerrilla leaders can only lead troops who share their convictions and who trust them because they have proven themselves in the field.

administration's willingness to deal with Sinn Fein comes not
from that party's having any legitimacy, democratic or otherwise,
but because they represent an armed force which, somehow, has
to be dealt with. The Americans are also fully aware of the danger
this presents of poisoning the peace process. When you allow
terrorists, or their representatives, to the negotiating table, you
have acquiesced in their planting their agenda on that table. It
then becomes a question of whether you are still truly negotiating
for a solution which can be accepted democratically by the
peoples concerned. Or whether it hasn't, actually, now become a
search for a solution acceptable to the terrorists – one primarily
designed to simply get them to stop their killing.[223]

---

[223]This is the very nub of the negotiating quandary: Physical Force
Republicans just do not see the conflict in Northern Ireland in the way normal
people do. It is not that they are psychopaths, though many clearly are – many
local IRA chieftains and their soldiers have all too obviously delighted in torture
and murder and extortion and, thus, correspond fully to Mafia gangsters in their
amorality – but the rest, and in particular the visible face of the Movement, are
men of honor (in the normal sense). They are not morally depraved, but, rather,
morally disordered; they are sociopaths. They truly believe that the IRA is a
legitimate guerrilla army engaged in a war of national liberation. They also
believe intuitively in the 'indisputable legitimacy' of Physical Force
Republicanism. Consequently, appeals to the will of the democratic majority are
so much irrelevant blather to them. And herein lies the dilemma: given that the
IRA cannot be militarily defeated (by the British) and given that the local IRA
commanders cannot be coerced not even by higher IRA authority (such as the
Sinn Fein leadership or even the Army Council) in that their ability to act is at
bottom dependent almost exclusively on the loyalty of their own gunmen, then the
only way of keeping them quiescent is to conform to their mindset – to the way in
which they see themselves and their 'struggle' – and to deal with them,
accordingly, as an undefeated 'national liberation army'. Thus, to keep the peace
intact – that is, to keep the guns silent – the IRA must keep their honor which
would mean keeping their guns (giving them up would be surrender which would
be the delegitimization of their struggle). And, thus, democracy in Ireland would
be poisoned at the source (cf., Dennis Kennedy 'Scramble to appease terrorists is
abasement of democracy,' *Irish Times*, 10 May 2000). How vitally this

But these are questions and concerns which go beyond the American role in the Northern Ireland peace process. They are, rather, the proper concerns of the involved parties, and I mention them solely to underline that Washington's involvement in the peace process is based, not on wishful thinking, but on tough-minded understandings. President Bush and his administration remain as dedicated to the cause of peace in Northern Ireland as President Clinton; but, at the end of the day, any American involvement can only be supportive.[224] It is up to the parties at the table to make the necessary judgments concerning trust and forgiveness. And the problem is one which can, ultimately, only reach resolution through agreement by the Northern Irish

---

fundamental operating-logic of Physical Force Republicanism has been destabilized by the IRA decommissioning begun in October 2001 remains to be seen. The certain hope, though, is that the poison – if kept quiescent – will be leached out through the daily application of democratic behavior.

[224]At the beginning of this chapter, I noted that this American involvement in Northern Ireland was 'now ranked by Irish observers as Clinton's finest foreign policy achievement'. In truth, this was just me being generous. What Irish observers have standardly claimed is, rather, that this involvement was Clinton's 'only major foreign policy success' (e.g., Paul Arthur 'Desire on ground for pact to succeed is a real sea change,' *Irish Times*, 18 January 1999). Again, we experience the embarrassingly parochial. Certainly, observers from most everyplace else in the world – from the Baltic Republics to the Middle East to Latin America to the Far East – would be highly surprised to encounter such an exclusionary and parochial (not to say smug) focus; see my articles, 'Glowing record drowned in smut,' *Sunday Independent*, 13 September 1998, and 'Clinton's legacy will stand the test of time,' *Sunday Independent*, 10 December 2000. As I have, in this chapter, contested many 'findings' by academics and others, perhaps I could best summarize my attitude towards feckless abstraction by this dictum: the professional knows, the academic surmizes, and the pundit fantasizes. Let us remember, then, that the core actors in this business were the professionals (the diplomats and government officials and politicians) and that their views should not be blithely treated as though the views of non-actors (academics and pundits) were of equal weight. Therein lie the pitfalls of bogus history.

themselves. After all, they are the people who will have to live with the consequences of any agreement.[225] Still, there are more than a few Americans who will be deeply satisfied to see the Clan na Gael and its ilk recede into terminal oblivion.

---

[225]Subsequent to my delivering the paper upon which this chapter is based – indeed, nearly coinciding with the delivery – The Good Friday Agreement of 1998 was reached; see George J. Mitchell *Making Peace* (London, 1999).

Seven

Sitting the Exam: The Real World and Irish Perceptions, with the Vietnam War as a Case-in-Point

This sidebar complemented a number of stories in the *Irish Times* of 29 April 1995, commemorating the 20th anniversary of the fall of Saigon which ended the Vietnam War. Presumably, the editors of that newspaper intended it to serve as a factual guide (*vide*, 'Factfile') to frame the accompanying 'news' stories. Such sidebars are normally picked up from a wire service. Identify points of factual or interpretative error in the six identified items and then assign your own grades for accuracy to its compiler (the editors of the *Irish Times*?).

FACTFILE

(*Irish Times*, 29th April 1995)

Population: 66 million

Area: 329,560 sq km

15th century: Europeans arrived. Portuguese, then Dutch, English and finally, French.
1897: French dominant

1940s: Occupied by Japan during second World War. Ho Chi Minh formed Viet Minh (1941), launched general insurrection (1945). Vietnamese Democratic Republic at war with returning French colonialists.

FACTFILE (cont'd)

1954 Gen Vo Nguyen
Giap, at battle of Dien
Bien Phu, broke French
morale.

1954: Geneva agreement
on withdrawal of French
troops, elections for 1956,
Viet Minh to withdraw
above 17th parallel. US set
up Ngo Dinh Diem regime
in Saigon (now Ho Chi
Minh city), in violation of
Geneva agreement, as
elections were prevented.

1. A curious version of events.[226] The
U.S. did not 'set up' the Ngo Dinh
Diem regime. Nor was his taking office
'in violation of the Geneva agreement'.
Diem was named prime minister by
Bao Dai in June 1954, a month prior to
the ceasefire agreements negotiated in
Geneva between the French and the
Viet Minh and brokered by Zhou Enlai,
Molotov, and Anthony Eden. As to the
canceling of elections, does anyone
today still seriously contend that honest
elections could have taken place in
North Vietnam (they were to be
nationwide, after all), where the Viet
Minh government was busy
'liquidating' thousands of 'feudal
landlords'. Afterwards, Ho Chi Minh
confessed the 'land reform' campaign
had been a 'mistake'.

---

[226]The literature on the Vietnam War is voluminous. Acknowledged as the
best single-volume history is Stanley Karnow *Vietnam: A History* (New York,
1983). Perhaps some day, after the Communist regime in Vietnam has followed its
fraternal Communist regimes into the dustbin of history, we will get an equally
honest account of the war from the North Vietnamese side.

FACTFILE (cont'd)

1960: National Liberation
Front (NFL), led by
Nguyen Huu Tho,
resisted successive
military governments in
Saigon. US troops arrived
(580,000 by 1969).

2. Curiouser and curiouser. The National
Liberation Front (aka: the Viet Cong)
was, indeed, proclaimed in December
1960 but organized Communist
insurgency had been going on in South
Vietnam since October 1957 when
Hanoi decided to set up thirty-seven
armed units in the Mekong delta. Nor
was this Front 'led' by Nguyen Huu
Tho, a French-educated Saigon lawyer
who was merely a figurehead, fronting
for the politburo in Hanoi. Admittedly,
Viet Cong activity was low-key at
first; the way they 'resisted' the
Saigon government was primarily by
assassinating South Vietnamese
government officials, rising from 1200
murdered in 1959 to 4000 in 1961.
Finally, no U.S. troops (as distinct
from advisers – see next item) arrived
in 1960. The first U.S. combat forces
arrived in March 1965 when two
Marine battalions came ashore at
Danang. But what's a mere five years?

1961: US aid increased.
16,000 military advisers,
$400 million in military
aid.

3. A minor inaccuracy. The figure of
16,000 U.S. military advisers is close
enough, but this peak was not reached
until after President Kennedy's
assassination in November 1963.

FACTFILE (cont'd)

1963: Buddhist flag
prohibited. Thousands
arrested. Buddhist priests
burned themselves to
death in protest. Viet
Cong attacks increased.
1966: US bombing of
Hanoi and Haiphong.

4.   Misleading. Air raids had been carried
out against the North since February
1965 (first, retaliatory and, then,
strategic), but Hanoi and Haiphong
were essentially off-limits until
Nixon's massive Christmas bombings
of December 1972. Even then, the
targets were still military, and total
civilian casualties were 1,318 in Hanoi
and 305 in Haiphong (these are
official North Vietnamese figures).

FACTFILE (cont'd)

1968: NFL launched offensive during Tet, the Vietnamese Lunar New Year holiday.

March 16th: US troops massacre more than 100 in My Lai village.

5. Simply perverse. The only item given a specific date in this entire 'Factfile' is the shameful and horrific massacre by U.S. troops of villagers at My Lai. But, not even a mention of the thousands of civilians, both Vietnamese and foreigners, deliberately and systematically sought out and then murdered by the North Vietnamese and Viet Cong at Hué during the Tet offensive a month or so earlier. Nor is there mention here or elsewhere that such summary executions, torture and rule by terror were standard operating policy pursued by the Communists throughout the war. Note, also, that North Vietnamese regulars were involved in the Tet offensive, though, indeed, the bulk of the estimated 50,000 Communist soldiers who were killed were Viet Cong – many of whose survivors came to believe that a primary objective of Hanoi in launching the Viet Cong into these suicide attacks was to eliminate their potential opposition to final control by Hanoi.

FACTFILE (cont'd)

1970: US and South
Vietnamese troops attack
North Vietnamese and
NFL groups in Cambodia.
1972: Further US bombing
of Hanoi and Haiphong.
1973: Ceasefire signed in
Paris.
1975: US troops quit
Vietnam

6. The final gross 'error'. No U.S. troops
quit Vietnam in 1975 – the fall of
Saigon did not involve the
'ignominious withdrawal' of the 'last
troops from the embattled US
embassy' (as the *Irish Times* put it in
their editorial of this same issue). The
last U.S. combat forces had, in fact,
been withdrawn from Vietnam in
March 1973 (all but a few thousand
had departed by the previous year).
But what's two years?

Final observation: the *Irish Times* ran on the front page of this
same issue a full-color photograph of a young Vietnamese
woman against a billowing red flag with a caption reading, 'The
youth of Saigon salute their heroes'. Anybody in favor of
bringing back into usage the old term of abuse, 'Communist
dupes'?

Epilogue
Marking and Grading

Having slain the monsters of self-righteous leftism, wilful misinformation, wishful thinking, and other denizens of the parallel worlds, what ought we to say, in conclusion, about American foreign policy and its motivations and how they ought, in fairness, to be portrayed in Ireland?

During my four years at the American embassy in Dublin, I put on standing offer, regularly repeated, my willingness to speak on this subject before audiences. My offer was accepted by Professor Paul Arthur for his class at the Magee College campus of the University of Ulster and by Professor Dermot Keogh at UC Cork. I also spoke on the subject to the command and staff course at the Curragh. No one at Trinity College or UC Dublin or any of the other third-level institutions, however, took my offer up. Nor did the Irish School of Ecumenics despite my frequent contact with the director of their peace studies department.[227] Among political parties, my offer was accepted solely by Young Fine Gael. While the politicians of the other political parties were quite ready to regularly lecture us on our shortcomings and 'immoral' behavior – particularly representatives of the Workers' Party and the Irish Labour Party – it seems that they couldn't be bothered to invite me or some other representative of the American embassy for a face-to-face debate. I can only conclude that they didn't feel

---

[227]This is hardly surprising given that his considered view was that the 'United States...is the most dangerous country on earth;' see *Ireland and the Threat of Nuclear War* ed. Bill McSweeney (Dublin, 1985), p. 44. However, to be scrupulously fair, he has modulated his views; see his book review, 'From the brilliant to the god-awful,' *Irish Times*, 12 August 2000, in which he refers to 'the immense store of wealth, innovation and decency which is a vital source of stability of the American empire'.

the need to. As I believe I have amply demonstrated, there existed (and still exists) among the Irish political class – the politicians, the academics, the journalists and other public figures who concern themselves with international affairs – a smug self-satisfaction about the innate goodness of Ireland's performance on the international stage. It wasn't just that the Irish were good people (which they are). It had to follow axiomatically that their efforts internationally were good – not just well-intentioned but good in their affects – and it followed further that this innate goodness blessed the Irish with an intuitive understanding of international affairs. They looked into their hearts and knew what was right.

There was, of course, the awkward reality of Ireland's comparative lack of influence on the international stage.[228] This couldn't just be due to Ireland's negligible size, for hadn't Ireland demonstrated time and again its ability to cut to the quick and provide the answers?[229] No, there had to be a villain and the villain was us. We were the bully on the block who wouldn't let Ireland play the role nature intended her to play. Why? Because where Ireland, internationally, was progressive and concerned with justice, we were right-wing and concerned with our own interests. Seemingly, the sole way to remain comfortable with Ireland's lack of power to influence events was to condemn American 'interventions'.

It may be that the simplest illustration of this judgmental tendency in public Ireland is my own case. I have regularly been accused by Irish friends – knowledgeable politicians and journalists and academics alike – of being right-wing or

---

[228]What follows draws upon a presentation, on 30 July 2002, to the John Hewitt International Summer School, Garron Tower, Carnlough.

[229]See, however, my review of Joseph Morrison Skelly *Irish Diplomacy at the United Nations 1945-1965* in the *Irish Review* 22 (1998), pp. 123-28.

conservative or, at the least, a Republican (the American-variety).[230] I am none of these. I have, for my entire adult life, considered myself a Kennedy Democrat – fiscally conservative, progressive on social issues, and strong on foreign policy. For someone, like myself, who not only does not apologize for American foreign policy but insists on defending its essential goodness – that is, its positive contribution to international peace and progress – to be equated with reactionaries like Jessie Helms shows just how skewed Irish perceptions have become.[231] Was Harry Truman right wing? Or Jack Kennedy? Or Bill Clinton? Of course not, and my positions have not varied in the slightest from the policies they projected.

In the seventh century, early Christian Irish mythographers sought to confer on the Irish language a special status, claiming that Irish was the first language brought out from the Tower of

---

[230] Personally, I greatly resent being thought a Republican. In the United States, Democrats are defined by the people they want to help; Republicans by those they want to get.

[231] When I published my article in *Studies* which, *inter alia*, defended in trenchant terms the motivations behind our foreign policy, this prompted a piece in the *Phoenix* which labeled me a CIA agent. This is a terrifying accusation for any American Foreign Service officer and caused me to file a libel suit, resulting in a settlement and apology; see the *Phoenix*, 10 September 1993 and 16 February 1996; my article in the *Sunday Independent*, 18 February 1996; anon., 'US diplomat wins libel action...,' *Irish Times*, 9 February 1996; Brenda Power 'Diplomat gets damages for 'unfair comment'' the *Sunday Tribune*, 11 February 1996; and Liam Collins 'The case of the spy who wasn't,' *Sunday Independent*, 11 February 1996. Throughout the case, I was concerned whether an Irish jury would see the matter as deadly serious as it truly was – a concern validated at a subsequent lunch with a highly experienced Irish political reporter. He mentioned that he had known my predecessor as political officer at the embassy quite well and claimed, 'We all knew he was CIA.' 'How's that?' I asked, knowing that the man in question was also a State Department Foreign Service officer. 'Because he defended American foreign policy so strongly,' the reporter replied, and he was being serious.

Babel due to its unique qualities of being comprehended beyond any other language.[232] This is an early example of Ireland shadow-flexing its intellectual muscles. Then as now, it was a self-compensatory attempt to project a superiority in the face of the undoubted dominance of another – that is, the Latin language – for, unlike other non-native Latin speakers such as the Anglo-Saxons, the Irish in those early Christian centuries did not make much headway with this new international culture. Their Latin efforts circled nearly solely around the Bible, and while, for instance, they produced a modest number of exegetical texts there was nothing from an Irish scholar to match the works of Bede in either quantity or quality. Even the Anglo-Saxon scholar Aldhelm, who learned his Latin from an Irish schoolmaster, rapidly outshone the Irish in the breadth of his classical and Patristic learning and, indeed, became anxious to distance himself from the taint of Irish scholarship.[233]

It would seem that national habits die hard. Certainly, Irish mythographers have been busily at work over the last two decades or so erecting another Tower of Babel-construct in which we evil Americans need be brought to heel and who better to do it?[234] What are the realities? Whose judgment has proven the better one? Here, it is useful to recall the adage that the future keeps telling us what the past was about. Was the American role in Central America in the 1980s (to grasp, once again, what was

---

[232]Michael W. Herren 'Old Irish lexical and semantic influence on Hiberno-Latin,' *Latin Letters in Early Christian Ireland* (London, 1996), XII, p. 199.

[233]See my article, 'Aldhelm of Malmesbury and the Irish,' *Proceedings of the Royal Irish Academy* 99C (1999), pp. 1-22.

[234]See, for a depiction of the consequences on Irish foreign and, in particular, defense policy of a 'public mythology' of Ireland as the 'moral conscience of an otherwise depraved, cynical, and egotistical developed world,' Eunan O'Halpin *Defending Ireland* (Oxford, 1999), *passim* and especially pp. 346-49; and my review in *Irish Historical Studies* 32 (2000), pp. 293-96.

for so long the very nettle of Irish lecturing and condemnation of
U.S. foreign policy) one of support for right-wing
governments?[235] Or was it as we claimed all along one of
resisting repression, whether from the right or the left, and of
nourishing democratic forces? Well, the future we projected has
arrived. The countries of Central America, for all their residual
problems, are at peace and governed by democratic governments;
and the countries of the Western Hemisphere have declared that
the maintenance of democracy in each of the countries of the
region is the common responsibility of all the countries – indeed,
in this San José Declaration we have established the right of this
Pan-American union of nations to intervene to protect democracy
should it be threatened in any of the member states.
Unprecedentedly, the nations of the Western Hemisphere are
(with the sole exception of Castro's Cuba) now engaged in
cooperative efforts to tackle the next enemy on our target-list –
governmental corruption.[236] This is the future which we foresaw
and battled for. The future which the Irish consensus-view
imagined was one of 'radical democracies'[237] (for this, read a
regional replication of the Marxist rule of Sandinista Nicaragua).

---

[235]As Conor O'Clery wearisomely regurgitates as late as 1996 (*The Greening
of the White House*, p. 83). He notes, p. 86, that the two American embassy
officers he particularly scorns in his book, John Treacy and Tom Tonkin, had
come to Dublin from Guatemala; it might have occurred to him that this was the
specific reason for their inability to suffer fools – they knew what U.S. foreign
policy in that region was – indeed, both had performed courageously in support of
our policy of stemming human rights abuses and bolstering democracy.

[236]See, for instance, the report of the Summit of the Americas, Miami, 1994.
This outcome is the result of an indigenous development of democratic forces
which were long-embattled by a contending political culture, particularly within
the Latin American countries of our hemisphere.

[237]See, as one illustrative example, Dermot Keogh 'The United States and the
coup d'état in El Salvador, 15 October 1979: a case study in American foreign
policy perceptions and decision-making,' *Central America: Human Rights and*

But, if our policy and actions in this particular region have faded as a neuralgic issue between our two countries, let me turn to the hardy perennial: U.S. policy towards Israel.[238] If any international issue can serve as a paradigm of a divisive split between American and Irish views (indeed, between American and European views in general), it is the Arab-Israeli conflict. During the two-plus decades I served as a career American diplomat, I had no direct involvement in U.S.-Israeli affairs or in Middle Eastern affairs. However, regardless of where you actually serve as an American diplomat, our relationship with Israel is inescapable. Everyone, it seems, has fixed opinions on the nature of this relationship and, when they learn that you're an American diplomat, they all want to tell you all about them. Perhaps the most vexed single conversation I had on this subject took place on the terrace of the residence of the American ambassador in Caracas – not exactly a place where the question of the Arab-Israeli conflict was front-page news.

Beyond such incidental encounters, there were two periods in my diplomatic service during which the question of our relationship with Israel was a recurrent concern. The first was the eight years, from the late 1970s on, in which I dealt with the United Nations, first in Vienna and then in Geneva, with a year in New York in between. On most issues, this was not a golden age

---

U.S. Foreign Policy (Cork, 1985), p. 38. Throughout this lengthy article, Professor Keogh repeatedly ridicules American diplomats as naive for their belief in democratic elections and their support for José Napoleón Duarte as a democratic leader. It might be useful to observe here that this article well illustrates the dictum that 'contemporary history' (that is, the writing about events in which the participants are, for the most part, still among the living) is not properly the province of historians but of the professionals – the politicians and diplomats and soldiers – who were the enactors of the events.

[238]What follows draws upon a talk given, on 29 March 2001, to the Ireland-Israel Friendship League, at the Progressive Community synagogue in Rathgar.

for the UN. As I detailed in chapter 3 above, the Non-Aligned Movement – or the Group of 77, as these developing countries termed themselves when the subject of negotiations was economic – pursued any number of wrong-headed or ideologically-bent objectives during these years, most often in an unholy alliance with the Soviet-bloc countries. We Americans got used to being roundly condemned on what seemed a daily basis. And regularly it seemed the only countries voting 'no' on these resolutions were the U.S. and Israel (on most the EC member-states courageously abstained). The virulent tenor of the times can be instanced by recalling the nadir of it all, which was reached in the 'Zionism is racism' resolution, passed overwhelmingly by the General Assembly. Fortunately, for the most part, that irresponsible period of the UN is now firmly in the past.

The other period in my own career where our relationship with Israel was a present concern was precisely in Dublin. My arrival as the Political Officer at the American embassy in the summer of 1988 coincided with a concerted effort, over the ensuing several months, by the Israeli government to finally bring to conclusion the long-standing discussions on the establishment of a resident Israeli embassy in Dublin. Along with many other friends of Israel, we at the American embassy had a tangential involvement in these efforts – tangential but substantial enough for me to acquire a thorough exposure to the prevailing Irish attitudes towards Israel. It was an eye-opening experience for me, but I don't wish to address these attitudes directly since I am not Irish but American. What does properly concern me, however, is the related subject of Irish perceptions of the nature of the American relationship with Israel – specifically, the assumptions which govern commentary on our policy towards the Arab-Israeli conflict.

The first is that American foreign policy towards Israel is determined by the influence of what is called the 'Jewish lobby' in the United States.[239] I would be unable to even estimate the number of times that this has been stated, to me, as simple fact. Commonly, there is an implication that this lobby enjoys the same sort of sinister influence often attributed to Opus Dei in Catholic countries. Often there are Machiavellian flourishes – for instance, I have been told, more than once, that all the key official players in the U.S.-Israeli relationship are Jewish Americans. In truth, it had never occurred to me, anymore than to any American, that any of the persons in question were, in fact, Jewish. For us they were simply Americans. Perhaps the most bizarre single incident I witnessed personally was to hear a former British foreign secretary state, in the presence of what I am certain he took to be several Irish people, that he understood, quite conclusively from his Washington sources, that the U.S. was being reined in from acting more forceably over the Oslo Accords by then-Vice President Gore who was doing so to protect his own electoral fortunes. The truth, of course, is rather different. However persuasive advocates for Israel might be in Washington, if they did not exist at all, U.S. policy towards Israel would remain the same. To put it bluntly, our policy towards Israel is based on an American reading of American interests. We and Israel are allies. For us, Israel is the sheet-anchor of our policy in the entire region. Like the U.S., Israel is a democracy based on the rule of law. It is the sort of country which we would wish to see replicated throughout the Middle East, indeed, throughout the world. Our friendship, based as it is on a mutuality of interests and the bedrock of democracy, is not subject to the

---

[239]See, as all-too-typical, Patrick Smyth 'Funding lies behind influence of Jewish lobby,' *Irish Times*, 6 April 2002.

whims of coups and so-called revolutions. We can depend on each other.

A second prevailing misperception is that the United States lends 'unquestioning' or 'uncritical' support to Israel.[240] This sort of canard ought to need no refutation. No one who pays even passing attention to the news can have missed the numerous instances, over the decades, of American anger at perceived Israeli stubbornness – or, indeed, of Israeli annoyance at American overbearingness. We have had our share of problems with each other. But what we don't do is question each other's good faith. Others do, however. We Americans have actually been accused, in Ireland, of supporting 'right-wing Israeli irredentism'. This has been said on public occasions, supposedly in all seriousness – in one instance, on a radio talk-show in which I was a participant, by a noted barrister who was subsequently raised to high office. Somehow, the American involvement in 'land for peace' – President Bush's endorsement of a Palestinian state, President Clinton's boosting of the Wye River agreement, Secretary of State Baker's initiative embodied in the 'Madrid Process' which led to the Oslo Accords, President Carter's brokering of the Camp David Accords, our drafting of UNSC Res. 242 – all of this, this historical track-record of consistency in policy, is apparently dismissed as no more than a hypocritical charade. In telling contrast, President Mubarak believes that the U.S. supports 'land for peace,' as did his predecessor Anwar Sadat. As did the late King Hussein and the present King Abdullah. As does every rational Arab leader. But not in Ireland. Indeed, it has become simply tiresome to hear Irish commentators, and even leading politicians, state that – unlike,

---

[240]Here I cite, as typical, Robert Fisk 'Gore choice a paper tiger for Mid East,' *Sunday Independent*, 13 August 2000.

for instance, our policy towards the regime of Saddam Hussein in Iraq – the U.S. has never attempted to force Israel to comply with a single UN resolution. Standardly, UNSC Res. 242 is then cited as the prime example of our culpability.[241] But what is never mentioned is that this resolution calls not just for Israel's withdrawal from territories occupied during the 1967 war but also for the right of Israel and all countries of the region to live at peace behind internationally-recognized and secure borders.[242] To spell this out for the slow learners, this means a negotiated withdrawal where *both* Arabs and Israelis must act to secure a resolution of their conflict.

A third misperception is that American policy in the Middle East or, specifically, in the Arab-Israeli conflict, is not 'even-handed' and that, consequently, an enhanced European role is required.[243] Europeans seem quite fond of claiming this but, somehow, it seems to me that decades of pandering to Arab intransigence and Arab irrationality is not the best background for playing the role of an honest broker (still, there is certainly a role for greatly enhanced funding of economic development in the region).[244] In the meanwhile, the U.S. will continue to deal with Arab and Israeli alike. Just to drive this point home, being 'even-handed' in a negotiation does not mean steering some sort of

---

[241]See, again as typical, my clash on television over this issue with Garret FitzGerald; 'We don't need lectures on morality, thank you,' *Sunday Independent*, 23 September 2001.

[242]This is the formula – 'land for peace' – which, inescapably, underlies every genuine attempt at a resolution of this conflict, such as the Saudi initiative in the late winter of 2002. See also below in the Postscript.

[243]Cf., Paul Gillespie 'Powell's Middle East mission widely recognized as a poisoned chalice,' *Irish Times*, 13 April 2002; or Raymond Deane 'Save Palestinians from US style of democracy,' *Irish Times*, 25 July 2002.

[244]Why are Europeans so fond of making such claims? Why do Europeans do what they do? See the Postscript below.

middle-course between the countervailing demands; it means, rather, supporting those demands which are just and workable.

A fourth misperception, and the final one I need mention, is that the Arab-Israeli conflict could have been solved decades ago if the U.S. had only coerced Israel into the needed concessions.[245] In the first instance, this bogus argument relies on the fundamental fallacy that peace lies entirely within Israeli hands. And, in the second, it is no more than the sort of weasel-worded assertion which is trotted out about American foreign policy most everywhere in the world: somehow it's always our fault. In the specific case of Israel and the Palestinians, it arises from a supposed dependence of Israel on the U.S., at least militarily. As with most such misperceptions, it is based on a high degree of historical amnesia so I will simply suggest that, for the past, people making this accusation ought to look back at the full track-record of Israeli military accomplishments and, for the present, they ought to look at the finely-calibrated nexus of the American military-assistance relationships in the region. They can begin, if they like, with Israel and with Egypt and with Saudi Arabia, but they ought, then, to look at the same military-assistance aspect of our relations with Greece and with Turkey. By such a comparative reading, they should understand how the objectives of security and peace are met by balance and by an objective evaluation of security needs.

But these are real-world issues, and what we have been considering, in examining this area as a paradigm for Irish views of U.S. foreign policy,[246] are perceptions which do not spring

---

[245]Marion McKeone 'So long Saddam, hello Arafat,' *Sunday Tribune*, 27 April 2003.

[246]What I have addressed here concerns Irish misrepresentations of U.S. policy towards the Arab-Israeli conflict. A recital of Irish misrepresentations of the conflict itself would fill a book; see the Foreword above.

from the real world but, rather, from the need of some people to give voice to their bias, however misconceived. Many, perhaps most, of the Irish people who voice such misguided views do so in good-faith. But others know full well how they are distorting the truth. Deliberately, they disregard the facts, source analysis, contextualization – all the tools of serious analysts and historians – and they twist casual links into causal linkages, coincidences into complicity, a relationship into responsibility. In short, they are morally-obtuse fantasists. So much, then, for the lack of logical clarity and, indeed, of reality prevailing in public Ireland in this as in other areas of American foreign policy. What about the Irish government?[247] In my Introduction, I characterized official U.S.-Irish relations as 'rarely less than highly cordial'. Can we presume, then, that, in contrast to the distorting predispositions among Irish pundits, the Irish government engages in a consistent good-faith effort to consider our policy positions on their merits? And that they are seen publicly to do so? What I have specifically in mind, here, is the professional's approach to foreign policy. This begins with an analysis which, in a logical manner, proceeds on the basis of demonstrable facts and

---

[247] I must say – even if only as an aside – that during my four years at the American embassy in Dublin I was appalled by the Irish government's behavior regarding the Arab-Israeli conflict; if anything, it was more reprehensible than the standard self-righteous posturing beloved of by European politicians in general over the last many decades. In telling contrast, Ireland's performance, once elected to the Security Council (or, perhaps, once a change in foreign ministers was effected), was marked by realism and responsibility. Perhaps Ireland's taking a seat on the Security Council had the equivalent affect that achieving high governmental office so regularly has on Socialist politicians. Being confronted with real responsibility – knowing, that is, that your actions and your words will now have real-world consequences – can work wonders. Certainly, the phenomenon of true-believing fire-breathing radical Socialists being converted, upon taking office, into statesmen of moderation is one that we have all witnessed over and over through the decades in country after country, including in Ireland.

draws conclusions in a fair-minded and reasonable fashion, and then, in formulating a resulting policy, asks how best national interest would be served.

It is clear, from the diplomatic record, that, whatever romanticized view might prevail popularly about Ireland's role in world affairs, Ireland's professional diplomats have been clear sighted in their approach to issues and realistic in their pursuit of the desired outcome.[248] This is particularly true in regard to Ireland's relationship to the various incarnations of the European Union. What about in regard to the United States?[249] Perhaps I could best approach this question by recalling the public debate in Ireland, beginning when George W. Bush's election as president was first confirmed, about whether a President Bush would continue Clinton's involvement in the Northern Ireland peace process. On this, the pundits covered the water-front, from personality differences to questions of partisan political differences between Democrats and Republicans to substantive policy differences. But the sole question was: would Ireland retain its influence with the incoming administration? And the sole concern motivating this question was about what Ireland could expect a new Bush administration to do for it. Not a single commentator – so far as I am aware – asked what Ireland could do for the United States. Indeed, not a single commentator even noted the one-sided nature of the discussion, in Ireland, about expectations concerning the incoming American presidency. But it didn't go unnoticed in the U.S. We had, notably, an article on this issue appearing in the *Irish Times* by Congressman Ben

---

[248]On this, see my review of *Irish Foreign Policy, 1919-1966* edited by Michael Kennedy and Joseph Morrison Skelly (Dublin, 2000) in *Irish Political Studies* 15 (2000), pp. 238-39.

[249]What follows draws upon a presentation, on 13 March 2001, to Fianna Fail's Dublin Forum in the Mansion House, Dublin.

Gilman, the chairman of the House Committee on International Relations.[250] Diplomatically phrased, his article warned against allowing extraneous issues such as nuclear weapons to dominate the U.S.-Irish agenda and called for a 'new, broader dimension' to our bilateral relationship, one that would involve Ireland working closely with the U.S. on the Security Council. In short, Ireland's national interest lay in finding ways to cooperate with the United States, not in continuing to lecture it in a morally superior fashion.[251] As one Irish commentator characterized it, the article's message was, 'Get real'.[252]

To be blunt, there has long been a lack of reciprocity in the official U.S.-Irish relationship. I first became aware of this during my consultations in the Department of State prior to my arrival in Dublin in the summer of 1988. The U.S. Foreign Service, like any diplomatic service, has a corps of inspectors and each American embassy undergoes an inspection every few years. The inspectors are primarily concerned that the embassy's officers are doing their jobs properly but they also take a broader look at the state of the diplomatic relations between the U.S. and the host country. Our embassy in Dublin had been inspected in the spring of 1988 and, as I read through the inspectors' report, the one item which stood out for me was a perceived lack of reciprocity in the American-Irish relationship. We were doing a good deal for Ireland, particularly on trade and civil aviation issues (not to speak of the $100 million we had already donated to the

---

[250]'Irish-US links at risk in post-North agreement era,' *Irish Times*, 23 December 2000.

[251]A tradition continued by David Andrews while foreign minister; see my article, 'Why Andrews doesn't cut the US mustard,' *Sunday Independent*, 11 October 1998.

[252]Colum Kenny, 'Money talks – with an American accent,' *Sunday Independent*, 7 January 2001.

International Fund for Ireland), but it was difficult to see what actually we were getting in return. In my last year in Dublin, we were again inspected and again we reported the same lack, with particular reference to Ireland's performance during the first Gulf War (here, we should recall that these were the years of all those U.S. immigrant visa programs almost tailored for the needs of the Irish during those pre-Celtic Tiger days).

So what actually would constitute reciprocity in this relationship? Perhaps the most fair-minded and perceptive public exposition of this issue was made by Sean Donlon, a former Irish ambassador to the U.S., in the address I have already cited, to the Ireland-United States Chamber of Commerce in Dublin on 21 November 1989. He began by noting that the working assumption in Ireland had long been that the 'United States [was] a staunch friend [which could] be relied on for support and help' whenever Ireland needed it. But, then, he felt compelled to warn of the tendency which had, perversely, emerged in Ireland which encouraged 'small interest groups to dominate the [foreign policy] debate and to set an agenda for the conduct of the Irish-American relationship which [was] essentially dominated by a spirit of anti-Americanism'. His remarks received widespread coverage in the Irish press, provoking extensive vituperation at the hands of the vociferous nutters who dominated media attention regarding America. Typically, they accused Donlon of advocating that Ireland adopt a slavish attitude to the U.S. in gratitude for all the benefits it receives. In doing so, they wilfully ignored a key paragraph of Donlon's speech:

> As a sovereign independent country we have a right, even a duty, to establish our own foreign policy agenda. An Irish agenda is unlikely to coincide in all respects with that of the U.S. and there may even be sharp differences

on specific issues. It is entirely right that when our interests do differ, we should not attempt to conceal the difference or be afraid to pay an economic price for a principled political position.

As a statement of principle, this is impeccable. But as an operating guide to Ireland's relations with the U.S., it begs the question. As a former career American diplomat, I find it impossible to envisage a price ever being exacted from Ireland by an American government. In regard to us, Ireland's foreign policy is literally cost-free; and the reason for this immunity is that the relationship is conducted not through the State Department but through Congress – a reality acknowledged, most likely inadvertently, by Taoiseach Bertie Ahern. In February 2001, he was widely reported in the press as saying of former Ambassador Jean Kennedy Smith, 'She overruled the State Department...more than once to help us...and they gave her stick for it, even after she was gone, and I want to thank Jean for all she's done for us.' What Ambassador Kennedy Smith actually did – and, according to press reports, this was a salient consideration of the inspectors general who investigated her alleged retaliation against career staff at the embassy[253] – was to seek to avoid any policy confrontation with the Irish government. If true, that's no way to run a diplomatic relationship.

During my four years at the American embassy in Dublin, it was a common experience for me, when I went over to the Dáil for foreign affairs question-time, to hear the Irish foreign minister read out, in his response, an analysis of a given foreign policy situation which was, in every particular, the same as ours. What

---

[253]See Richard Gilbert 'Dissent in Dublin,' *Foreign Service Journal* (July 1996), pp. 28-35.

was not done was to carry this congruity of views into public. For instance, just over a decade ago – as I detailed in chapters 2 and 5 – both the Irish and the American governments, in the debate then on-going in the United Nations about how to bring peace to Cambodia, adamantly opposed any return to power of the Khmer Rouge and said so, publicly and vehemently and formally. Both governments voted in the UN in support of the strategy to resolve the conflict sponsored by Cambodia's neighbors, the Association of Southeast Asian Nations. There was not a sliver of difference between our two governments in their analyses of the problem and its workable solutions. But when the demonstrators gathered outside our embassy to castigate us for the horrors of the Khmer Rouge, the Irish government said nothing. And, a decade later, they again said nothing as the demonstrators gathered, again, in front of the American embassy when the Indonesian militias ran riot in East Timor.

Am I suggesting, then, that the Irish government – as a gesture of gratitude and reciprocity – do our work of public diplomacy for us? Not at all, though this is, indeed, an area where, regularly, we are truly damned if we do and damned if we don't. Yet, once again, to cite but a few examples from the last decade or so: if we make public attempts to explain our positions on agricultural trade, an Irish minister for industry and commerce angrily accuses us of 'bullying'. I mean that literally. If we promote a seminar on NATO, neutralists accuse us of attempting to 'bully' Ireland into abandoning its neutrality. If we request clarification of state involvement in the granting of a certain communications license, the Irish businessmen concerned – as well as financial journalists – accuse us of 'bullying' and trying to treat Ireland like a banana republic. Disparity of size does carry its built-in liabilities. Still, we're big boys. But what I am suggesting is that every democratic government has an obligation to explain to its own citizens its own reasons why it has taken any given position. The Irish government can do this superbly when it is a question of, for instance, ratification of an EU treaty. It would be helpful if they would do the same when it is a question of their holding the same views as the U.S., particularly on contentious issues. It would also be helpful if, when our views differ, the Irish government would acknowledge, publicly, that it is a question of honest difference and that the U.S. is acting in good faith. In short, a relationship of reciprocal respect – just as the U.S. shares with Israel.

I want to be clear about this. Accordingly, in order to demonstrate how this so-devoutly-to-be-desired relationship of reciprocal respect would work out operationally, let us take the salient issue of the UN sanctions imposed on Iraq consequent to the Gulf War.[254] Here, Foreign Minister Brian Cowen, from his very early days in charge of Iveagh House, was explicit in enunciating Ireland's position. Despite the best efforts of the Irish media to depict an Ireland 'distancing itself' from the U.S. and Britain, Cowen insisted – in Washington, D.C., in Moscow, in Paris, in New York – that Iraqi compliance with the UN sanctions was not negotiable and that Iraq must so comply before the sanctions could be lifted.[255] What was not done was to fully justify, for the Irish public, the reasons for this policy stance.[256]

---

[254]What follows draws on addresses made as a guest-speaker, on 2 February 2001, during a debate of the Literary and Historical Society at University College Dublin and, on 6 November 2002, during a debate of the Historical Society at Trinity College, Dublin.

[255]See 'Iraq must destroy weapons for sanctions to be lifted – Cowen,' *Irish Times*, 24 February 2001 and the accompanying articles on the same page.

[256]In October 2001, Minister Cowen did, finally, address this issue in a statement to the Dáil. However, though he made the same salient points which I will be setting out in the text, his statement was not oral but written; see Deaglán

The received wisdom in the Irish media – and, presumably, among the Irish public – remained that the sanctions were an utter failure: not only was Saddam Hussein still in power but the sanctions were achieving nothing but the infliction of great suffering on the Iraqi people. But the official UN reports detailed a very different truth (as was well recognized by the Irish government). At the time of the ceasefire in 1991, it had been projected that Saddam's weapons of mass destruction could, with the cooperation that the Iraqis had pledged themselves to, be eliminated within six months. But when, in that summer, it became clear that Saddam had opted, instead, for a policy of obstruction, of lying and bullying, in order to conceal and preserve his ability to construct these atomic, biological, and chemical weapons, the Security Council proposed the oil-for-food program as a means of relief for the civilian population. Saddam rejected the offer outright for four years and then dithered on its implementation for nearly another two years. It only finally began operating in March 1997. The program provided for Iraq to sell oil under UN supervision with 72 percent of the earned revenue used by the UN, pursuant to Iraqi purchase orders, to purchase food, medicine, and other humanitarian supplies for Iraqi civilians along with spare parts for the oil industry and other sectors such as electricity and sanitation (of the remaining 28 percent, 3 percent went for overhead and 25 percent for reparations for the destruction wrought by the Iraqi military in its invasion). Despite bogus Iraqi claims, its oil production under this scheme soon exceeded pre-war levels and the earned revenue provided more than adequate means to purchase needed food and medicine and spare parts (as Minister Cowen explicitly noted in

---

de Breádun 'Cowen says Saddam fails to feed people,' *Irish Times*, 22 October 2001.

his Dáil statement). Why, then, were the needed supplies not getting through? According to the head of the UN humanitarian program, it was due to the Iraqis themselves who were persistently under-ordering the needed supplies, particularly in the health sector. This was the structural break-down point in the oil-for-food program. Short of replicating the Iraqi national marketing system – which, even if Saddam would ever have permitted such a superseding of his control over his population, would have involved crippling expenditures by the UN to put in place and support tens of thousands of marketing and distribution personnel with all the infrastructure they would require – there was no alternative to relying on the Iraqis to, first, determine the needed food, medicine, and other supplies and, then, to see to their proper delivery. This they singularly failed to do. The only logical conclusion is that Saddam was deliberately provoking and exploiting the misery of his own people, particularly children, in order to con the gullible into supporting his demand that the sanctions be lifted without his having first delivered up his weapons of mass destruction. The UN also reported that Saddam was deliberately withholding medicine, hoarding up to half of the medicine supplied in warehouses and actually re-exporting such nutritional supplements as baby milk to sell for hard currency – money which he then diverted to re-building his military and to constructing 'palaces,' nearly half-a-hundred since the end of the Gulf War, structures which the head of the UN inspectors described as the 'sites from which his programs of mass destruction were designed and operated'. UNICEF specifically laid the blame for child malnutrition and death on Iraqi 'mismanagement' (their diplomatic euphemism) – in telling contrast, in Kurdish northern Iraq where the UN directly administered humanitarian assistance, child mortality rates fell below pre-war levels. These were all publicly available facts upon which, I can only presume, the Irish government based its policy position. Why has the Irish government not spelt them out for the Irish public?

I had my say, in the Introduction above, about why I thought the Irish have seen things the way they have so I will say no more on the subject. I will conclude, rather, by simply speaking of why we Americans see things the way we do.[257] 'Immoral' is a favorite epithet of the critics of our foreign policy. I'll let them answer for the philosophical basis, if any, of their attribution of morality. I will also let those who want to believe in eternal truths and the natural law.[258] For the rest of us, we need seek no human-transcending basis for values. All values derive from our simple existence as human beings, and it is from our living together that we take our purpose.[259] Thus, political morality is what works; it is that which we have learned from human experience enables us to live together in peace and prosperity. The United States was the first country specifically founded to incarnate an ideological polity – a mutually-reinforcing set of beliefs about the nature of man and of how men can live together in society to the common good – and my country has proved to be, over the two-plus centuries of its existence, a forcing-ground of the human

---

[257]What follows draws upon a presentation, on 6 November 2001, to Young Fine Gael at Trinity College, Dublin.

[258]The noted American theologian John Courtney Murray, S.J. *We Hold These Truths* (New York, 1960), pp. 109-23 and 295-336, does his best to uphold fundamentalist Catholic teachings on natural law and its divine origins, but his American cussedness keeps breaking through to demonstrate (however subconsciously) that, in truth, natural law is what experience has demonstrated works because it accords with human nature (see particularly p. 116).

[259]Cf., Thomas Jefferson's letter, of 13 June 1814, to Thomas Law; and D. Vincent Twomey, SVD 'Plurality should not deteriorate into ambiguous pluralism,' *Irish Times*, 27 January 2003.

experience.[260] Politically, we Americans have embodied our sense of morality in the American creed: individual liberty as the focus of the polity, equality of opportunity and legal respect, private enterprise. This creed may – to take one aspect of American life – have resulted in the United States being the developed country with the greatest inequalities in terms of wealth but it has also made the U.S. the most dynamic in job creation, productivity, and per capita real income.[261] Internationally, we think it would be no bad thing if other countries would be as us.[262] Certainly, we feel that the peoples of other countries would be better off and, assuredly, we know that we, at home, would benefit if the United States were one in a world of democratic nations.

If others can not see our history in the glowing terms we mostly use when we speak of it,[263] then we would ask that they, nevertheless, understand that human beings are fallible and that

---

[260]See my review, 'Empire of liberty – an American tale,' *Sunday Independent*, 19 September 1999.

[261]Seymour Martin Lipset *American Exceptionalism* (New York, 1996), pp. 55-73.

[262]Spare me, please, any acerbic comments about Americanization and cultural imperialism; I refer in these observations solely to the beneficial import of democracy, however local historical experiences might wish to implement it (though, I am driven to add, the McDonald's corporation could well serve as a paradigm for the positive manifestations of modern industrial democracy: high-quality food and service, entry-level training in work-attitudes and discipline, well-lighted centers of cleanliness and security in blighted neighborhoods – not bad for a fast-food joint which has replaced the greasy spoons and ptomaine palaces of the past).

[263]The American domestic exceptions, of course, would be found in the language of leftist or rightist intolerance, marked by paranoia, anti-intellectualism, bad faith, and contempt for ordinary people; in America, leftist intolerance is nearly the sole prerogative of academic intellectuals, while rightist intolerance holds sway among the white supremacists and militia-groupings. Unlike in Europe, both in America are marginalized from power.

politics involves hard and imperfect choices about the uses of power.[264] There must also be the commonsensical recognition that, until human beings turn into angels, there remains the ongoing need for violence. Human rights are secured by the rule of law which is secured by enforcement. For us, political morality means keeping one's commitments,[265] and we ask from others maturity in evaluating what we have done and why we have done it – the mature judgment exhibited, for instance, by the Irishman, Edmund Burke, when he observed of the American colonies, that 'the American constitutions are to liberty what grammar is to language'.[266]

---

[264]See Linda K. Kerber 'Teaching American History,' *The American Scholar* 67/1 (Winter 1998), pp. 99-100. Despite the Platonic belief of academics and like-minded pundits that factors in international relations are real if they exist in the minds of theorists (cf., Bill McSweeney *Security, Identity and Interests*, Cambridge, 1999, *passim*), such factors are not real (that is, they possess no real-world validity) if they do not affect the deliberations of the professionals involved. To give a specific example, the occupation of Haiti by the United States 1915-1934 was Great Power behavior conditioned by the understanding of international norms of the times; it was not a factor in the deliberations of President Clinton and his advisers seeking to resolve the crisis of the restoration of President Aristide.

[265]Aristotle termed this the 'virtue of justice' (*Nicomachean Ethics*, V, 1).

[266]Edmund Burke 'Speech on Moving Resolutions for Conciliation with the Colonies,' delivered on 22 March 1775.

Postscript

Farewell to Foreign Affairs
Fecklessness

A dozen years ago at the time of the first Gulf War, I was the First Secretary for Political Affairs at the American embassy in Dublin.[267] The coverage of that war in the Irish media – particularly in Ireland's leading daily newspaper, the *Irish Times*, and on RTE, Ireland's state-owned television and radio service – was marked by an anti-Americanism which was so hard-edged and nasty that I eventually wrote at length about it all.[268] It wasn't that anti-Americanism in Ireland came, at that time, as a surprise. It was, after all, a phenomenon which, though recognition of it always did come as a shock to newly-arrived American diplomats, had long been noted by international observers and, by the time Saddam invaded Kuwait, I had been in Dublin for long enough to know well what to expect. Still, it was embittering to witness the presentation, on a daily basis, of Gulf War One as a morality play in which Saddam Hussein was David,

---

[267] Though largely written in Dublin, as is evident from references in the text which I have let stand as written during the course of the war, I began this piece after I had determined to leave Ireland and return home. A decade and a half of incessant anti-American bias in Irish public life had worn me out. But it was the intensified nasty-mindedness of the anti-Americanism on prideful (in truth, shameful) display during the lead-in to the war in Iraq that had, finally, convinced me that Americans who, unapologetically, believe in the essential goodness of America were unwelcome in Ireland. It was time to go to live where rationality in the foreign policy debate was the norm. Finally, I should note that, written a good deal after I had completed this book, this is a stand-alone farewell.

[268]'Ireland and the Gulf War: A View from the American Embassy,' *The Recorder* 14/1 (2001), pp. 113-31.

the hero of the Arab world (rather ironic, that!), facing up to the Goliath, the United States as international braggart and bully.

This time around, things were somewhat different. For starters, I was now retired and, hence, was able to appear on Irish radio and television, free from diplomatic restraints and free to speak out (I was the designated war-monger). More pertinently, the tone of presentation across the Irish media had changed; anti-Americanism was not the driving-force it had been. Certainly, the lead items chosen for each morning's newspaper and each broadcast were still perceived American set-backs – friendly-fire incidents, alleged civilian casualties, 'fierce' resistance, the post-combat looting – but, for the most part, the actual news coverage was as good as in the media of other countries. Unlike during the first Gulf War, this time Saddam's propaganda was not written up as representing the 'Arab View'. Could I actually claim that my hammering-away on this issue for a decade had had some effect? But if the news coverage had woken up to its responsibilities, the commentary – editorial and punditry, alike – was as slanted as ever.

Perhaps the first thing I was told when I arrived in Ireland in the summer of 1988 was how seriously interested the Irish people were in international affairs. That could well be, though from the very beginning I certainly saw little evidence of it in, for instance, the letters-to-the-editor page of the *Irish Times* where crackpot letters sometimes seemed to set the prevailing tone. Indeed were one to judge from those letters to the *Irish Times* regarding U.S. foreign policy, Ireland would seem to be almost exclusively populated by paranoid leftists. However, as polls and other indicators demonstrate, this is decidedly not the case – the Irish people are as commonsensical as people everywhere. And those Irish who are professionally serious about international affairs – the members of the Irish diplomatic corps and the Irish military and diplomatic historians such as Eunan O'Halpin – are as good at their jobs and as clear-headed about their business as the professionals of any country.

So why the puerile nature of so much of the commentary on the U.S.? The short answer is that this simply reflects the lack of genuine informed content in what passes for public debate on U.S. foreign policy in Ireland. This is a 'debate' whose forcing-ground is one of factually-bogus premises: Irish 'neutrality,' the 'UN target' for Third World aid, the iniquity of the 'equality gap'. Baseless bromides which go virtually unchallenged.

Even on the best of the current affairs programs – RTE's 'Questions & Answers' – there seems no recognition that responsible debate is conducted in the mainstream – and that, consequently, the Greens and Sinn Fein should never be invited to 'contribute' to an international affairs debate (anymore than you'd invite Socialists to a serious debate on economics). There is no recognition that this cavalier attitude towards foreign affairs debate is utterly lacking in professionalism. There is no Jim Lehrer in the Irish media.

Of course, Ireland is not alone in suffering such a degradation of public discourse on foreign affairs. To some degree, this is a problem common to all our countries. Its origins lie in that sea-change in the intellectual's perception of international affairs that took place during the Vietnam War period – a transformative lurch in normative values from the resolve to resist Communist subversion of democracy over to a self-regarding and condescending scorn for democracy. It was an abdication of intellectual integrity – a *trahison des clercs* – on a herd-like scale.[269] In Europe, this cognitive degeneration is, quite self-complacently, nurtured by a much older – indeed, centuries-old –

---

[269] As I noted in chapter 4 above.

mental aberration: European intellectual and cultural condescension towards Americans. Americans, you see, are crass and ignorant and ill-educated, while Europeans have an intuitively superior understanding of all things serious. If you find it impossible to credit that educated men could indulge themselves in such a childish caricature, then take a look at some of the judgments concerning Americans made by Garret FitzGerald: 'simplistic and shallow,' for instance, is how he characterizes American reporting on international affairs.[270] Other Irish commentators have actually put forward as a serious contention the claim that, unlike the Irish, Americans don't understand history (worked wonders in Northern Ireland, didn't it?).

'Simplistic' is, of course, the standard derogatory term applied by Europeans to the American approach to most any foreign policy issue. Americans see things in black and white, the wise Europeans claim, while they themselves readily recognize that the world is more complex and solutions more nuanced. That the European are correct in their 'analysis' is readily apparent from the lengthy string of diplomatic successes Europe has enjoyed: such as Srebrenica? Or, perhaps, the ongoing funding of anti-Semitic children education programs in the Palestinian territories? The simple reality, of course, is that we Americans not only take the lead, by default, on every major international crisis but also take time out to clean up various messes in the Europeans' own backyard, such as the armed conflict between Spain and Morocco over an uninhabited rock off the North African coast. The truth is that the American view of the world is clear-headed – we see things the way they actually are – because we are prepared to take

---

[270]'Disaster may bring US closer to rest of world,' *Irish Times*, 15 September 2001.

responsibility, while the European view is wilfully blurred to justify a cop-out from having to actually do something. A shower of weak sisters who use up all their courage 'standing up against the US' does not constitute a viable force for the enforcement of international law.

In practical terms this European fecklessness has long taken a more pernicious turn than just self-righteous posturing leading to abstention from action. In effect, the European Union, in its councils, does not tackle a crisis with the goal of working out how best to resolve it, but of how best to project EU influence over it. The determining motivation of the EU is, in short, one of obstructing or side-lining any American lead in order to enhance Europe's standing by diminishing that of the United States. This is the 'French disease' which has systemically infected the body politic of the EU, and its classic manifestation was the warning delivered to the U.S. by then-EC President Jacques Delors to 'stay out' of the crisis engendered by the break-up of the former Yugoslavia: this was a European problem, he declared with the full backing of the EC member-states, and the Europeans would solve it. Didn't they ever? Their solution to the ethnic war in Bosnia was to impose an arms embargo and then send in lightly-armed infantry to oppose Serbian tanks. The American response was to recognize, in our simplistic way, that the core cause of the war was Serbian aggression and our solution was to knock heads at Dayton to achieve an accord with minatory enforcement provisions. Our own contribution to the peace-enforcement troops subsequently sent into Bosnia was an armored division.

Elsewhere the EU has worked diligently (and successfully) to engineer an isolation of the U.S. in one international negotiation after another, from the land-mine ban on to Kyoto. On the land-mine treaty, for instance, the EU effectively put paid to the U.S. signing up to it by saying 'no deal' to the American need for a once-off time-limited exemption – to ensure against North Korean adventurism. (Would these European negotiators still, today, claim as then-Irish foreign minister David Andrews did that, in this instance, land-mines 'serve no military purpose'? Yes, they probably would.) And on Kyoto, once the U.S. had been forced into withdrawal from the implementation conference, the EU – in order to keep other countries like Japan and Russia on board – agreed all the concessions which the U.S. had requested. All of this simply to allow the EU to posture as the champions of all progressive causes – while actually doing little if anything of substance. It's the U.S., not any EU member-state, which is by far the largest contributor to de-mining operations, with our personnel and resources being deployed in some forty countries. And is any EU country even beginning to meet its Kyoto-mandated target on gas emissions?

Of course not, because the purpose wasn't to actually address the problem of global warming but to disguise the Europeans' own deficiencies in the environmental area by talking down the U.S. The United States is, in most every aspect of human endeavor with global import, the one indispensable nation, and Europeans just can't stand it. But you would have thought that, somewhere, the penny would have dropped. That somewhere, in the world of Irish policy-making, someone would have taken a look at the actual track-record of U.S. accomplishments in environmental protection – the first clean air and water legislation under President Johnson in the 1960s, an Environmental Protection Agency established in 1970 by President Nixon, mandatory unleaded gas introduced in the 1970s – as compared to the track-record of European states and then have asked whether there wasn't, just perhaps, something to be learned from the American approach. Sticking a finger in Uncle Sam's eye in order to feel better about yourself isn't a very promising foreign policy approach.

The simple truth is that all these duplicitous diplomatic maneuverings have been attempts to delegitimize American power by portraying the United States as operating outside international law, and the most egregious such villainous charade was, precisely, the French-orchestrated campaign to stymie American-led military action against Saddam Hussein's Iraq. What the French (and the Germans) were (and remain) up to had nothing to do with peace or the rule of law. It had everything to do with cynically exploiting a target of opportunity to undermine American-led enforcement of international law as mandated by the UN. In the German case, it must have seemed a God-sent opportunity to legitimize internationally Chancellor Schröder's gutless domestic opportunism, his blatant electoral appeal to anti-American bigotry. For the French, it was a simple continuation of their decades-long policy of attempting to drive a wedge between the U.S. and Europe, but, still, it constituted a sustained display of bad faith, astonishing in its bald-faced hypocrisy even for Chirac. The French and the Germans claimed that a peaceful solution was possible because the inspections were working. But, as even the dogs in the street recognized, that the inspectors were achieving any success at all – indeed, that they were even back in Iraq in the first place – was entirely due to the minatory build-up of American (and allied) forces in the Gulf. And not only were France and Germany not contributing in any way to this military presence, they actively sought, throughout the crisis, to gut it of its very credibility – that is, the certainty that if Saddam did not comply, then force would be used to compel him – by despoiling this military force of its legal right to enforce the will of the UN Security Council: Germany by declaring that they would not contribute to a war even with a UN mandate, France by declaring that they would veto 'under any circumstances' a resolution authorizing a resort to war. Saddam Hussein couldn't have asked for better allies.[271] If President Bush had not made it clear, over and over again, that the U.S. would, if necessary, ignore the French-paralyzed Security Council and lead a 'coalition of the willing' to disarm Iraq, Saddam could have just stalled the inspectors forever, secure in the knowledge that his good friends, the French, would prevent a UN-mandated enforcement. The result of this Franco-German posturing was a delegitimizing not of American power but of the rule of law; and, rather than becoming the axis of an European counterpoise to American power, France and Germany ended up isolating themselves within Europe – let us not forget that, within both the EU and NATO, a decisive majority supported the United States.

Figuring this out wasn't rocket science. Unless, of course, you're one of those analysts determined on finding the U.S. guilty no matter what factual or logical distortions you have to resort to. Standardly, Irish analysis continues to refer to France as leading the 'pro-peace' opposition to the United States, while Fintan O'Toole of the *Irish Times*, in one of his mother-of-all-bile masterpieces, contended that it was the 'breathtaking stupidity' and 'political incompetence' and 'astonishing arrogance' of the Bush administration which was responsible for '*forcing* France and Germany into open defiance'.[272] How does he – so consistently – manage this stuff with a straight face? In the meanwhile, the most politically-contentious single issue in Irish reaction to the war – believe it or not – has been the use of

---

[271]As noted by the new foreign minister of free Iraq who, in his intervention before the UN Security Council on 16 December 2003, termed them 'appeasers' of Saddam.

[272]My italics. 'No room for democrats in new Iraq,' *Irish Times*, 18 February 2003.

Shannon airport by planes ferrying American forces to the Gulf. Apparently, this is felt to sully the purity of Ireland's neutrality. Demanding that the use of Shannon should be denied to the U.S., the major opposition party in the Irish parliament, Fine Gael, has resorted to legalistic pedantry to argue that the war is 'illegal' (the Irish Labour Party considers it 'illegal, immoral, unjust, and anti-democratic'). Fine Gael claim they are adhering to the principle of upholding the primacy of the United Nations. Po-faced obtuseness isn't in it. Typically, Fine Gael's long-standing leading intellectual light (and former prime minister), Garret FitzGerald argues against America's 'arbitrarily' using its power by claiming that 'it is hard to see much good coming of an Iraq war, but one can readily envisage it generating a lot of evil'.[273]

And then there's Paul Gillespie, who informs us that Iraq developed its chemical warfare program 'under the direction' of Donald Rumsfeld.[274] When challenged for his evidence in support of his stating as simple fact such a defamatory accusation, he says blandly that it's 'in the literature,' meaning that some dippy academic published a half-baked piece in which baseless conjecture is substituted for logical analysis. But if you ask for real-world evidence or confront him with logic – such as, if any such thing were even remotely true, why didn't the Iraqis parade this evidence of American complicity? – then there is no answer.

Why do such baseless condemnations of the U.S. go unchallenged in so much of the Irish media? Why is Robert Fisk, for instance, permitted without the slightest challenge to claim on 'Morning Ireland' that the war in Iraq would be 'all about oil, nothing to do with humanitarian concerns, nothing to do with

---

[273]'Iraq crisis bound to leave messy situation,' *Irish Times*, 17 March 2003.

[274]'Rationale missing for a preventive war against Iraq,' *Irish Times*, 25 January 2003.

weapons of mass destruction'? Perhaps it was because he offered such wondrous proof. It seems that an American oil company with which Condoleezza Rice was once associated had just launched an oil tanker named after her. Well, let's hope that the first American oil tanker to pull up to the docks in the post-Saddam Iraq will be the 'S.S. Condoleezza Rice' so that Mr Fisk can use a photograph of her for the cover of his book exposing the hitherto wholly unsuspected existence of the international oil market.

Why, in short, is there such a prevailing lack of genuine debate? For starters, there is the corrosive effect of Irish 'neutrality'. Or, to be precise, the shameless pretense that such a thing exists. Irish 'neutrality' is intellectually bogus, politically gutless, and morally obtuse. Neutrality can't just be proclaimed, it has to be defended (witness the Swiss or the Swedes). That this is the case has been openly acknowledged for decades by rational Irish politicians (mostly to be found in the ranks of the Progressive Democrats and Fine Gael), but Fianna Fail – despite the rationality of its current defense policy as manifested in its signing up to the Partnership for Peace and its firm support of the need to disarm Saddam Hussein – continues its electoral cowardice of crouching behind this fiction, instead of confronting its supporters with the truth. And the truth, readily apparent to international observers, is that 'neutrality' is a semantic facade from behind which the nutters on the Irish political scene launch their obsessive tirades of condemnation. There's the adolescent posturing of the Greens in the Irish parliament, morally equating the U.S. with Saddam's Iraq. There's presenter after presenter on radio and television claiming – against all the evidence of the last war in Iraq – that this war would not be aimed at Saddam but at the people of Iraq. And there's the Irish Labour Party's spokesman on foreign affairs, Michael D. Higgins, in an op-ed piece in the *Irish Times*, arguing that the UN sanctions-regime was responsible for the misery which the Iraqi people were suffering.[275] As Foreign Minister Brian Cowen stated to the Irish parliament in October 2001, the UN oil-for-food program provided the means for the Iraqi government to meet 'fully' the nutritional and health needs of its people; it was Saddam's cynical manipulation of the program – his diversion of revenue and imports to sinister uses – which was directly causing the widespread misery.[276] And, in the first Gulf War, innocent civilian casualties were not in the hundreds of thousands, as so regularly claimed on RTE, but in the low thousands,[277] and it was well established, in advance, that the targeting this time would be exponentially more precise. But such commentators are impervious. Even as the Americans moved into Baghdad and our television screens were full of scenes of smiling welcoming Iraqi faces – as in Kosovo, let us remember, as in Afghanistan – they persisted in their absurdities.[278] All, of course, in defense of Irish 'neutrality'.

Here, for instance, is how Eddie Holt, writing in the *Irish Times*, put it, on the third day of the war after scenes of the jubilation of the ordinary Iraqi had appeared (on British

---

[275]'In Baghdad a desperate "what can we do?" But there is time to stop war,' *Irish Times*, 5 February 2003.

[276]As I detailed in the Epilogue above.

[277]As even the *Irish Times* recognized in an article reprinted, 14 March 2003, from the *Washington Post*: Walter Russell Mead, 'Bush is right and war is best of appalling options'.

[278]See for two typical examples of their adolescent refusal to own up to their wrongheadedness – a basically petulant obstinacy as intellectually perverse as their 'arguments' are self-delusional and the language of their abuse of those who disagree with them is venomous: Matt Cooper 'The end justifies the means? Tell that to the maimed and the dead,' and Diarmuid Doyle 'How the peace movement won the war,' both in the *Sunday Tribune*, 13 April 2003.

television): George Bush was ordering American 'soldiers to blast, burn, butcher, slaughter, massacre, dismember, leave starving, render homeless – basically 'destroy'...– poor people, as though they were vermin'.[279] What, in God's name, could you possibly say about a newspaper that seeks out such commentary from its writers? Throughout the war, coverage in the *Irish Times* depicted the conflict as one of fierce support for the regime by the Iraqi people and as involving heavy civilian casualties at the hands of the coalition forces. On the very morning following the fall of Baghdad, its featured analysis managed, in a relatively short piece, to work in 'ruthless' no less than three times (as well as its being the lead adjective in its headline) to characterize the Americans' use of firepower, stating that the 'influx of civilians [into Baghdad hospitals] told its own story'.[280] Unfortunately for this fearless analyst who was sitting at Central Command headquarters in Doha, Lara Marlowe – whose reporting from Baghdad was a revelation for its objectivity and courage – actually visited these hospitals and noted in the same issue that 'there were so few women and children [though] doctors kept insisting that most of the victims were civilians. "They often don't survive, so they don't come to hospital,' [the Iraqi doctor] answered, unconvincingly'.[281]

It would undoubtedly have been more politic to have explicitly said the following at the beginning of this piece, but I do not – at least, in general – have any quarrel with the Irish government. Not now that there is a responsible and intelligent

---

[279]Eddie Holt 'Ask not for whom the bombs toll,' *Irish Times*, 22 March 2003.

[280]Deaglán de Bréadún 'Ruthless, relentless air power of US far superior to antiquated Iraqi artillery,' *Irish Times*, 10 April 2003.

[281]'People power overwhelmed defenders of the regime as the final drama unfolded,' *Irish Times*, 10 April 2003.

foreign minister. But it would be nice if there were more forceful, more pro-active interventions on international affairs. No one is better than Brian Cowen at arguing the government's case – that is, arguing the facts – in media interviews and in the parliament. But there seems an unwillingness to take on the nutters in a definitive manner by forcing a public debate on the essential principles informing Irish foreign policy.[282] Part of this, of course, is due to the already-noted electoral cowardice of Fianna Fail over 'neutrality'. Much of the rest is to be found in narrow Irish interests. The government defends, for instance, this charade of the 'obligation' to meet the 'UN target' of 0.7 % of GNP in official development assistance because it serves, so self-righteously (indeed, hypocritically), to artfully conceal the reality that what the developing countries actually need to effect their economic development is not aid but access for their exports in our markets[283] – a reality which would mean dismantling the EU's import-restrictive Common Agricultural Policy with all that that would portend for the Irish farming sector. Never say the Irish are defending selfish interests when they are so magnificent in their contribution of Third World aid!

In its recovery from the irresponsibility of the 1960s, the responsible left has shed its obsessional fanatics (that is, those with a flat-earth mentality who, in cognitive defiance of the evidence, continue to argue such inanities as making 'the economy serve social ends') and has returned to its traditional core concerns with raising the well-being of the marginalized and the disadvantaged by promoting economic growth. It has recognized that the market is not inimical to social concerns – it is indifferent, it is an economic mechanism – and that,

---

[282]Cf., my observations in the Epilogue above.

[283]See chapter 3 above.

accordingly, economic decisions should be made solely for economic reasons, with any untoward social consequences being addressed by social measures (which, of course, can only be funded from the tax revenues accruing from economic growth). So whom do the Irish pundits choose to glorify? None other than the discarded remnants of 1960s leftism gathering themselves in the so-called anti-globalization movement.[284] These are considered as the 'new hope,' when, in fact, their ranks are made up of no other than the same adolescent smart-asses and recidivist lunatics every generation seems to throw up. We know what would happen if you stop globalization. The first era of globalization – that is, the linking of national markets internationally via information technology – was halted by the Bolshevik revolution. Of course, here the Irish political class must share much of the blame. They, too, continue to worship at the shrine of that economically-meaningless sacred cow, the 'equality gap' – in every intellectually meretricious way, the economic mirror-image of 'neutrality'. The latter a refuge for Irish Republican ideologues and their fellow-travelers; the former a recipe for producing an economic sink-hole.[285]

So what hope is there? The sad answer is that there is little that can be done, so long as responsible Irish intellectuals continue to distance themselves from the public debate and they will continue to do so so long as the media continue to allow the nutters to dominate this debate. I have myself participated in dozens of Irish television and radio talk-shows and I could not begin to estimate the number of times I have been confronted, by the presenter, with an assertion straight out of the fantasy world

---

[284]Peadar Kirby 'More humane form of globalization shows current model not inevitable,' *Irish Times*, 16 November 2003.

[285]Cf., the Introduction above.

of paranoid leftism and been asked to respond: Isn't this all about oil? Isn't the Security Council controlled by the U.S.? Isn't it really American foreign policy which brought on 11 September?

Indeed, what about 11 September? You would have thought that the sheer evil behind the terrorism of that day would have jolted some rationality into the Irish debate over American foreign policy. Indeed, President McAleese's unscripted response, on the day, was to characterize what happened, with dead accuracy, as 'crazed hatred unchecked'. More typical was one talk show presenter who compared it to the bombing of Dresden and claimed that now Americans would be 'baying for blood' – thus neatly setting the tone for what would prove to be prevailing themes in Irish commentary: that we Americans had it coming and that our reaction would be far worse than anything the terrorists did.[286] Perhaps I can best illustrate how infantile this is by pointing out that the corresponding response of right-wing nutters was to claim it was God's punishment on America for legalizing abortion. If I were to appear on one of their talk-shows, I would undoubtedly be confronted with, 'Isn't this proof that George W. Bush is continuing Clinton's conspiracy to deliver the U.S. into the hands of the UN?'

And now, as I write, the Irish airwaves and press are filled with 'experts' asserting that the end result of this war will be an American puppet government in Baghdad, one that will adhere to a 'whole new Israel-friendly Arab order'.[287] Indeed, the most damning proof these pundits can think to put forward in demonstration of the sinister intent of the U.S. is that we will

---

[286]See fn. 3 above.

[287]David Hirst 'A regime change with potentially enormous consequences,' *Irish Times*, 10 April 2003.

soon see an Israeli embassy in downtown Baghdad![288] Oh, yes,
God forbid that rationality and peace should break out. So, in
final illustration of this malevolent phenomenon of anti-
Americanism in Ireland, let me end by reverting to one concrete
example in this connection of a falsehood concerning U.S.
foreign policy, which, while hardly unique to Ireland, is much
loved there. It well illustrates the sad truth that it is not, as so
standardly claimed, American policy which is at fault but the
venomously-distorted characterization of it which drives the
critics of our policy from unreasoning resentment to irrational
hatred. This is the canard that the U.S. permits Israel to defy UN
resolutions.[289] There can hardly be an Irish commentator who
hasn't stated this as simple fact (not to speak of such politicians
as Garret FitzGerald). Well, no, as a matter of fact, the claim isn't
true, not even remotely. All UN resolutions concerning the
Arab/Israeli conflict mandate actions by *both* the Israelis and the
Arabs. In particular, UN Security Council Resolution 242 – the
governing resolution passed consequent upon the 1967 war –
calls on Israel to withdraw from territories occupied during that
war *and* calls for all the countries of the region to live at peace
behind secure and internationally-recognized borders. In short, a
negotiated withdrawal based upon the premise of 'land for peace'.
Egypt acceded to this mandate by agreeing a peace with Israel at
Camp David in the 1970s and, in return, the Israelis withdrew
from the Sinai. It is, then, patently clear that the Israelis are not
the ones defying the UN. It's the Arabs, both the Palestinians and
the rejectionist Arab states who, intransigently and irrationally,
refuse to come to terms with the existence of the Jewish state of

---

[288]Robert Fisk 'Fall of a tyrant: Saddam sidelines,' *Irish Independent*, 10
April 2003.
    [289]Cf., in the Epilogue above.

Israel. PLO leadership has proven a disaster for the Palestinian people, leading them up the blind alley of violence. In this, they have been aided and abetted by the EU which locked the Palestinian people into PLO control by their Venice Declaration of 1980, and it is the EU which has continued to underwrite Palestinian terrorism by their massive funding of the PLO. Arab, indeed Muslim, hatred of the U.S. is not consequent upon any U.S. policy; it is self-generated by their own scapegoat-seeking self-deception in reaction to the failures in their own societies[290] – a systemic mendacity given succor by far too many Irish commentators.

7 December 2003
Sacramento

---

[290]See Bernard Lewis *What Went Wrong? The Clash between Islam and Modernity in the Middle East* (London: Weidenfeld & Nicolson, 2002), and my review, 'Why the West and Islam are in conflict,' *Irish Catholic*, 1 August 2002.